1912/2000

The Horse Adjutant

A Boy's Life in the Holocaust

The Horse Adjutant
Leon Schagrin
Stephen Shooster

Leon with Maciek, Artist's Rendition

Leon Schagrin and his horse Maciek

Shooster Publishing, LLC
South Florida

Limited Edition 2011
Associated with ISBN 978-0-9830319-1-8
USA copyright 1-601102291
Leon Schagrin / Stephen Shooster
The Horse Adjutant; a Boy's Life in the Holocaust
Key terms:
Holocaust, Jewish literature
Jewish non-fiction - History
Grybow in the Holocaust
Leon Schagrin

Printed in the United States

Warning - This book contains mature materials and was
not written for young children.

This book is dedicated
in memory of my
beloved family and
over *200* relatives
who were brutally murdered
during the Nazi
Holocaust

September *1st to 3rd,*
1942 at Belzec
Poland

A Living Legacy

Carly Shooster &
Leon Schagrin 2010

When I was twelve, prior to my Bat Mitzvah (Covenant with God), I was designated by Leon Schagrin, a Holocaust survivor, to represent him at the 100th anniversary in the year 2045. I'm sorry to say he will be gone, my dad will be in his 80's and I will be 45 at this momentous event. Thus is the nature of history, by choosing a young person, me, Leon can carry his living message as far as humanly possible.

While spending time with Leon and his wife, I inescapably am drawn to the panther tattoo that poses in a running stance on his forearm. Hypnotized by the power of the cat, while listening to him speak in a Polish accent, thick as it is authentic, he tells stories about his life. Listening I am stunned, he endured feats I can only begin to imagine.

I would expect him to be bitter, full of hate but this is the furthest thing from his demeanor. He does however say boldly, "I have a complaint with God." I don't blame him. Where was God when his life was turned upside down? How could God condone The Holocaust? or any genocide?

Leon and Betty do not have kids. So when he was faced with the mortal question of every man, How to create a legacy, he decided to adopt one, me! I hope I can measure up to his standard and tell the world his simple message so aptly recounted during the 60's - Make Love not War! Stamp out Hatred!

Like Paul Revere urgently speaking of pending battle the Horse Adjutant rides shouting, Find a way to make peace.

Join me in 2045,

Carly Shooster

Carly Shooster 2011

The Horse Adjutant
Leon Schagrin
Stephen Shooster

With Remembrances from .... Morris *Moshe* Katz

Max & Rose Blauner

Eli Sommer

Writer / Editor .... Jim Boring

A Special Note .... Carly Shooster

Grybow Research .... Kamil Kmak

Forward .... Frank Shooster

Interviews by .... Malcolm Rosenberg, Jaime Shooster, Kamil Kmak, Stephen Shooster, Frank Shooster, Moisey Abdurakhmanov

Graphics .... Steve Mizejewski

Special Mention .... Diane Shooster, Cassidy Shooster, Carly Shooster, Jason Shooster, Michael Shooster, Robert Field, Dahris Clair, Rose Diamond, Sherman Frank, Bruce Rosen, Fran Klauber

Photographers ....Kamil Kmak, Jolanta Kruszniewska, Courtney-Coliflower-Ortiz

Artist .... Shoosty

Audio Editorial Consultant ... . Inez Geller

Audio Engineer .... Joe Beard

Audio Facilities .... Joe Beard Productions

Why We Tell These Stories ... .Danny Lieberman

JRI-Poland Town Leader.......... .... Deborah Raff

Student's Perspective .... Moisey Abdurakhmanov

Frank Shooster

The Possibilities

Frank Shooster, esq.
Civil Rights Attorney

I have never been given a greater honor, or a graver responsibility than to have been asked by Leon Schagrin to write the forward to his first-hand sworn testimony of his Holocaust experience from the moment Germany declared war on Poland until his final liberation from Auschwitz, only to have to overcome anti-Semitism all over again upon his arrival in the United States.

Leon Schagrin is a genuine hero in his own right. Understanding that nobody is born to hate, Leon has willingly subjected himself to relive his Holocaust experiences in hundreds of school auditoriums. To date he has spoken to more than 10,000 middle-school and high school students throughout South Florida.

Leon's testimony may well be the single most chilling reading experience you will ever have. It reads like a thriller that will keep you up all night, but you may need to put it down from time to time to catch your breath, wipe a tear, or work up the courage to turn another page.

You cannot read this book without becoming traumatized by its unforgettable images of horror and cruelty. As you accompany Leon Schagrin to the depths of hell and beyond you will be stunned, shaken, and speechless. No artist of fiction, no Dante, no Kafka, no Orwell, no Marquis de Sade has ever been able to envision, let alone depict, a more horrifying inferno than the mechanized mass murder personally witnessed by Leon Schagrin. That he survives at all is amazing itself. Sometimes survival was a matter of luck, if it's proper to use that word at all to a prisoner-slave in a concentration camp. Sometimes it was quick thinking and sharp judgment. Most of all, Leon survived because he looked like the idealized Aryan: tall blond and blue eyes. Ironically, racism almost killed him, and racism probably saved his life.

In the midst of his chronicle of unparalleled cruelty, there are moments of tenderness from the kindnesses of strangers at the risk of their own lives, to the sacrifices of so many for the sake of love, duty, or honor. Unfortunately, these moments are just tiny flickering sparks of light in a dark sea, incident after incident of murder, cruelty, and humiliation, naming names, dates, times, places of perpetrators, collaborators, victims, and bystanders. The events are now more than sixty-five years old, but Leon Schagrin has been blessed (or cursed) with an almost photographic memory.

If this were the sad fate of only one man, it would be terrible enough. But from the dawn of so-called 'civilization' to the present day, countless people have experienced the kind of suffering borne by Leon Schagrin, and countless more have no doubt suffered worse, from the Inquisition's rack to the 'advances' of modern civilization such as gulags, death factories, and IEDs. Yet, only a minute number of people have lived to tell about it. If a novelist, or a screen writer, needed a character who could tell the story of the Holocaust in Poland, they would be hard put to find a better character than Leon Schagrin, if only because of his *Zelig* or *Forrest Gump-like* presence at so many pivotal moments.

It's easy to say why this book had to be written. First and foremost, we live in a world where Holocaust denial is rampant.

Every witness account is a brick in the bulwark of historical truth. Every witness statement helps to fill gaps in the historical record, and enables historians to corroborate, verify, or rule out specific allegations. The philosopher, George Santayana, once said, "Those who fail to remember the past are doomed to repeat it." Holocaust denial is a political weapon used to demonize Jews, and delegitimize the Jewish state. There are many other good reasons for writing this book that Leon has asked me to share with you on his behalf, which I outline below. But, before going there, let it be clear, commercial success is not among them. This is important, because Holocaust denial exists alongside its self-contradictory twin: 'Holocaust exploitation.' This despicable doctrine admits the truth of the Holocaust but asserts that the Jewish people and the Jewish state have used it for political and financial gain. Each twin is the child of anti-Semitism, and though they are both contradictory, they are both advanced by the enemies of Israel and the Jewish people to incite hatred, terror and war.

Any author would like to see their book become a bestseller, but Amazon.com lists 2,000 Holocaust memoirs and biographies, so only a fool would write another Holocaust memoir thinking it was a ticket to fame and fortune. Besides, in writing this book Leon wants nothing for himself. He and his wife Betty, herself a surviving member of Schindler's List, have formed the Leon and Betty Schagrin Foundation for all proceeds originating from the sale of this book or any derivative works. This foundation is a 501(c)(3) not for profit organization dedicated to promoting anti-hate education. I am sure he would be satisfied if every last copy of his book were given away with the hope it would be read and its lessons learned.

While it's easy to say why this book had to be written, it's not so easy to say why it should be read. Why one would want to be part of Leon Schagrin's struggle to survive. Why experience his nightmare, even if only vicariously? If you are a Holocaust scholar you won't want to miss it, if only because Leon witnessed so much with his own eyes.

I have been a student of the Holocaust for fifty years now. I have been fighting anti-Semitism throughout my career as a civil rights lawyer in private practice. I sit on the state and national leadership boards of the Anti-Defamation League (though I speak here solely in my personal capacity.) I count over three hundred books in my personal library about the history of anti-Semitism. Not one of them packs the power of Leon Schagrin's narrative.

Before exposing a child to this story, parents and teachers should exercise caution. It's not necessarily a bad thing. I am convinced that for my children, and me, our exposure to the Holocaust at an early age was a life-changing event—in a positive way. I don't know what child psychologists have to say about exposing kids to mass death and destruction, but in my case it led directly to my decision to practice civil rights law as well as my involvement in the ADL.

I have my own twins: Jay and Lauren. When they were ten years old we visited Dachau, where we saw the torture chamber that housed Pastor Martin Niemoller. He's responsible for the famous speech about the cowardice of German intellectuals opposing the Nazi path to totalitarianism:

They came first for the Communists and I didn't speak up because I wasn't a Communist. Then they came for the trade unionists and I didn't speak up because I wasn't a trade unionist. Then they came for the Jews and I didn't speak up because I wasn't a Jew. Then they came for me and by that time no one was left to speak up.

Or, as this statement attributed to Edmund Burke says:

All it takes for the triumph of evil is for good men to do nothing.

Today, Leon is eighty four years old and suffers with macular degeneration. It's become quite difficult for him to read and write as he can only see out of the corner of his eyes. He can no longer drive, and it's hard for him to get around. He has asked me to articulate his thoughts about why it was so important to give his testimony while he can.

First, Leon wants to honor the memory of all the victims of the Holocaust, especially his father, mother, four sisters, and infant brother who were gassed in the Belzec death camp, September 1st to 3rd, 1942. The best way he knows how to do that is to tell the world what he knows about it.

Second, Leon wants to honor each and every person who saved his life—and there are many of them whom you will come to know in the pages that follow.

Third and foremost, he would like to see something good come from this book. He has already succeeded in performing a public service for posterity. Yet, if you ask Leon, he will say that the best thing that could happen from this book is if it encourages leaders of national and international institutions and organizations to enact laws that will make it possible to indict, apprehend, extradite and try persons who advocate or incite genocide—before the killing starts.

Under current international law, war criminals can be prosecuted after the fact, but by then it is already too late. The UN Convention against Genocide is 50 years old. Since that time the world has experienced a mind boggling number of new genocidal and ethnic cleansing campaigns, at least 34 separate events killing at least 12 million people. Only a few of the perpetrators have ever been brought to justice. These figures exclude mass deaths from war, disease, or famine. The Rome accords of 2002 have led to the new

International Criminal Court with the power to prosecute crimes against humanity. Most scholars of international law have concluded that incitement to commit genocide is illegal under customary international law, but the ICC has not issued a formal opinion endorsing that theory and creating binding legal precedent.

Whether the ICC will deter future acts of genocide has never been tested. The record of intentional institutions thus far has been dismal. We can hope that some day humans will have evolved beyond their capacity to dehumanize one another, but until that happens we can only hope Leon's dream will become a reality.

Reading Leon's testimony you will notice that the full panoply of human vice and virtue are on display, and not always attached to the good guys or bad guys respectively. You'll encounter Jewish police and kapos, every bit as repugnant as their Nazi overseers. This point is crucial, because it demonstrates convincingly that no race or nationality has a monopoly on virtue, which is another way of saying that any one of us could find ourselves succumbing to the same moral weaknesses we observe throughout the book.

We will never eradicate hate until we accept that any one of us could be deluded into believing our neighbor is less than human. As long as any group believes it is incapable of succumbing to barbarity, they risk becoming barbarians themselves.

So, if you are Jewish as am I, join me in a little introspection. Forget about current events, because they are too emotionally charged. Let's go further back. One of the most disturbing accounts of genocide from antiquity can be found in the Torah, where we learn that God ordered the Israelites to slaughter the Amalekites and Midianites and enslave their women.

The Israelites were persuaded into believing they were acting with God's blessing, and they followed God's orders without question, killing tens of thousands, as part of the conquest of Canaan. We are their descendants, with many descendants to be proud of, so we were able to overcome our own history.

In many ways, the modern world should be less susceptible to mass media manipulation because of the explosion of the internet. That may bode well for the future, but for now several generations of Palestinians have been educated from Kindergarten on portraying Jews as an evil, satanic force bent on world domination. The vast majority wasn't even alive in 1948. I am told that this practice has diminished in the West Bank, but it will probably be generations before the kind of visceral hatred that motivates people to become suicide bombers shows any appreciable decline.

So, the Horse Adjutant's mission must go on. Leon's mission must become our own. Every generation needs to teach its children about the price of unbridled hatred.

Frank Shooster

Leon Schagrin at Riverside Elementary School
Mrs. Berger's Class. Carly Shooster front right
fig 151

A Guide Through the Inferno

Stephen Shooster, Co-Author

President of the Leon and Betty Schagrin Foundation

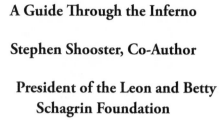

I am humbled by this project. Taking the responsibility of capturing the story of a Holocaust survivor is something I never expected. This is especially true since the story of Leon Schagrin is not a simple one and perhaps the most horrible I have ever heard. But the thing that resonates most with me is that while learning and documenting his malignant adventure how quickly a whole race, my own race, came to the brink of total extermination. It is unthinkable that a rich culture with roots in every European country could be singled out and decimated in only a few short years. Yet, that is exactly what happened.

In places this story is written from a first-person point of view. In order to accomplish this I had to become Leon. It is a difficult role to play. There were days I pondered the decadence to which he was subjected and felt dizzy. I have tried to imagine what he felt and must still feel every day. Most people would block these horrors, as I know he must have as well in order to have lived a long, productive, and loving life. But, now with the urgent frailty of age, he is compelled to capture his story in writing, for all time. Asking me to help, I resisted at first, finding every excuse, but when I finally listened I was captivated. I hope you will be too.

A first person narrative is fraught with the potential for error and I accept responsibility for any found in this book. Every effort has been made to insure accuracy but memory and skill being human attributes they are inevitably flawed.

Leon escaped death on many occasions only to face new life threatening challenges. The more you learn, the more you will realize Leon is not just telling a story but acting as a guide, like Dante's Virgil, not just to share his story, but his love for the safety and well-being of all mankind. In doing so, he is on a sacred mission and he wants everyone to join. When you have read his story it is his hope that you will exercise vigilance and become a guardian of freedom. To do so you *must* promise to bear witness and protest against xenophobic hatred, and support those people and organizations that stand for the highest values of mankind against the evils that always threaten them.

Unlike most stories written about *The Holocaust* this is a modern work completed during the age of the internet. Because of this, I had unprecedented access to research materials and people, both near and far, who were ready and able to help. Early on, I happened to seek out on the social networks help from someone in Poland and was surprised how quickly I found one, a young college student, Kamil Kmak, who incidentally grew up in Leon's hometown of Grybow (Gree-Boov). Kamil took hundreds of photos of the area, read the early versions of the manuscript multiple times, introduced me to his friends, and sought out local people who are still alive to collect old photos and stories. His personal perspective opened my eyes to the broader conflict and being gracious he was always within an e-mail distance away to keep me on track. I found myself sharing messages with him constantly for the past few years. I am sure because of this I have found a new lifelong friend.

Using the internet allowed Kamil and I to communicate instantaneously, sharing images and text. In this way, I was also able to coordinate a conference between him, representing the new Polish generation, and a survivor, Leon, to talk in their native language, Polish, about their mutual hometown. This, in and of itself, was a modern miracle.

I need to mention two other people who were instrumental in making this happen, Malcolm Rosenberg who's willingness to take the time to meet with Leon frequently jump started the project and Jim Boring who took upon himself before anyone else the over arching mission to make this a reality. I may have gathered all the stones but Jim polished them.

Let me add a special note of love and appreciation to my wife, Diane and our kids, Jason, Jaime, Carly and Cassidy. Putting this book together was a work of sincerity and devotion that took much time away from you. However, I believe, taking this time and completing this project is one of the greatest gifts I will ever be able to give. Thank you for your patience and understanding. Each of you is the love of my life.

Stephen Shooster

The Horse Adjutant

Contents

Introduction

Leon Schagrin

By telling you the story of my life, at my late age, it is my hope to leave behind a true and accurate testament for future generations. It is my hope that you let these writings serve as a warning against tyranny and hate. What I want you to take away from my life story is just how important it is to defend your freedom, at all costs. Experience has shown me that *if you lose your freedom, you are condemned.*

Every day, I am sorry to say, I still feel the shadow of evil following me and it will probably remain until the end of my life. However, perhaps if we all share the lessons of the Holocaust it will not be repeated by future generations. It is my sincere wish that future generations will be on extreme alert surrounding the dangers of a dictatorship and any type of Fascist thinking, which, I am sorry to say, still exist today. I can't stress this enough, by all means, protect your freedom and pursue a course that reduces and finally stamps out hate.

I vowed to my father a long time ago, before he was forcibly taken from our home, with my family and our entire neighborhood, soon after to all be brutally murdered, that I would tell the story of my life to everyone who would listen. Not because I am important, but because if my story is lost to the ages, then what happened to my family and me could be repeated. It is not easy to tell you my story. It is painful for me to recall such memories. Once you get past the pain and realize the miracle of my survival you may be ready to think about the bigger ideas, like what it means to be free, and why if you lose your freedom you lose everything. If things were different my father and mother would have grown old together and my brother and sisters would have had long lives. I hope things are different for you and all the future generations.

Many years after the war I visited Belzec, Poland and confronted my greatest nightmare. It was incomprehensible to me that in a small field covered in volcanic rock rest my mother and father, my four sisters, and my baby brother, along with some 600,000 other souls from all of Upper Galicia (Southeast Poland). It is not just the number of people, which is appalling but that they were all destroyed in a period of a single year. My own family was among 12,000 - 15,000 people who were killed in *only* three days by the deadly gas chambers.

It is difficult to imagine a hellish nightmare of this magnitude, such a thorough and methodical annihilation of a race from all parts of Europe. And yet, as large as this tragedy was, we were not alone. There are many other places like Belzec in Poland and Germany and elsewhere around the world. But there is a difference. Belzec is one of the only pure extermination camps ever to be built. Today, we are only aware of one survivor of this place. From him and a few of the soldiers we learned that the people who were brought there, my family included, sat waiting in a field for their turn to be subjected to killing by deadly gas then carelessly tossed into a pit.

My anger knows no bounds when I think about it. I have found, the only way I can channel my energy appropriately is to warn each and every one of you, and to share my love for all of mankind, including my forgiveness for those that acted on their twisted irrational thoughts. This is my extreme shout to the world - if it happened to me, a 12-year-old child living in a modern mixed community, who would presume to say that you and your family are safe? It is my secondary wish that the world, especially the March of the Living include Belzec in their many excursions to visit Auschwitz and the other camps.

Today, I am 84 years old and I live in South Florida with my wife Betty, who is also a survivor. She survived due to the kindness of a man named Oscar Schindler, and is a member of his now famous list with her two sisters. In fact, her sister Helen was brutalized by the despicable Commandant Goth as one of his maids at his home. She bravely protected her sisters by accepting this abuse. Many years later, after the war, Helen met with the surviving daughter of Goth, in the well-documented and award-winning film, *Inheritance*.

The story of my childhood is one I wish upon no other person. The fact that I survived in many ways was just luck combined with boyish bravado. I went through a storm of the greatest dimensions. It was a political storm that has come to be known today as *The Holocaust* and because I was only twelve when it started, I can hardly understand why it began. What I do remember is that I was a happy child and that my childhood world suddenly turned against me and seemed to conspire to force me into poverty, then a homeless laborer without any family, and last a starving slave prisoner with four weeks to live; all of this before I turned eighteen.

During most of this time, my job, the one thing that kept me alive, was to care for a horse. And with this horse I met some of the most notorious characters of the war. By hooking him up with a carriage I became the driver of the top Nazi official in the Tarnow ghetto, Hauptsturmfuhrer Blache. I also used my horse to collect bodies that were once my entire world and on more than one occasion was forced to step on the blood of my relatives as it spilled in a senseless river of horror that went on for years. It seemed that it would never end. Yet, throughout it all, I tried to remember that I had a normal childhood before the war and I lived in a culturally rich and enlightened time of history going to school with children of many ethnicities and cultures without incident. When I was lost in the political maelstrom of the German occupation it was these guideposts that kept my world in focus - that reminded me of home. Because of a good upbringing I knew somehow that goodness and peace were possible and must still exist in the world.

My story is full of pain. Many times I was a breath away from my last, but somehow I survived. Please carefully read my story and remember what I am telling you with a sense of urgency. We must keep such horrors from happening ever again.

To those who helped me tell my story I have only the deepest gratitude.

Leon Schagrin   2011

The Panther

Jim Boring

Leon Schagrin with Jim Boring
Kabassa, Beer and the Manuscript
2011

The tattoo is faded with age and the leaping panther is no longer a glossy black but a more muted darkness on the old man's arm. Still it speaks of a time long ago when a young man marked himself with the image and the spirit of the creature. The panther covers a still earlier tattoo, a set of numbers that once seemed to mark a young boy for certain death.

We sit together, side by side, on Leon Schagrin's couch – a yellow legal pad in my lap, a small ottoman before us that drifts back and forth as one or the other of us rests our heels on it. Nearly every Friday for a year and a half we sit like this, enduring unendurable memories. Behind us the window looks out onto a parklike setting and a tennis court – always empty. The small condominium apartment is neat and clean. The nameplate on the louvered door reads, Leon and Betty Schagrin.

Here live two unlikely survivors of a great man-made horror, the attempted extermination of an entire people. The history of that attempt is well-documented and preserved in both collective and individual memory. The poignant eloquence of Anne Frank and the vivid remembrance of Elie Weisel among so many others have created a tapestry of cruelty, terror and also humanity that humbles us before the awful and the wonderful possibilities in human nature.

This is one more of those horror stories – different only in the particulars from the plague that descended on all of Europe at a time not so very long ago in historical terms but now nearly past the lifetimes of the survivors of the generation that lived through it.

We are far enough from those times and events to know that whatever lessons they might have taught us have not been learned. The hope that social institutions would be formed to prevent and deter genocidal atrocities has not been realized. The blindfold of Justice seems now to prevent her from finding her way to those who so desperately need the impartial fairness that same blindfold once symbolized. And yet we work and continue to hope that one day our better angels will prevail. Indeed hope is the belief that we have better angels. This is the story of Leon Schagrin, a boy visited by both demons and angels.

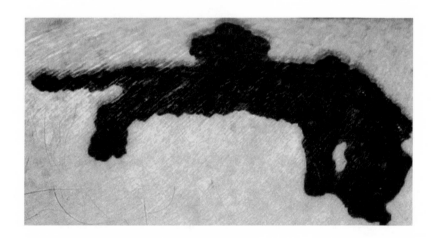

The Panther
Leon Schagrin's Tattoo

fig 147

32

The Horse Adjutant

Leon Schagrin
Stephen Shooster

Leon with Maciek, Artist's Rendition

Leon Schagrin and his horse Maciek

33

34

Chapter One

The Tyroleans

Late 1939, twelve year-old Leon Schagrin stood on the side of the road and waved and cheered with his friends as Tyrolean troops roared into town. The colorful soldiers with their feathered caps, their horses and motorcycles, their belt buckles with the words, "God is With Us," emblazoned on them – all this was heady stuff for a boy.

But this victorious army was not returning to its own but occupying Leon's town of Grybow in a region in southern Poland known as Galicia. Still the excitement of the military movement overcame any resistance Leon might have felt. The soldiers were friendly, tossing candy to the children, and waving as they passed in parade. Leon even got a bowl of soup from their mess.

Six of the soldiers were to be bivouacked at Leon's home. One of them turned out to be an old comrade of Leon's father, who had served in the cavalry of the Austrian army in World War I. The soldiers were kind and polite during their stay. Simply being allowed to touch their rifles impressed Leon. He dreamed of a day when he too would be a soldier.

Leon's preparation for this invasion had been a sudden move on the part of his family from their home in Grybow to his grandfather's farm some thirty miles away, near the city of Tarnow, when the German attack began. Leon's father, a self-taught veterinarian, had left the family, which included Leon's four sisters and his pregnant mother, in his father-in-law's care while he attempted to join his reserve unit of the Polish army. But the war was over quickly, even before he found his unit. Leon's mother then gave birth to her sixth child, Leon's brother, Naftali. When Leon's father returned from his unsuccessful attempt to join his unit the family returned to Grybow.

The almost festive arrival of the Tyrolean troops was misleading. These ordinary soldiers were soon moved east and by the end of November they had been completely replaced by German SS and Gestapo assisted by Polish police. The nature of the new regime was soon clear. The synagogue was turned into a stable, an open ghetto was established and the movement of Jews was restricted to one kilometer. Jews were allowed to walk only on designated streets. White armbands bearing a blue Star of David were required to be worn. All businesses owned by Jews were confiscated. Leon was no longer allowed to attend school and as his thirteenth birthday approached, preparation for his Bar Mitzvah was forbidden along with all religious observations. Beatings, humiliations and shootings became an ordinary part of daily life.

Suddenly, and without any reason a boy could understand, the world transformed from one in which the greatest obstacle to be avoided consisted of household chores and the greatest trial was attending school, to a world in which his very existence was threatened on a daily basis. He saw, for the first time, adults whom he respected, among them his own teachers, shot dead in the street. Anyone, Jewish or otherwise, who resisted the Nazi regime in the slightest, was targeted. Very soon the atmosphere in Grybow became thick with fear. No one was safe.

Living in such a world became a matter of life and death decisions made instantly on the basis of what was happening at the moment. And the correctness of those decisions could not be anticipated; everything became a matter of luck – one lived or died at the whim of men whose motives could not be understood. Why these men killed with such ferocity, such enjoyment and so mercilessly was so far beyond the experience of any of their victims that effective reaction was impossible. Murderers had taken all the power of the state and they used that power with ruthless efficiency. The world had gone mad.

In such a world the ordinary bonds of community broke under the strain. The institutions of government, the schools, the religions, the day-to-day connections of business – the shops, the markets, the places people gathered for entertainment or work – every convention was shattered. The familiar became a threat, neighbors became enemies, the trust implicit in all the usual transactions and activities of daily life dissolved and was replaced by fear, and every action was taken with dreadful anticipation. The simple act of walking down the street required courage.

Yet this was Leon's home, his town, the place where he had played stickball with his friends, where every Monday market day he had moved among the townspeople and the peasants from the farms bringing their pigs and chickens and vegetables, the Gypsies hawking their copperware, the Yuvanim, (also known as the Lemkos) from the mountains with their leatherwork, all the Jews and Gentiles with their variety of cultures and skills mixing easily in one festive event. Leon would look for work he could do for vendors at the fair, working the grinder on the ice cream maker was his favorite. How ordinary it all was then and how it now seemed a memory of Eden.

The town of Grybow is in the foothills of the Carpathian Mountains. Organized around a town square dominated by one of the most beautiful Roman Catholic churches in southern Poland: an agricultural town whose only industrial operations were a brewery and a lumber mill; a town of small shops, of craftsmen, of butchers, bakers and tailors, all serving the townspeople and the surrounding peasant farmers in the countryside. On the roads in encampments lived Gypsies who made copperware pots and pans. In the mountains lived the Yuvanim (of Ivan), said to have been driven out of

Russia into the mountains by Ivan-the-Terrible many years earlier. They worked in leather and created many useful items sold in the market. They also were notorious smugglers from their isolated border homes in the mountains. Grybow had a professional class, the intelligentsia, consisting of politicians, lawyers, teachers, and businessmen. The clergy of the dominant religion, Roman Catholic, were prominent and influential.

Grybow was also the gateway to the health spas and resorts in the nearby mountains. Tourists from all over Europe would pass through Grybow on their way to these places. Leon and his friends would earn a few coins by cleaning dust from their cars. The women with their furs and cigarette holders, the men in their big cars, all made an impression on Leon.

Somehow that seemingly solid world no longer existed. The men of the intelligentsia once honored and deferred to in the streets, were now being dragged out of their homes and summarily killed. Killing became such a usual occurrence that it became necessary to have bodies removed from the streets and Leon was one of those chosen for the grisly task. As a member of a family with horses and carts Leon was a natural choice. And, because it was much more dangerous for a grown man to be among the Nazi murderers, as a boy Leon was safer doing the job than his father. Besides, Leon's appearance was such that he looked like the Germans and was inconspicuous as a consequence.

One day Leon was ordered to bring his horse and cart to pick up the body of a prominent lawyer who had been killed. The man lay on the street, his fine clothes seeping blood. The incongruity of one of the leading citizens of the town lying so well dressed in a pool of blood on the street was disorienting. Leon focused on the man's polished and well-made shoes and could not absorb the full reality of what was happening. The numbing effect of such horror had only begun.

38

The Nazis called for a collection of all fur coats. One woman, an American citizen married to a local Polish man, protested – waving her passport and demanding her rights as an American citizen. The Nazis dragged her and her husband into their front yard and shot them both.

In another instance the Nazis called for 100 "volunteers" to be turned over to them as hostages and directed the newly formed Jewish Committee to gather up these people from the Jewish community. Not surprisingly there were no volunteers. In retaliation the Nazis gathered the men of the Jewish Committee and the Jewish police and shot them all. Leon gathered bodies of adults he knew well from the site of the execution. The sight of these bloody bodies with their stricken familiar faces, the task of lifting and moving them onto his horse cart, began the process of preparing Leon for horrors yet to come. He was becoming inured to the sight of slaughter and the smell of human blood.

What Leon could not understand was the why of such brutality. He and his family were simply ordinary people. The fact of their religion set them apart from the majority but in nearly every other way they were like everyone else in Grybow. Roman Catholics were different from Eastern Orthodox Catholics, Gypsies were different from Lemkos, Poles and Russians and Germans all were different from each other by nature of circumstances. What justified the particular hostility shown toward Jews? Why had it arisen so suddenly out of nowhere? What crime had Jews committed that could justify the cruelty of the Germans? Leon could fashion no answer to these questions. Whatever motivated the Nazis was beyond him. He did understand that the Nazis were the real evil and not the Jews or the other victims of their inexplicable rage. He understood that survival would consist of dealing with the behavior of the Nazis as it occurred and not in puzzling over their motives.

Old Grybow from Church Tower
Orthodox Synagogue Bottom Right
fig 2.

40

Chapter Two

Green Hills

When I was a boy, I was just a boy. I did not enjoy school. The only subjects that interested me in the slightest were history and geography. Both were more important than I realized at the time. However, even with those budding interests I was neglectful. I would frequently go to school without doing my assignments, leave my books at home or just stare out the window, dreaming. Thinking back, when I was growing up, I was far more afraid of my teachers than policemen or anyone else.

This behavior led to stern warnings from my teachers to my father and me. One time, my teacher said to my father, How can your son learn without books or doing his assignments? My father simply shook his head and later pulled me aside and chastised me, If you keep this up, you will be lucky to grow up to be a dogcatcher.

I tried not to let it bother me, especially when I was on my own, which seemed to be most of the time. How was I to resist the temptations that lay all about me? There were so many things I liked to do. I would explore the hills and forests of the mountains towering above me, wade in streams and rivers filled with frogs for catching, play around the old high railroad bridge that arched like a Roman aqueduct across the river near my home, harkening stories of far away places. I would raid the neighbors' apple or pear trees or play stickball with my friends.

Up to the age of twelve there was no question I had many better things to do with my life than sit around a boring classroom getting knocked on the head. Just about the only good thing I can remember while sitting in class, was that on any given day, I could imagine a breeze blowing down from the mountains calling me away from duty and schoolwork. The only trouble was this idyllic vision was often interrupted with a whack on the head.

To put it mildly, my school was strict. All the children, re-gardless of racial or ethnic background went to the same school, although girls and boys went to separate classes. The rules might have been designed with good intention, but the teachers had the authority and the inclination to beat students and too many times, I was on the teaching side of that stick. I may not remember the lessons they taught me, but I have an uncanny memory for names, dates and faces. So, even though I went to elementary school over 70 years ago, I never forgot my teachers' names or their painful lessons.

Foremost, was a husband and wife team, the Salachas. He was a Polish teacher and she was a Math teacher, they would both beat me for the slightest infraction, and then there was Professor Głąb. He would not beat me, instead preferring to pull my ears, which was just as bad. It's a wonder I still have ears, at all. For these teachers, punishment was a normal part of teaching and they used it liberally to instill order (terror) in the classroom.

But, as much as I developed a disdain for the way I was treated in school, it was nothing compared to the storm that was brewing outside of my country, in Germany. Overall, however, the school must not have been that bad, because I was still a dreamer, lost in my own thoughts, as much as they tried, they could not beat that out of me.

I am sorry to say, besides my lack of interest in school, I also had no interest in helping my father to take care of horses. It's not that I was a lazy child, because I did what I was told, but I just found working with animals sickening. My father, conversely, seemed to like what he was doing, earning a reputation as a veterinarian and natural healer. I think he learned these skills from his father, my grandfather, who also worked with horses and also while serving with the Austrian Cavalry during WWI.

My father was a hard worker scratching out a meager living,

barely supporting our family. But, at least he earned enough to own a home within the City limits of Grybow, not an easy task, since the Jews were required to pay taxes greater than their gentile counterparts in our community.

The only language we spoke in school was Polish. But, being Jewish, my parents spoke Yiddish at home, a unique combination of Hebrew and German. So, I had to learn both. In fact, one of the most interesting things about the Jews throughout Europe is that they spoke the native language of whatever country they happened to be in, plus Yiddish. In many ways their connection to Hebrew through prayers, the common language of Yiddish and their strict adherence to tradition made them a nation-within-a-nation no matter where they found themselves. This is especially true, since they found themselves frequently in hostile circumstances within their host nations, both in the form of abuse from violent pogroms, and being told to leave their homes and communities sometimes after generations of living in the same place, sporadic violence or, in my dad's case, excessive taxation. Yet, no matter where they lived, they found ways to thrive, raising children that would abide by the Sabbath, lighting candles and praising God and family. I was too young to understand any of this prior to the German occupation, but Polish history and European history is replete with atrocities and hardships upon the Jews.

My hometown of Grybow is located in the southeastern tip of Poland near the foothills of the Carpathian Mountains. It is nestled along the River Biala, or the White River. The river earned its name from its fast moving water. It was far more suitable to white water rafting, or a trout filled mountain stream than boat traffic. During some months it was deceptively placid, but during others, when the snow melted it would become a raging, *white*, potentially destructive torrent.

In 1934 when I was about 8 years old I remember being on top

Boys school room.
Grybow, Poland prior to 1939.

Front row, third from the left is commissioner Leszek's son.
The professor, Jachowicz, in the back of the room.
He was also in charge of the gym and had two kids in the school.
Leon Schagrin in back left side. fig 3

of the old Roman arch bridge with my friends looking down at the raging river. We were amazed at how violent the white water was. I saw horses and cows caught in the torrent and even parts of house crashing through the rocks. It was terrible. Down below the fireman were trying to do whatever they could to help rescue the animals. Today, you might find it odd that I being an 8-year old was on top of a bridge that the raging water was flowing beneath but back then

44

The White River   fig. 1

it seemed normal enough for me to be most anywhere in our small town with my friends. Since the bridge was so huge and designed for rail traffic I did not expect it to be affected by the water below so I felt safe as I watched in horror the wild scene below.

While I was growing up my community thrived. Looking back, I think I lived in a winter wonderland. Snowfall averaged up to one meter per year, and temperatures reached and stayed below freezing degrees for an extended period. This produced snow that was 'perfect' for sports, rarely turning to slush. Conversely, the extreme cold temperature was also dangerous. So, it was critical to be prepared ahead of time. To do this, during the warmer months, firewood needed to be cut, coal gathered, food prepared and winter clothing tended. Overall, this was the type of climate that makes for strong hearty people, which is exactly what our towns' folk were made of.

During the winter, it was common to see people wearing full-length fur coats, not for show as much as for warmth, but they

The White River Swollen with Spring Floods
Notice the Crest of the Bridge   fig. 144

looked good too. It was also common to see fur hats and gloves, scarves and more. We knew how to live in the cold weather.

As you might imagine, tourists loved our climate. Because of this, tourism was enabled with good roads, fast trains and world class resorts. The closest resorts were located nearby in the famous town of Krynica. Krynica had a ski lift, making it easy to enjoy skiing down the mountain. So, our region became a favorite destination for sports clubs from the big cities and this increased traffic was good for business in Grybow. Our town supplied them with all kinds of things including basics like, eggs, butter, milk and chicken. Many a horse and carriage would travel up the hill and into the valley next door with deliveries. In its role of supporting Krynica, Grybow was a gateway town, the last stop before the resorts in the mountains.

People came from all over to enjoy a little of the region's splendor. One of the more exciting things tourists could do was take

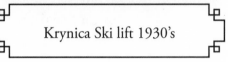

Krynica Ski lift 1930's

the ski lift to the top of the mountain and glide all the way down one of the trails towards Krynica, a full six miles! It was quite a spectacle to see. I remember seeing some of those tourists on their skis. They were easy to spot, unmistakably dressed in fancy winter clothing. Since you could glide all the way down the hill that also meant merchants going to Krynica had to take their horse and wagons up hill all the way the other direction and on the way home, these poor merchants had to go downhill, which was not nearly as elegant as the tourists on skis, bordering on comedy.

Even though I am describing my life in the 1930's, I lived in a nascent modern world, the kind that could let your imagination soar. Radios and Telephones were beginning to be deployed, and engines of all kinds powered planes, cars, and giant machines. One of the highlights of this industrial society was a high-speed train system that ran through Grybow where it slowed to climb up to its destination in Krynica, *The Lux Torpeda*. It was a national treasure, a train that could approach speeds of 115 miles per hour! Painted white over red, with our national colors, it was something that made all of Poland proud. To me, standing on the side of the tracks while the train went by, the color I saw was a blur, because it moved so fast. This train was the state-of-the-art in rail services with an interior that was something out of a fancy magazine. The result was easy access for the elite to visit the beauty of our countryside while being served in luxury. I always wished I would have had a chance to ride in one of those trains, or at least clean its windshield.

Tourism was good for business, so the local people loved the tourists. I felt like Grybow was a perfect place to grow up, except for school, because I loved the outdoors and everything it had to offer. But, Grybow wasn't just a winter wonderland, it was also a beautiful place in the warm months. During the springtime, wild flowers grew abundantly. I remember during these months stumbling across large fields of purple; wild violets with their unmistakable fragrance. Breathing deeply, I enjoyed those fields immensely. Sometimes, I would even take the time to lie down in the bed of purple and ponder the sky. Surrounding this purple quilt, the bedposts were forests filled with trees of all kinds. They had distinctive smells too. Among them, in abundance, were chestnuts and lilacs. It's no wonder I had little interest in school.

Summer brought tourists as well. Those folks were attracted to the health spas; the center attraction was the springs, rich in different kinds of minerals. They were said to be good for a variety of ailments. Others, found their own reasons to visit, like hiking and fishing. For those travelers that arrived by car, it seemed every one of them would stop at our only local automotive station to fill up with benzene. It was the smart thing to do because we were the last stop before the ride up the mountain and this is where you could find me on many a day. As the cars lined up, my friends and I, the local urchins, would beg to clean their windshields. We gladly did this with the hope their owners would reward us with some loose change, but the real reward was simply seeing all of those exotic people – the women with their cigarette holders and furs, the men confident and rich. Incidentally, this is where I first became familiar with different types of cars, including, Fords from the USA, and Tatras from Czechoslovakia, each one seemed to come from another world.

As modern as my hometown seemed, not everything was tame. We were surrounded by a vast wilderness. Many wild animals made their homes in those places. I could hear wolves howling in the

Lux Torpeda - exterior
Artist rendition interior
circa 1930's fig 5 + 154

Grybów   Jarmark w Grybowie

Grybow Jarmark pre-war
fig 6

winter or easily wander upon a snake while hiking in the summer. Sometimes, a black bear would come close to the town and create a commotion among the people and while all of this was happening on the ground, hawks controlled the skies. With their sharp talons, these perfectly proportioned birds-of-prey successfully hunted from over-head. As a child, I could easily appreciate their grace and beauty. However, the locals hated them, considering them pests, a threat to livestock. We were taught to hunt them with not one thought cross-ing any of our minds that in a few years controlling the sky would mean something vastly different.

The Jarmark

My boyhood world was simple. I played with my friends,

50

roamed the hills as much as I could instead of doing chores, and avoided schoolwork like the plague. Besides all of this freedom, my favorite day each week was Monday, the day of the weekly Jarmark, or Market Day. Each Monday the people converged to the center of our town, bringing all sorts of things to sell, creating a circus-like atmosphere.

The center of town was an open courtyard, framed at either end with two circular pools of water. Many years later, talking with my old friend Max he reminded me how those two small pools were filled with the promise of the region, crystal clear water. He was 92 at the time we discussed this, proving how memorable and mesmerizing those pools were. Evidently, I wasn't the only person who appreciated their refreshing wonders. All-in-all this was a perfect location for local commercial activity.

On market days you could see the strangest things at the Jarmark. The sellers would set up boxes and tables of goods with all kind of items for sale while horses and wagons idled nearby. The wagons filled up a large portion of the square. There were so many of them, it created a traffic jam full of work animals, manure, carriages and their keepers. My father could easily be among them. Meanwhile, for me, if this was not enough stimulation, I remember one odd fellow who sold dried mushrooms that were tied in a string around his neck. With this costume, he would dance around trying to draw attention to his strange produce. There were also Gypsies in colorful clothing selling gleaming copper ware, metal they carefully banged into useful shapes that the townspeople favored.

Our clothing was mostly handmade, there was no such thing as a department store. But, at the Jarmark you could find some finished pieces for sale. For instance, I saw leather goods in all shapes and sizes - whips, saddles, belts, shoes and boots.

As a child, I wandered around this fair with many other poor kids. All of us were looking for jobs to earn a little change. My fa-

St. Catherine's Church, Grybow
fig 7

vorite job was having a chance to turn the grinding machine on the ice cream maker, a rare treat.

This is also where I had a chance to hear and practice many languages, as well as become familiar with the cultures associated with them. Among the cultures, it was common to hear Polish, Yiddish, German or Russian. We weren't far from that strange land. As I wandered around, for some reason, I excelled in understanding all of these languages. Maybe, it was for the practical purpose of just earning a few coins? I'm not sure. Or maybe my language skills were advanced because I spoke two languages from a young age.

Grybow thrived on a combination of tourism and the Jarmark. There were other fairs, as well, in other towns. One, not far away was held in Jaslo. It specialized in horses. My father and his best friend, Tadeusz, would visit that one together, and once in awhile return with a good find on four hoofs. My father's best friend was a Polish Catholic. They got along great, earning each other's deep friendship in the cavalry during WWI. Now they lived around the corner from each other, raising families and running similar businesses.

For me, I feel what public school was lacking, I learned in the marketplace and the most important lesson I learned was that to get what you want in this world you have to be nice, respectful, willing

The Grybow Jewish Orthodox Temple
Still desecrated as of 2010.
Photo Kamil Kmak fig 8

to work hard and be able to communicate. As you can imagine, the Jarmark was one of the highlights of my week. Plus, it was a great training ground for a commercial future, far more interesting than school and its associated learning by punishment.

But, as idyllic as I may have painted an image of my little town, it was far from perfect. Most of the people were just barely making a living. The surrounding area didn't help much because of poor soil quality. Fertilizer was needed to grow agriculture, which was no easy task to gather and deploy in our mountainous region. Therefore, our produce was very limited and most had to be imported. What we did produce in mouthwatering abundance, however, was some of the best apples, cherries, plums and pears you ever tasted. I found myself up many a tree grabbing the little globes of joy and learning the hard way how I had to be quick to avoid their care-

Grosze
fig 9

takers who carried big sticks. I think running away from those tree shepherds may be how I learned to run so fast. Regardless of the poor conditions, many small subsistence farmers surrounded the town trying to grow whatever they could.

I have always believed the town of Grybow was special. St. Catherine's was the second largest church in all of Poland, second only to the one in Krakow. But the most interesting fact to me is how directly in the shadow of the church stood the small but stately Orthodox Jewish Temple, the Grybow synagogue, and how, like the church, it was built to last. When I ponder how these two pillars of ethics and morals stood side-by-side for so many years it doesn't take a big stretch of imagination to see how they must have found a way to get along.

In the Orthodox temple, the men dressed in distinctive black outfits and would chant the prayers in the ancient tongue of Hebrew, rocking back and forth, davening in praise of God. Here they would also open the Torah scroll, read from it and even sing from it, and then discuss every aspect of the text until late at night. And, when they were finished, they would go to bed, wake up the next day, and do it all over again.

As a child I wasn't very religious. So, when I walked by the Orthodox temple the thing that stood out the most to me had nothing to do with religion. Instead, it was the smells of the nearby bakery, and whenever I think of those smells, I recall the owners of the bakery and their sons, the Eisens. But the memories aren't great, because their son, and one of his friends, a boy named Reinkraut, both tried to bully me whenever I was near. These kids were a little older than me too, making this a dangerous place to be. I'm sure, from their demeanor, I was not the only one they bullied. I would move past

54

them quickly and then come upon one of two gymnasiums, these were not athletic centers as Americans consider gymnasiums, but trade schools producing carpenters and electricians. The electricians particularly interested me. At the time they were training to run the generators used by the giant saws at the local wood mill. Anybody who had an opportunity to see that wood mill would have been amazed. It had saws for every purpose, giant cutting machines, and over in the corner, working on one of them, with his lunch box by his side, was my cousin Jrichem Goldberg. The noise, productivity, and mystery surrounding the electric power, and whirling machines, hypnotized me so much so that years later I would overcome my aversion to school and earn a degree in a related field.

I liked exploring *my* town. I still remember many of the Jewish owned stores and their owners. One of the most popular was Graifman's Bakery. It was on the main street, but you could smell the bread cooking from far away, and unlike the Eisen's, I did not feel threatened to visit, on the contrary, you couldn't keep me away. I used to loiter around there for hours hoping to hold the horse of a rich man like Franciszek Paszek, the owner the local brewery. He rode a fine steed. It was a tremendous horse, tall and handsome, full of vim and vigor. If he were to show up, I would jockey with the other kids for a chance to hold the reins while he went into the bakery. For this, one of us might get a quarter Groszy (coin), just enough for a bakery treat.

The bakery was second to everyone's favorite store, Shein's Hardware. Shein's was full of functional things, and always had lots of visitors with all sorts of reasons for being there. My reason was simple; I couldn't afford anything, so I would walk around, look at the items and imagine how to use them. Maybe, one day I would have a need for a wrench or some pipe, a saw or some glue and sandpaper.

Nearby the hardware store was Mendel Fink's Beer Bar. This

is where I could find my father on occasion. When he was there, he could sit and drink beer for hours. Beer seemed to soothe the nerves of a great number of the people in the community, as the beer bar was always full. This is where he would have the opportunity to be with the rest of the men of the community, trade business talk or just idle the time away for a rare bit of personal pleasure. Whenever I tried to wander in and join them they would shoo me away, No kids allowed, Son. My father wouldn't even have been bothered, as the nearest person to the door would take care of the riffraff.

I'd leave and stumble upon the next little business, Lipczer's Clothing & Materials store. Besides the store, their family had four children, all boys. I once heard those boys were considered "one of the flower beds of the city." I am sorry to say, three of them ended up in Auschwitz concentration camp with me, the other went to Russia. All of them were older. When I was twelve, the youngest, Usher, was about 20 years old, and the oldest, Joshua, must have been 25 years old. I don't know much about the one that went to Russia. The rest were all in the Polish army prior to the war. I remember them coming home at the end of 1936 for the Jewish holidays. They showed up mounted on fine steeds with sabers dangling from their side. Being a child, all I wanted to do was to draw their swords and ride one of those steeds. I thought I *will* make a fine gallant young soldier, with gleaming buttons and adventure painted all over my face. I tried to touch one of their sabers, but they wouldn't let me. I always admired those boys. Besides being soldiers, they also had specialized bicycles designed for the mountains. I admired those bikes greatly, too! Thinking, One day I will be just like them.

Moving along the street I came upon Herbach Unger's stores. He had two of them, one that sold flour and the other that sold fabrics. It was their son, Simon, who would help to save my life in Auschwitz. And, off the main street, over on Sądecka Street, the Hirsch family had a kiosk selling cigarettes. I went to school with their son,

David, and we played stickball together. His home happened to become the demarcation denoting the beginning of the Jewish ghetto when the German occupation came to town.

My tour of Grybow would be incomplete in the eyes of a child, unless I mentioned the candy and variety store owned by a Catholic family. Their candy store was not located on the main street with the rest of the stores but instead near the river, under the bridge. I remember this well because my very close friends Moshe, Roman, and Max Blauner, three brothers, and the rest of their big family, lived nearby. If I were lucky when I went to visit them I would buy a candy. Most of the time I could not afford to buy anything, so it was torture to walk by the store on the way to the Blauner's, and since I used to eat dinner there at least once or twice a week I often thought of those candies.

My own experience as a boy was one in which I felt no particular discrimination from our Catholic neighbors nor from the community at large. On the contrary, I considered many of them my good friends. I attended The Adam Mickiewicz School. The school was directed by the esteemed Director Korzeń. We were not separated by race, nor was there any need or thought of it that I was aware of. I stayed in the back of the class, and hoped I would not be called upon or hit. As far as I remember we were just one big happy class getting yelled at equally. They punished all the kids, I never felt ostracized for being a minority. The only place my religion even came up in the context of school was when Catholic subjects were taught. During those times, the Jewish children were given the choice to be excused from class. I, of course, had no problem with this practice, as I was always glad for any reason to be excused from school.

Everything seemed normal enough for me, but I had a very limited understanding of how such subtle discrimination prepares the groundwork for more extreme practices. I was soon to learn just how extreme those practices could be.

Looking back no one would have guessed that my world was as fragile as crystal. It did not take much for everything to shatter. It started with the authority figures in my life. They became weak and helpless, seemingly overnight. Then, before long, my race was despised, ridiculed, restricted from basic essential products, like food and soap. Finally, to be killed at random, deported and concentrated like rats into ghettos only later to be treated far worse. With all of this my somewhat peripheral awareness of myself as a Jew suddenly became my most defining characteristic.

149 Hungarian Street, Grybow, Poylan

My home was a small house made of wooden logs with clay forced between the logs to seal the house from the cold. This made for a sturdy building with four rooms, an attic and a cellar. The construction method was common for the area. The only thing different about our house was a roof made of tin that made rainfall a clattering symphony.

Our home rested on a quarter of an acre of land with a small attached stable where my father kept six to eight horses, all of which were for sale, except for one my father used for his own purposes. On the opposite side of the stable was the outhouse that drained into a cesspool below ground. Luckily, we did not have to go too far in the cold of winter to use this. But, more likely we would just use a chamber pot inside the house and throw it out in the morning. The heart of the home, like most homes, was the kitchen, and the main feature of the kitchen was a brick and clay stove that doubled as a heater. We spent many nights gathering around that small heater. I was born in this home on October 30th, 1926.

When you first walked into the house there was a foyer. It provided a little bit of protection from the cold and snow, and served as a place where we could hang up our coats and take our snow-covered shoes off, so they wouldn't make the house a mess. This front entrance served a dual purpose. There were two doors on the floor, under the welcome mat, that you could pull up to access the Underground cellar. This is where we kept the food supplies. At the time there was no such thing as a refrigerator in ordinary homes, so we just placed the food into the cellar to keep it from freezing in the winter or spoiling in the heat of the summer. This did a good job of taking care of perishable food especially during the cold months. The only exception was that once in awhile when we had to buy a block of ice wrapped in sawdust from Krieger's if it got too warm during the height of the summer.

Our home had all of the amenities that were common for our area in the 1930's. My mom's pride and joy was our furniture. It was made from mahogany and was covered with an expensive French varnish. We also had our own well for water. All we had to do was turn the crank to lift the wooden bucket, and as if by some miracle, we had fresh water. This was far better than walking to a common well and carrying heavy buckets. Next to the well we planted a small garden where we grew string beans on long poles, tomatoes, radishes and onions. They grew well because we could fertilize them with horse manure and provide a little extra water from the well in the event of a dry spell.

To counter the darkness of night we had a few lamps that burned kerosene. Reading by the firelight and sitting near the heat of the stove made for a cozy home. My parents' bedroom also had a heater to keep it warm on cold nights. Inside both the heaters we would place a brick to help maintain the warmth. The wood would burn and the brick would get hot. This added an extra measure of heat for the room once the fire burned out.

On the side of the house we had an overhang to give a little protection for the carriages. This open-air room had a tarpaper roof.

We kept all of our tools under this roof, as well as enough wood and coal to last the six months of winter. The little bit of protection it offered helped keep the wood and coal dry and ready for use while extending the life of the carriage. When I was growing up I thought there was only one thing missing from our house, fruit trees. We did not have a single fruit tree, but at least one of our neighbors, the Gorskis had a few. My mother used to send me to their home to buy milk and eggs that they produced on their farm outside of town. I think to this day they still own that place. I remember this family well since I was not such a good boy and I would steal fruit from their trees causing their sons to go after me and if they caught me I caught a beating from them. This did not stop me from trying again as that fruit was beyond tempting and as you might imagine this made following my mom's orders to buy milk and eggs put me into potential harm from those same boys. Also if those boys did not catch me somehow my father would find out about my transgression and he would beat me too.

A few years before the war, the Polish government, made life for the Jews more difficult than any other race. The worst of these actions were decrees drastically increasing taxes only upon the Jews. My parents, already financially on the edge had a hard time with this additional burden. To ease the situation, they rented out one of our two bedrooms, mine. So, I slept in the family room and my room was rented to a woman named, Rachel Grubel. She was mentally impaired, but harmless, and loved to play with her cats. She had four of them. I think she was supported by her sister in the United States. The reason I believe this to be true is because she did not work, and would receive letters with lots of interesting stamps from far away in America.

My family, had relatives in America as well and every year we would receive a very large package from them. Inside we would find clothing for my parents and all the kids, plus dolls for the girls.

I used to scour that box for a toy or anything that would interest me. My parents would send them things too. One of the most precious is a still photo of my family. This is the only photo I have of them.

Spitz fig 11

Meanwhile, having a renter may have helped financially, but it was still not enough money to make ends meet. So, the local government magistrate sent an officer to our home, and he glued a certificate to each piece of my mom's precious, French varnished pieces of furniture, showing that they now belonged to the state. It was sort of a lien, to settle taxes. After the tax man left my dad explained what the certificates were, and I got so angry I ripped 'em off. I guess you could consider us as lower middle class bordering on poverty, but prior to the taxes doubling, we were living a reasonably happy middle class life.

Our horses needed lots of attention. To help manage them my dad had a dog named Spitz. His name, also, matched his breed, a *Spitz*. I don't remember how old he was, but at some point he had a strange look on his face and started to foam from the mouth. This could only mean one thing, rabies, a disease that manifests itself with uncontrollable anger and frenzy. It was scary. I noticed something was wrong so I told my father, and in response he went to the local magistrate. They, in turn, sent a policeman to our house. I knew the fellow they sent, Oleksiewcz; he lived near my friends, the Blauner's, over by the candy store. Oleksiewcz, was not a member of the Blue Police who handled crime in the city but the court police, the same ones who also beat the drum to announce the news for the city and that slapped the lien on my mother's furniture. When he arrived, I could tell by my father's and his expression that something was very wrong. I stood by my dad while they were chatting until my father asked me, Can you fetch a glass of water for our guest? I left, doing as I was told. Within a few moments, when I was out of sight, I heard a shot.

As soon as I heard the abrasive noise, I ran from the well, and saw Spitz on the ground. Red marked his white fur. His mouth quivered and then it froze. I was shaken, but I knew he was dangerous, and understood why they had to destroy him. Working dogs were a common part of the community and the rules were very strict on having them. One rule for certain was that dogs were not allowed to roam freely in the town. If they were found loose, without a master, they would be captured by the local dogcatcher and brought to the pound. This was a job, according to my father, that suited me well for my future.

The population of Grybow in the 1930's was about 6,000 people, most of whom were Catholic. However, a sizable proportion of about 2,000, a third of the population was Jewish. This Jewish population was further split between secular (not very religious) and Hassidim (Orthodox - or very strict in their traditions). The Hasidic Jews dressed very distinctively with beards, payess (side-curls), and long black clothing with fur hats, all of which set them apart from the community. As you might imagine you could find them congregating around the Orthodox temple. They spent much of their time around the temple. To them, learning Torah was a sacred task that required tremendous time and energy.

I found records showing the Jewish people arrived in this region in the 1400's. So, before my life story there was about 500 years of history. By 1930 over three million Jews lived in Poland and many more lived in Germany and throughout Europe. During this time they created a very rich and unique culture with their own language, customs, literature and more. Some might even have called the 1930's the 'Golden Age of Judaism.' But that was before the tide changed so dramatically.

Musicians would come from Tarnow once in awhile. They would bring their fiddles, accordions and clarinets and play Jewish music like the Hora and Klezmer, they would also play the Polka, a Polish classic. When my cousin Malka Schagrin got married in 1937 to Irichem I saw the musicians up close. It was a private affair held at a large house. The ceremony was Hasidic, under the chupa right outside the party place. The couple settled on the other side of Grybow near Biala Nizna. I do not know if they survived the war. Since my sisters

Malka Schagrin
Goldberg[30]
fig 160

were much younger than me they did not go to the wedding. Instead most likely my neighbor Tadeuz's wife Mary would baby-sit them.

Apart from the Hassidim, on the other side of the town, you could find the secular Jews. This is where I lived. Unlike them, we dressed like the rest of the Polish community and went to temple only on occasion. On those special occasions we would go to our own temple and one of the Orthodox rabbis would come to lead our prayers. So, even though we were not as fervent in our religious practice we embraced the same teachings. Whenever there was a happy occasion, like a bris or wedding, or a sad occasion like a funeral, it was always one of the Orthodox rabbis who would perform the service.

Religion mattered little to my father or to me. It was more important to my mom. She would enjoy the comfort of being with her friends. Whenever we went to temple the men would be separated from the women. So she would have plenty of good company.

On my street I had neighbors of all denominations, Hasidic and secular Jews, as well as Polish Catholics. For instance, the Weiss family was Hasidic. They lived nearby with their two sons, only one of whom survived, Aaron. His family sold chickens as well as delivery to the resorts in Krynica. I remember how their old horse and carriage was loaded frequently for trips up the mountain. They also sold eggs and butter. The packaging of the eggs fascinated me. It was an art. They used special wooden boxes with straw to protect the eggs. I am sure whatever they did they had to be extra cautious since the roads were very bumpy.

Once, I saw an event that seemed to harken far back in time. One day the Rabbi from Bobov came to town with an entire entourage of Hasidic Jews, a long stream of men dressed in black. It was most likely the great Ben Zion Halberstam himself coming to visit his counterpart in Grybow to discuss the Torah long into the night. When he came to town it was like a parade of Orthodox Jews. But the thing that stood out to me was how they were carrying him on a platform, like a king. It was like something out of a storybook. When they passed the giant Cathedral of St. Catherine's the procession stopped and the famous rabbi waved in recognition of the Catholic priest. In return, the priest did the same. No words, just two religious leaders acknowledging one another peacefully with respect.

This period started to unravel around 1935 when Poland began to pass laws that discriminated against Jews. The passing of these laws foretold a great tragedy. Each law was a small step onto the slippery slope of disaster. It all started with a series of laws, one worse than the next, until the rights of the Jews were negligible.

Even though the Jews were directly in the cross hairs of these laws other minorities suffered as well. To the south of my home lived a people we called Yuvanim. These were people who, according to local lore, were chased out of Russia by Ivan-the-Terrible in 1560. And even though to my family we knew them as Yuvanim in actuality they represented many sects. By the time it was over no one was untouched by terrible consequences.

Grybow

Farmland outside of Old Grybow

fig 15

Grybow

Old Grybow
fig 14

Grybow

Orthodox synagogue, far left on the street, from the nearby view of the church.
fig 13

Grybow

Grybow. Rynek.

Grybow, Poland pre-war. Children wandering in the streets.   fig 18

68

Grybow

Grybow, Poland, Mansions 1939 fig 20

Grybow

Children playing near bridge. Grybow
fig 157

Grybow

Roman aqueduct style rail bridge. Grybow 1938
fig 16

Jarmark

Jarmark w Grybowie.

Jarmark in Grybow, Poland, before 1939   fig 21

Jarmark

Jarmark in Grybow, Poland, before 1939   fig 17

Grybow Local Life Pre-War

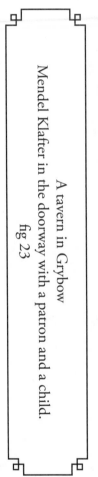

A tavern in Grybow
Mendel Klafter in the doorway with a patron and a child.
fig 23

Grybow Local Life Pre-War

Grybow Midwife's home - front left   fig 22

Grybow Local Life Pre-War

Location of Sheins Hardware (3rd from right) 1945
Next to Magistrate
fig 150

Grybow Local Life Pre-War

Krieger's Store
fig 24

Religious Life in Pre-War Poland

Church Procession in old Grybow
fig 25

78

Religious Life in Pre-War Poland

Church leader in old Grybow
fig 26

Religious Life in Pre-War Poland

Tsadik of Bobov Ben Sion Halerstama (Halberstam)
Daughter's wedding Procession
fig. 27

Religious Life in Pre-War Poland

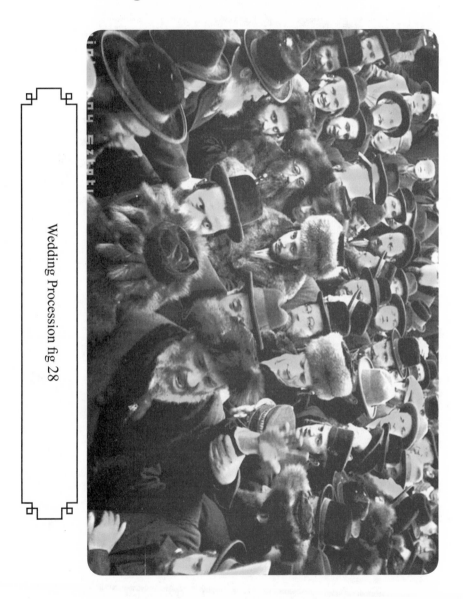

Wedding Procession fig 28

Leon's Neighborhood in Grybow

Leon's Neighborhood, Grybow Poland   fig. 151

Chaja Braw Schagrin — Hersch Schagrin

fig 133

Chapter Three

Everyday Life

My parents, Chaja and Hersch Schagrin[29], worked hard. Together they had eight children, however two died in early childhood. I don't even know their names. I was the eldest child after them and at the age of three, I became ill, deathly ill. Because of this, my mom feared her family was cursed. She could not bear the stigma of losing another child. Thankfully, I recovered, and grew up to be strong and agile, proving we were not cursed and over the next few years my parents had five more healthy children. After me, Henna came four years later, then came Golda followed her, and the twins Gitle and Toby born 1937, last, my baby brother, Naftali, arrived. He was born in September, 1939. This date, September, 1939, would also turn out to be the birth of World War II.

My dad was a horse trader and a sort of self taught veterinarian while my mom took care of the house. Together, they took care of their property, fed and cared for animals, and built a small garden, all the while six kids wandered around. My father's father, my grandfather lived nearby, too. His name was Josel, (Rojte Josel – The Red Josel – He had fiery red cheeks). My grandfather had moved from Nowy-Sacz to Grybow before I was born. My grandmother, his wife, Tobi, was the leader of the house.[28] She died when I was ten years old. I stumbled upon her lying on the floor when she died. My father was there with his brother. I was ten. They were measuring her. I think she was about 6 feet long. I asked my father why she was so long? And he told me people stretch when they die. My grandfather would receive money every month from America. He would go to his small chest, open it with a key and unwrap a leather purse to give me some change for candy or other treats.

My grandfather was sort of a veterinarian too, just like my father. The little I know about my grandfather is that he must have been good at taking care of animals, because the peasants he helped gave him his horse. He died without any warning when I was nine years old. Many people were in attendance at the funeral, including folks from all the religious and cultural denominations of the area, not just Jews. I was not allowed to go to the funeral since I was not yet 13 years old. But I followed along any way. The procession snaked through the streets, my grandfather's body laid in a buggy leading the way. Eventually it passed through the gates of the only Jewish cemetery in Grybow. Inside, the men's headstones were separated from the women's. The Orthodox Jews controlled the cemetery. A hole was dug and a plank was laid into the space. When they were ready the Chewra Kaddisha (the men that handle all of the funeral arrangements) became the pallbearers. The body was wrapped in fabric and placed on top of a plank that they all held. Then the body

84

Grandfather
Joesel Schagrin
fig 32

was placed on top of the plank within the freshly cut earth and prayers were spoken followed by the people present putting a broken piece of glass or a small pebble onto the body. When the body was laid to rest Kaddish was spoken. The people moved to the side while the Chewra Kaddisha buried the body and they had a little vodka with some cake. The reason I know all of this is that I did not stay home, instead I found myself sneaking up the side street out of sight and then through the bushes at the graveyard to the small chapel. Here I watched the whole thing and stayed out of view.

I became quickly bored with the proceedings and started to wander around the headstones with my eyes. While doing this, I saw some with dates hundreds of years old[1] and even stumbled upon one stone with two entries. I stopped cold at this one, because it read 'Schagrin' in Hebrew, my own last name. I saw my mom with a tear placing a small rock on top of the headstone. These were my two older sisters, they died very young. They were placed together in the same grave.

The thing I remember about my grandfather's death was how it was handled in an honorable way. That was the important thing, to give honor to your forefather. During this event I learned to recite the Kaddish, an ancient tradition meant to honor the dead. I did so many times over the next few years... *Yitgaddal veyitqaddash shmeh rabba...*

I loved my grandfather and when I think of him I remember the pony that used to follow him. He liked to spoil it with treats. Like a dog that small horse would stay with him all day long. I remember the treats very well, too. They were made of pure sugar. I even remember there were two types of sugary treats. One was imported, and shaped into cubes, while the other was an organic yellow bar. I liked sugar too, so I probably followed right along with the pony.

My father, Hersch, was born in 1899. I would characterize his childhood as *hardscrabble*, rough and poor. In 1917, as World War One raged, he turned 18 and was immediately drafted into the Austrian cavalry, where he continued to work with animals. He never told me about his wartime adventures, except that this is where he met his best friend, and our neighbor, Tadeusz Skrabski (see photo).

When the war was over he got married and settled back in his hometown of Grybow. And, like his own father, he cared for animals. This made him an asset to the community, many of whom were poor peasants. These peasants did their best to pay him or give him something of value in trade. I remember my dad received gifts of firewood, potatoes or wheat. I even remember one of those peasants specifically. He was a Yuvanium who lived south of us in Banica on the border with Slovakia. This poor man would come all the way to Grybow with gifts of wood and food, so my father would care for his animals. They seemed to be old friends.

I wish I could say, I helped my father all the time, but I was a kid and loved to play instead. I far more preferred to wander the fields and hills than to work with animals. I guess he could have forced me to help him more, but maybe he wanted to give me an innocent childhood instead. Or, maybe because I was sickly when I was young, he was just happy to see me run around knowing eventually I would have to grow up. No matter what, I detested working with animals. To me the animals were nothing but endless hours of hard work and I thought they were something to be avoided just like homework. It definitely did not help my attitude towards them to watch my father perform one of the more gruesome and unpleasant

86

tasks required to do his job, which was to turn stallions into geldings. This is when the testicles are removed from the male to make them more docile. It doesn't take more than one time witnessing this to never want to see another horse castrated.

Living as we did in the 1930's there was no escaping chores. No matter how many times I tell you I explored the woods, I did what I was told by my parents first. I remember once taking one of our chickens to the kosher butcher for slaughter. This sickened me too, but it made for a fine dinner. I can't put my finger on it, but I am sure my father and grandfather taught me something about horses just by watching them, and more importantly I believe the little I learned from them most probably saved my life.

I will never forget my mother Chaja's restrained beauty. She was always busy with kids or cooking and cleaning. I was never told how she met my father. All I knew is that she was raised on my grandfather Papa Joe Braw's, farm about 12 kilometers east of Tarnow, and that she had a big family that all lived there.

My father had family as well. Together, between my mom and pop there must have been close to 200 relatives all living nearby. My father's older brother Izrael was one of them. He also lived in our town and rented a house near the River Biała, over by the candy store. In his little house he raised a large family of seven sons and two daughters. Izrael was about 10 years older than Hersch. He was strong and handsome, and although I don't specifically remember all of his kids, I do remember playing with them. Only one survived, Elizer. He found safety in Russia and then later after the war immigrated to Israel.

Overall, I felt we lived in balance with many different races in a safe and civilized society. However, when I look back through the books of history, I realize war loomed over this region time and time again. But, compared with what ended up happening in my lifetime they were mere skirmishes. Before I would turn 19 the entire Jewish community would be gone and the entire region of Galicia would be almost Judenrein, a German word that means without Jews. My entire world would be destroyed, father, mother, sisters, brother, relatives, community, region and state.

It is incomprehensible to think that my entire extended family was wiped out in only three days! But this is exactly what happened in Belzec extermination camp, on September 1st-3rd, 1942. During these few days my family was not alone. 10,000 - 12,000 local Jews were also murdered using the same method. Except for a few survivors like me almost the entire region of Galicia was destroyed in this way in a period of a single year. The number of deaths is an unconscionable 600,000, close to 50,000 people per month.

From my hometown fewer than ten Jewish people survived. What is left today at Belzec has finally been turned into a world-class museum. When it was commissioned, leaders from all over the world went there and gave speeches. I was appalled years earlier when I visited this site to see its disrepair and personally helped to establish the museum.

Belzec is example of the worst humankind is capable of, it was solely an extermination center. No one was supposed to survive this hell. Only one Jewish person did survive, a grave tender. Aside from him there are only a few of the Nazi henchmen who, today, are willing to talk freely about the atrocities. I found it very hurtful as a survivor when I visited the museum to see one of these despicable men telling their story on an endless loop, over-and-over again. But I am getting ahead of myself and the story of my life.

"Your Boy Will Outlive the Entire Family"

When I was a small child I became deathly ill with pneumonia. Getting sick and eventually getting better was a huge part of my family's history, but because I was so young I can't tell you much

88

about it. However, my friend, Max Blauner, who was 8 years older than me was able to explain what happened. He told me, Leon, your oldest sister died before she even turned one year old.

When I heard this I imagine my parents were newly married and my mother was pregnant. Eventually she has her first baby, It's a girl! My parents must have been excited to show all their family and friends their precious first child and as all parents, they took turns waking up day and night to give the baby attention. Then after about a year of bonding and cuddling, she suddenly dies and even though infant mortality was common in those times, no talk of statistics would sooth a grieving parent. It must have been devastating. So, when she got pregnant again, soon after, it was another little miracle and again there is a celebration, Mazel Tov! She turned out to be healthy, living past that critical first year, where they had such bad luck. I can only imagine the baby starts to crawl and then walk and even say a few words, capturing the young lovers' hearts. When again, with little warning, at the age of only 18 months, she dies and another small casket is carried to the cemetery where the Kaddish is read giving honor to the deceased. This must have been devastating, but eventually they try again, and again she is pregnant.

This time it is a boy, and they have a bris, removing the foreskin from his penis, a Jewish tradition going back to the beginning of recorded time. During this ceremony, they bless the child, and give it a name, Leon Schagrin, that's me! I mature normally until I'm a strapping boy of three years old, when something terrible happens. Once again, sickness raises its ugly head in my home. I become deathly ill and my mom shouts hysterically toward the sky, This can't be happening again!

Doctor Kohn (pronounced Cohen), our local doctor, comes to our house and tells my parents, I do not have any miracles for your child. I have checked the boy, he is very ill, and I am afraid he may die. My parents must have been heartbroken at this news, as he continued, I have one last resort. *They* are not pretty but it's a chance. My parents knew exactly what he was referring to, shaking their heads in approval, feeling all hope is lost and with their approval, the good country doctor placed leeches on my neck, and coaxed them to latch on. While doing this he said, I hope this brings his temperature down, we will see÷, his speech trailed off. Hersch thanked the good doctor as my parents brooded and my life hung by a thread. While the leeches worked candles flickered around my home to illuminate a vigil that had begun. If the leeches would not save me perhaps prayer would. Looking back, I'm not sure if any of this helped or hurt. What I do know is that leeches were used for thousands of years as a cure for many ailments and prayer never hurts. Being good conscientious people, my parents could not solely rely upon the doctor's cure. So, they also prayed fervently to God. If the good doctor could not provide a miracle, perhaps God would be kind enough to grant life to Chaja's and Hersch's child. To achieve this goal, continuous prayers were said for me day and night. This was a grave situation.

Many years later, Max Blauner explained:

When I (Max) was about 10 years old I was at temple with my parents. It was the day that the people were praying for a small sick child. It was you, Leon, who they were praying for. It was crowded at the temple that day. The people from both the Orthodox and Secular synagogues congregated together at our temple, the Secular synagogue. This was something I have never seen before. Like always, the ladies would climb the stairs maintaining separation from the men and the women, on the lower floor would run the service, read from the Torah, chant the songs, and daven to God as they prayed fervently. The women followed, and everyone was rocking back and forth in a singsong fashion with great passion just as they were taught by their forefathers, who taught them in the traditional way of prayer. But this day was different than most because the women were agitated. I heard them crying, Why God? Why can't you let Chaja have a family? Why? Why? Why? Followed by, Please, forgive us, God. The women were making such a racket that they started to disturb the whole building, and then uncharacteristically they descended the staircase and walked through the men directly to the Torah. Together, they surrounded the sacred text. The men were shocked. Normally something like this would never be tolerated. However, the women were not to be trifled with on this day. They took charge of the service, and read directly from the Torah, while continuing their pleas, Why God? Why can't Chaja and Hersch have a family? Tears and crying continued which knew no bounds. It was a spectacle to see that I will never forget.

Prayer can be a mystical thing, especially for the fervent, like the Hassidic Jews. They have an expression, *Zol Trefen*. It means, *to will something to happen*. Here, my mom and her friends were doing exactly that, conjuring the mystical, so that I should live by the shear intensity of their prayers. When the results were positive it was considered a miracle, and the word would be spread near and far. When the results were negative it would be the will of Hashem, the will of God, and nothing could change destiny.

Looking back this was the cauldron of spirituality that I came from. My family may have been secular, but if they had a serious issue they would always defer to the Orthodox temple. Meanwhile, despite all the attention, slowly, one step at a time, I recovered. It was a *miracle* I Survived at all. I did not know it then, but it seems this was the first of many *miracles* of Survival, for me. This is why, as soon as I was well enough, my parents took an extra measure to ensure my long-term survival. They took me to the local Rabbi, and asked him if he would bless the child. They did not want to go through something as heart wrenching as this ever again. They asked the rabbi, "How can we ensure our child will have a long life?"

Tsadik Rebbi
Bobover
Halberstamm
fig 33

The rabbi told them, "To give the child the strongest blessing you need to take the boy to our spiritual leader, The *Tsadik* (charismatic rabbi) of Tyczyn. He will know what to do to protect the child and ensure him a long life." At that moment they made up their minds to take me to the famous *Tsadik*.

It was a long ride to Tyczyn, about ninety kilometers away. As soon as I was well enough, we took the horse and carriage and went on a pilgrimage to seek the widely respected prophet, himself. My mom wasn't going to take any chances with her third child.

We left early, and arrived tired from our journey. Because we were excited to see the esteemed rebbe we went right to the temple where he was busy praying. Once his prayers were completed, he came out and met with us.

After a short introduction he asked my parents, "May I spend a few moments alone with the child?" My parents agreed and I found myself alone with the venerable rebbe. To be in his presence and have his full attention was a great honor. He did not say much to me. He touched my face and placed his hands on my head as he prayed. Then he looked at my arms and asked me to stick my tongue out. Satisfied he asked me to turn around.

Finally, he spoke to me, "What do you want to do when you grow up?"

I had no idea, so I shook my shoulders and smiled, making the motion of being unsure.

He said, "All right, you may go to your mother."

When he met with my parents he intoned, *Chaja Braw, daughter of Joseph Braw of Tyczyn, wife of Hersch Schagrin.* She

92

motioned that he was correct. He continued, *Hersch Schagrin, son of Josel Schagrin of Grybow.* My father bowed as a way of agreeing without interrupting the *Tsadik. Your boy will outlive the entire family.* He paused and let them absorb the strength of this statement. Then he said something enigmatic, something that still defies interpretation today. *Be lenient with him. He might belong to a special breed of people.*

My mom was puzzled. But his eyes were convincing. They had a mystical quality of knowing something that was impossible to explain. With little emotion and much confidence he added, *You should not worry. This child was born under certain letters. The date of his birth has letters, which I can not discuss with you. These letters can only be discussed with God.*

When in the presence of a venerated *Tsadik* your mind fills with the possibilities. So from this point forward I was blessed.

Rabbi Ben Tsiyon Halberstam second from right, The Bobover Rebbe in Krynica with followers. 1937 Krynica
fig. 34

Thinking back, I wonder if this is why my dad gave me plenty of space to explore, and just be a child when I was growing up instead of making me help him?

Before long, not only did I get better, but I grew strong, and had many friends. In fact, I felt very well integrated into the whole community. I spent most of my time between the Blauners and the Skrabskis, but I also spent endless hours with one of my good Catholic friends, Adam Nalepa. He was in my same grade. Religion did not matter to either of us. All we both wanted to do was play. We did everything together. Like going to local parties, playing stick ball, spending time at the park or even going to Sokoł, in English this is translated as Falcon; a local house of culture and recreation that charged an entrance fee.

I had to ask my father for a little money and permission for this one. He let me go, a generous token considering our financial position. Incidentally, to play stickball I took my mom's old broom and cut the head off. This made a nice heavy uniform stick to play the game. Unfortunately, this can also be used as a weapon, and my mom was very upset when I ruined her broom. That stick, and others like it would prove to haunt me over the next few years.

I was so well-liked by my Catholic friends that I used to celebrate one of their holidays with them, Three Kings, otherwise known as the Epiphany. To do this, I went with the local Catholic kids house-to-house, singing religious hymns, Christmas carols. It still is a tradition in Poland, to this very day, and I enjoyed it immensely. A few of the Orthodox Jews knew of my friendships and celebration of the Catholic holiday so, needling my parents, they told them, We're not sure if your son knows he is a Jew. I am sure my father dismissed those remarks as out of hand, because he never said a negative word to me about it. Besides, he was given an edict from the *Tsadik* of Tyczyn, Be lenient with me.

When I look way back, I know I was a dreamer, and the outdoors was my *real* home and I also know that schoolwork was the last thing on my mind. As a child, I had no patience for it. Luckily, I was smart enough to associate myself with Henry Ziołko. He was a good student, and willing to help me. Without him, I would have had raw knuckles, or red ears, much more frequently. He helped me with my Math homework, or should I say; he *did* my Math homework, instead of me.

I think, when I was growing up, my favorite thing to do was to play with my next-door neighbor's kids. I felt like I lived there. I ate dinner with them frequently and stayed to all hours of the night with them. I'll never forget the graciousness of Tadeusz Skrabski, my dad's best friend or his son Marion who was my age and two daughters, Jadwiga and Janka, and their baby brother who was born in 1938. Tadeusz and I are still friends today. They also had a little brother named Marion, he was born in 1932. Our families were so close that our horses even shared the same yard. I am sorry say that Stanislaw died in 1938, (1927-1938) before the war. He was only 11 years old. I will never forget his funeral the sadness is much more profound when a child dies.

One of my fondest childhood memories was going with Tadeusz and his kids to visit two parcels of land he owned nearby. He grew cabbage on one and potatoes on the other. Since they needed to be tended and picked he would put me on his carriage with his kids and we would go out for a few hours. I loved touching the earth and it was rewarding to help him for nothing more than appreciation. Eventually, we would go back out and pick the vegetables. Eating them reinforced my appreciation for nature. I have always loved getting my hands dirty and helping out my neighbors at the same time, plus his kids were my best friends.

I will never forget the birth of my baby twin sisters. My mother was at her full term in pregnancy and she happened to be taking a bath. While in the tub the baby came out! I knew this because my mother shouted for me, "Leon, help!" When I ran to her I saw lots of blood and a baby in her arms. I helped her as best as I could but she did not want my help instead she said, "Run, run right away and get the akuszerka (midwife), Ms. Olszewska. Tell her to come immediately."

I was scared. I ran as fast as I could to the midwife's home and when I arrived I said something that makes me laugh to this day, "Please come to my house right away. My mother has one baby in her arms and who knows how many more will come?" It was 1937. I was 10 years old.

After things were cleaned up the next day we celebrated with a little cake. This same old lady delivered me when I was born. The babies slept in my parent's bedroom.

I didn't have to be best friends for acquaintances to make a life or death difference in my life. For instance I knew a fellow from school, Zbigniew Mordarski and although I don't remember much about him, what I will never forget is the kindness of his cousin, Victor Mordarski. Before the war Victor (Wiktor) was a local attorney in our town. Later however, during the occupation he was considered a menace to that new authority. You see, he was someone that could fully understand the depravity of the situation and do something about it via the law, with his voice or in politics. For this, he was sent to a political indoctrination center. The center he was sent to was an almost unknown place to the world prior to WWII. It was toward the west of Poland conveniently located along main supply routes, Oswiecim.

The entire region was once owned by a Hassidic Jew[2] but the Germans converted it to a series of concentration camps. Once completed these would become the largest concentration camps in the world. Victor became one of the first prisoners there. You can tell because his tattoo had a low number. And somehow, he also became a blockmaster for its infirmary. Being in this position, even as a prisoner, gave him some access to camp records, and allowed him to help out the other prisoners with passes and medicine. It turns out that is exactly what he did for me, in my most dire need. Without Victor, I surely would have perished, on more than one occasion. There should be a memorial for him in Auschwitz for all of his effort. One of the highlights of my preparation for this book was finding a couple of photos of him, saved by his family who are still in Poland.

I had lots of friends. I remember many of them like it was yesterday. Henry Ziołko, the son of the train signaler, and Mendel Scher from Siołkowska Street. Mendel was one of the first Jews to be taken hostage from Grybow. And Simon Unger, who ended up with a tattoo in Auschwitz, that was three numbers behind me 161747, I was 161744. The Blauner family, Adela, Hudes, Thema, Romek (Roman), Moshe (Morris), Shia, and Hiam, and Max the eldest. They lived on Węgierska Street or Hungarian Street near Biała Wyżna. They were a big happy family whose father was also in the horse and carriage business like mine.

Because I was only twelve prior to the German occupation, my knowledge of the world was very limited. But up the street, at the Blauner home, Max, the eldest, was 20. He was born in 1919 and his impressions as a survivor, years later add other dimensions to my own understanding of my hometown.

Max Blauner: *I used to play with the local kids, too. And once in awhile all my friends would get together and play a big soccer game with the non-Jewish kids. In fact, it took most of the town's kids to get a soccer game going, and when they could get a game, the teams always ended up Catholics vs. Jews. But, the thing that stood out was that every single time we played together there would be a fight along ethnic lines. It did not stop the next game, as they all liked soccer, there was just no way around it. We would play hard and fast, and invariably someone would get bothered leading to a*

97

small fight.

The older Jewish kids were all part of the local Zionist organizations. And in our small town there were three of these organizations. I belonged to Honer Hazim, a progressive youth movement. Others belonged to Poalej Syjon, (Youths of Zion) and a third was Ha'shomar Ha'tzair, the Working Organization. There were very few Jewish youths who were not organized into at least one of these groups. My group was politically right leaning and I was able to grow and learn with them for only six or seven years before the occupation. They were training me to be a scout, as well as, to live in Israel. I was learning about far away lands, full of deserts, mountains, oceans, and a sea that is so salty nothing can live in it. A few of my Hebrew schoolteachers were in this same organization with me as well. All of them had visited Israel when they were young. I always enjoyed listening to their far away stories, too. In many ways, I was playing army, but the only talk of war, was the looming war with the Arabs in that part of the world, which we all thought was imminent. No one planned on or expected the Germans to rise up as they did, nor did we portend anything threatening to our fellow Polish citizens.

Kids grew up quickly in Grybow; I guess being poor does that to you. So when Max was 13, he left to become a tailor. The shop was in Nowy-Sacz, so he had to live there, away from his family for an extended period of time. This was the custom of the time. When a child was old enough, if he was also lucky, he would become an apprentice of someone in a profession, learning from the bottom up. All kids that were apprenticed worked the long hours required of the trade, for little or no money, just to learn something useful. By the time he turned 20, and his apprenticeship was over, he moved to Krynica, started his own business as a fine tailor, and had a girlfriend. It seemed he was well on his way to a successful career.

One bright fall day everything changed. I was just about to

turn thirteen years old. This was the year I was studying the Torah for my Bar Mitzvah. I found my Jewish studies as tedious as I did my ordinary schoolwork. Perhaps, I would have appreciated both more fully had I any indication that very soon education would be denied to me. Worse, the rest of my race would be marked as no longer considered fully human.

The war between Germany and Poland arrived as an announcement by my father, "We must pack. We are leaving our home immediately and moving to Papa Joe's farm." Soon after we were packed and on the road. The roads were dusty and chaotic. I saw many people with a look of panic in their eyes. Entire families passed by us with horses and carriages some shouting ominous stories of rape and killing. Most were headed east. Only the roads in the towns were finished all the other roads between towns were just dirt.

Within the next 30 days, World War II was in full swing, and Poland became ground zero for the initial German attack. Once we were out of harms way, at the farm, my father left to report to his unit in the Polish cavalry. When he left we settled in quickly at the farm. My mom was a full nine months pregnant. The apples on the trees were still green. It would not be until late October, or early November when they would ripen.

Shortly after we moved in, the Jewish holidays were upon us. To pay homage to the holiday I remember going with my grandfather, just the two of us alone, to a neighboring community. We did this so he could pray with his friends. But, I'm sure they also spoke about the foreboding future. Since he lived in the countryside, there was no temple for prayer. So, instead, we went to a friend's home, where we met the other country people. I barely remember this stay with my grandparents. It was so brief. What I do remember, however, was seeing all of my mom's family. If I had known this would be the last time I would ever see them, I am not sure if I would have acted differently.

Polish Cavalry - no match for the mechanized Germans fig. 36

Chapter Four

The Short War

Before my father left to seek out his cavalry unit, I saw him neatly dressed in his uniform. At that moment, to me, he looked like a hero. I remember it as if it were yesterday because I was gazing long and hard not knowing if I would ever see him again. After an extended goodbye, he left. At first I was sad, but my grandfather was very nice and soon I was busy playing. Only a week or so later my father returned, riding tall, astride his horse. He was full of life. My family was both elated and relieved to see him.

Thankfully for us, the war was over before he could even find his unit. Poland was completely overwhelmed by the German

Painting of German tanks on the move in Poland fig 37

army in less than a month and surrendered on October 6th, 1939 at Kock. Our army offered resistance without hope against the massive 'blitzkrieg' that Germany mustered. Years later, I learned, the pride of our army, *The Polish National Guard*, moved east away from the German advance instead of west towards it. They ended up retreating all the way to Russia where they expected a safe haven until they could figure out how to counter Germany's might. These were very confusing times. As Russia saw what Germany was doing, it swarmed to counter the offensive but then something happened that no one expected. Stalin and Hitler made a non-aggression pact, a peace treaty called the Ribbentrop-Molotov pact just prior to the invasion. Russia may not have been ready for war with Germany, so a treaty was convenient. Meanwhile, they did not know what to do with the Polish army. Regretfully, instead of enlisting the remainder of them to help attack Germany, the Russians first held them in

Soviets Entering Poland September 17, 1939 fig 38

a makeshift detention camp and then, before long, executed all of them. In this way 14,589 of Poland's finest troops were destroyed in Katyan. It was covered up for years.[3]

Soon war would be in full swing. The Russians attacked Poland on September 17th of the same year. It was like a stab in the back. One thing was certain; even though there was a treaty, the Russians would never allow Germany to be uncontested. The ideologies of these two countries were diametrically opposed. In many ways this is why the Jews were tortured. They were grouped with the Russian Bolsheviks as the Germans most hated enemy. The Nazis were shaping the war to surround their ideal of *herrenvolk*, or a master race, with the pure Germanic Aryan features being the ideal, and everything else to be destroyed like the Jews and Bolsheviks, or turned into workers for the State like the Slavs. The Church continued to operate under this regime and was either cowed into submission or complicit by their silence.

While all of this was happening on a grand scale, at the farm where my family and I waited on events, the danger seemed to subside enough for us to consider returning to our home in Grybow. In fact, during this time the only thing close to war I heard, was my mom screaming. Her water broke and she gave birth to my baby brother, Naftali. He was born at my mother's parent's farm outside of Tarnow in September, 1939. And with his birth, what should have been a time of great joy and celebration was instead filled with dreadful anticipation.

After a few days the baby was settled, and we made ready to return home. Luckily, we waited though, because right before we left, something happened I *will* never forget. Directly in front of the farmhouse, on the highway about 200 yards away, my entire family and I stood dumbfounded as the largest military movement of people and machinery I have ever seen crossed our very doorstep. On that day, I saw a parade of horses with men in full uniform flanked by single seat motorcycles buzzing along. This was quickly followed by the clumsier heavy-duty military bikes with sidecars that could carry three soldiers. Those three soldiers per car stood out with red stripes emblazoned on their pants. Following up in the rear were two columns of foot soldiers and mules loaded with supplies. There were hundreds of soldiers neatly dressed, each holding a rifle. The line stretched for miles. That day everyone and everything was moving east, towards the new border. I'm glad we were not on the road when

Three Man Motorcycle. fig 41

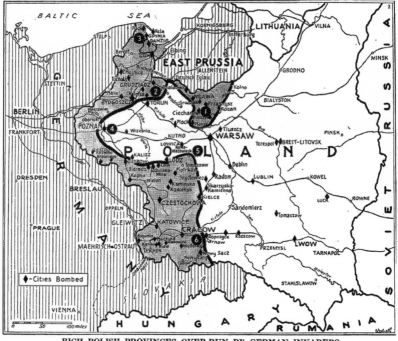

RICH POLISH PROVINCES OVER-RUN BY GERMAN INVADERS

The German armies driving into Poland extended their gains yesterday in various zones, but the most dramatic struggle was taking place north of Warsaw (1). There East Prussian forces were reported to have driven within twenty-one miles of the capital.

In the Torun zone (2) other forces pushed across the Torun-Brodnica road. This operation was said to have effected a liaison between the Polish Corridor troops and those driving west from East Prussia.

Farther north, the Westerplatte, munitions base in Danzig Harbor (3), was surrendered to the invaders by a small force of Poles who had been holding out since the war began.

In the Poznan region (4) the Germans were closing in on the city of Poznan from three sides. They were within eighteen miles of that center after the capture of Oborniki.

Another advance was made by the forces that have conquered the Silesian industrial region. They drove past Lodz (5) to Rawa-Mazowieck (5). In the Far South, near the Slovak border, Nowy Sacz (6) and other towns were captured.

The German fronts are shown approximately by the heavy lines enclosing the shaded areas on the map, drawn on the basis of a special dispatch to THE NEW YORK TIMES.

New York Times 1939
fig. 161

they descended like locusts.

Very soon these troops were gone. I didn't know what to make of it. One day I went to bed in Poland, and the next day I woke up in Germany. I knew Poland was an area that had often seen its rulers changed by the fortunes of war, but I thought the people just kept doing what they normally did, work. War was for big people, generals and politicians.

It was only a little more than twenty years since Poland

gained independence from the Austria-Hungarian Empire. Now, suddenly, most of it belonged to Germany and the rest to Russia. Since I was in the German zone I thought I would become a German citizen. However, I had no clue at the time that the German laws declared that all Jews had lost their citizenship. It would not be long before I understood we were in a country that did not want us.

When we left Grybow, before the war, we were not alone. Among the others who left were many of the town's leaders. One of the first that I knew who did this was our family doctor, Dr. Henryk Kohn.

He went east to Russia with his brother, Emil, leaving his large home near the park abandoned. Soon, his house would become the office of the local Judenrat or Jewish committee and it would be their tortured job to abide by the dreaded Gestapo.

We, on the other hand instead of leaving for good, returned to our home ahead of the new regime and expected things would return to normal soon enough.

For me, things were so normal that before I knew it I was back in school, bored, miserable, and staring out the window dreaming. And again, once in awhile, the teacher would slap my hands with a ruler to help me maintain my attention on the lesson. As usual, this inspired me to hate school even more. Meanwhile, my dad went right back to taking care of the horses. We weren't gone for long. I guess it was as if we went on a short vacation.

We returned home to the same place with a new baby and a fresh perspective except for the nagging thought of what would happen next.

Because my baby brother was just born, according to Jewish tradition he needed to enter the covenant with God by having a bris (cutting the foreskin from the penis). Normally, this would be a celebration and everyone would be invited, but because of the fear surrounding the occupation of Poland, my parents did this in secret so none of us saw the joyous occasion.

Eventually, the Germans entered our town. From my perspective it was a painless, almost festive event that took place with a sense of civic pride combined with disbelief. First, I saw musicians on horseback. They were followed by Tyrolean Mountain Brigades, from Austria, who were wearing brilliant feathers in their hats. Like most boys, when I saw this, I fantasized about being a soldier one day, myself. I also hoped that the prized German culture would now extend to our poor nation and my town. How foolish this thought turned out to be. The only imposition I recall was the requirement to billet half a dozen soldiers at our house. All this meant was they would set up their tents in our yard, and we would give them food. We did not have to cook the food, just bring it to their field kitchen and let them prepare it themselves. Having soldiers at our house must have been a burden, especially for my mother with a newborn baby but for me it only meant a chance to talk with real soldiers and, if lucky, be allowed to handle their rifles.

After spending some time among the soldiers in my yard, they gave me no reason to dislike them; on the contrary, they were very likable and went out of their way to be respectful to my family and make friends with me, besides they frequently gave me candy. One of them even knew my father from the last war. They were both in the Austrian cavalry. From my perspective, their visit with us seemed less like an invasion and more like a special occasion. I would even have to say that I genuinely liked them. They seemed like good enough fellows to me who took care of their horses and equipment, and since much of it was shiny and new. Their equipment was an endless source of interest for me.

It's great to be twelve years old. I could easily walk among the soldiers. They spoke German, so I could easily understand them. I saw nothing foreboding or ominous in their stay at all. The only clue of their disdain for my race was the way they treated our temple. This, they turned into a stable, as soon as they arrived. Because of this, I should have felt infuriated, but at the time, I did not comprehend the magnitude of what they were doing.

The only place I heard alarming reports was from the remote and sparsely populated hills and mountain regions surrounding my community. These hill people created the biggest panic. But, it was hard to tell if they were just worried about rape and pilfering or if it really was happening. In fact, for much of the occupation it was hard to know what or whom to believe.

One small thing that intrigued me though, was the glimmer on the soldier's belt buckles. It seemed incongruous with warriors. I saw a phrase written in German surrounding a symbol of their state. The symbol was a kind of windmill looking thing called a swastika and the whole thing was made of stamped brass. Since the swastika was something I had never seen before, I could not associate it yet with anything evil. However, what drew my attention were the simple words, *God mit uns* or God is with us. It was just another reason to think we must have nothing to fear; after, all we believed in God too. And not just any God, the Jews believed in the same God as the Germans, they just approached the traditions differently. Anyway, to me, these must be good men who understood the word of God. They

God is with us
fig 39

must have been taught good versus evil and right versus wrong, just like us.

Looking back, I realize this belt buckle was a Trojan horse proclaiming innocence, but intending something sinister. I think it was deceiving for both the wearer, giving him visions of God on his side, and the victim thinking these are God fearing people.

1940

In early 1940, a few months after the invasion, the Tyrolean soldiers left us and moved eastward towards the Russian front. I never saw them again. I wish they would have never left because what replaced them was a nightmare. When these new troops arrived, they set up three distinct police forces. First was the *Blue* or Polish police. One of our local police officers from before the war became its commandant. His name was *Kubala*. I remember him well. His son, Bolek went to school with me. I remember when I was young he condescendingly asked me to clean his boots as he stood in them. The thought of doing anything for him was disgusting so I turned my nose and ran away. The rest of the staff for the Blue police did not come from my hometown but from other territories within Poland that were already Germanized. They adopted Nazism and the new regime readily, even with zeal. After the war all of these men would be considered collaborators and treated harshly, but as the occupation was just beginning, they were extremely dangerous,

especially Kubala because he knew many of the Jews by name and he knew where they lived.

The second police force was German. It began with the foot soldiers, but was later augmented, and then replaced by the SS Gestapo, (Geheime Staatspolizei or Protection Squadron), the official secret police of Nazi Germany, wearing their signature tall black leather

Jack Boots fig 40

108

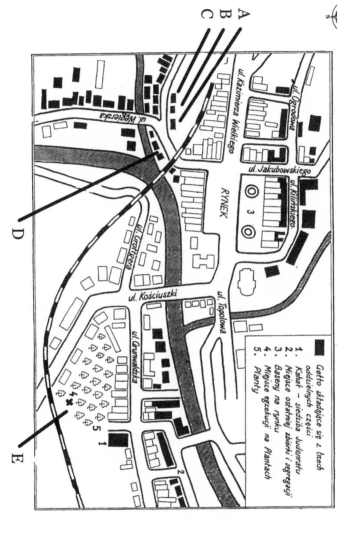

Open ghetto of Grybow 1942, Grybów. Studia z dziejów miasta I regionu fig 43

A - Schagrin Home   B - Mother's Brother   C - Goldman   D - American Shot   E - Judenrat Execution

A
B
C
D
E

RYNEK

ul. Ogrodowa
ul. Kazimierza Wielkiego
ul. Węgierska
ul. Jakubowskiego
ul. Kilińskiego
ul. Grottgera
ul. Kościuszki
ul. Topolowa
ul. Grunwaldzka

Getto układające się z trzech oddzielnych części:
1. Kahał – siedziba Judenratu
2. Miejsce ostatniej zbiórki i segregacji
3. Baseny na rynku
4. Miejsce egzekucji na Plantach
5. Planty

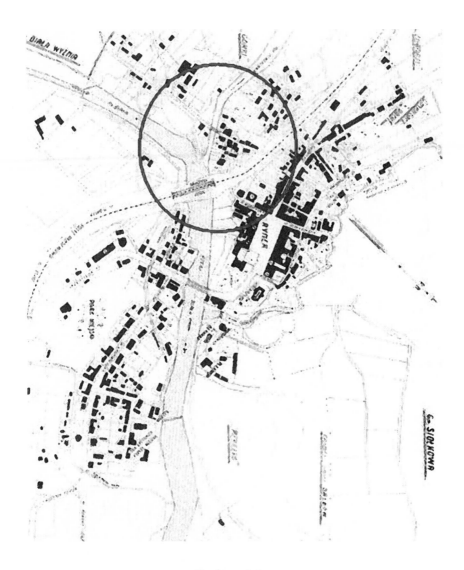

Grybow Map
Dashed line is railway.
Area in the circle is Leon's neighborhood (near the railway bridge).
Black polygons are buildings.
fig 44

jackboots. Those boots were common back then but today they are associated with totalitarianism. This police force was considered the internal police or enforcers of the Nazi ideology. The Gestapo characterized themselves as the hammer of Nazi ideology, It did not take a long time before I came to the realization that if they were the hammer, it also meant that we, the *Jews*, must have been the nails. These troops always worked side-by-side with the Blue police.

If this was not enough police presence in my little community, the new regime also created a Jewish committee to oversee a 3rd police force, the Jewish police. In this way they made the Jews themselves responsible for carrying out the harsh laws imposed upon them.

The war was just beginning. Poland was conquered and Germany was at the throat of Russia. The British and the French declared war on Germany and thinking the Russians would follow were surprised when they learned Russia had made a treaty with Germany instead. Because of this the Russians marched into Poland and took sizable amounts of territory. These years were marked by deprivation and hunger bordering upon starvation for my family and our community while my father and the rest of the Jewish men toiled with backbreaking menial work the Germans celebrated their victory. The only good news was that we were all still living together at home. And as long as we were home, we could take care of each other and pray together. So, we all prayed the same thing, God, please make this war short.

Even though the Jews were marked for especially harsh treatment by the Germans it was immediately apparent that the Nazis intended to first eliminate any political, intellectual or cultural resistance by the Poles themselves. As far as I could tell, their plan was to methodically decimate the leaders of Poland and reduce it to a slave state. Russia was clearly in their sights too but that was still a year or more away. My own history teacher was one of the first to be singled out and killed.[4] My friend's cousin, Victor Mordarski, the attorney, was deported. Individual by individual the leadership of the town was eliminated. The lucky ones escaped before the occupation. But nothing was certain. Even the people who left on their own were not sure that where they would end up would be a safe place. Our mayor was one of those that left of his own accord. He was promptly replaced with a German collaborator, as was the magistrate of the court. I have no idea what happened to either of them or their families.

After the soldiers arrived, my formal education ended. Jewish children were no longer allowed to go to school. My first reaction was relief. I no longer had to put up with getting my hands slapped or the long dreary hours learning things that were keeping me from playing outside. But it did not take long for my parents to properly orient my understanding to a sense of outrage. Suddenly, I realized I was not even worthy of an education in the eyes of our new rulers and uncharacteristically, I think this was also the first time I began to truly appreciate an education.

Being excluded from learning did not stop at the public school. The religious preparation for my Bar Mitzvah also ceased as well as any religious ceremonies at either of the Jewish temples. Now, I understood clearly that using the temple as a stable was the Nazi way of showing exactly what they thought of us. We were less wanted than their horses.

As the occupation wore on, edict after edict was passed. It was all bad news for the Jews, some worse than others. There was nothing we could do to satisfy those in power. They had made up their minds that we were a dangerous pestilence in their midst.

The stranglehold on my community took its course slowly, one step at a time. I believe, in some ways my survival depended on this slow, steady, decline. It was the slow speed of these worsening events that also toughened me up and gave me experience to handle

112

the terrible events that would happen next.

The German occupation turned out to be vastly different than anything in the past; for the Nazis this was a war against the Jews. Unlike war where there is a victor and the defeated their intentions were far more sinister. I clearly understood, even as a young child of twelve, that we could not withstand this poor treatment for long. We were sliding towards a tragedy of epic proportions. We were on a collision course with one of the worst crimes ever to be committed by humankind. The only hope would be rescue and it had to be soon.

It seemed hopeless; the world news was all bad. The British were defeated at Dunkirk and forced to evacuate the mainland of Europe while France fell to the Germans in a quick defeat. Germany was gaining territory by leaps and bounds. They seemed unstoppable. The only place it began to unravel was when they attacked Russia causing a two front war. Russia at first almost succumbed just like France but slowly with massive casualties it turned the tide.[5] Meanwhile, we were trapped behind enemy lines.

It is hard to believe, but all of the initial restrictions although strict were relatively mild. Since they didn't separate my family and we still found ways to fill our pot with something to eat. Plus we were already poor, so we were used to living on very little and did not expect much. It was not until massive numbers of the Gestapo arrived in Poland that things turned toward the unspeakable. With those troops the Germans established bases in every county within Poland, including mine. Once securely in place all the Jewish businesses were taken forcefully and our misery accelerated.

For me, luckily, I was too young to report to work. The cut-off age was 13. This gave my family a lifeline, as I could use my time at home to plan how to find food and then go and get it at night.

As much as the Nazi occupation was pressing us another even more immediate and ominous killer also was brewing, winter. So, even though the German's were a nagging problem, it was winter that demanded our immediate attention, and the winter of 1940 was shaping up to be brutal. Temperatures were reaching dangerously cold levels for extended periods of time. This caused us to suffer from the cold not just the hunger. And worse, as the Germans were also caught in the cold they compounded our misery by an edict requiring the Jews to give up all their fur coats. Without warm fur, we were feeling naked, in the dead of winter. That year the cold would go deep into our bones making us miserable and subject to sickness.

Regardless of the weather, my father and all the Jewish men reported to the area outside the magistrate's office every morning for his daily orders. Here they assigned him jobs. I remember his job was to remove the snow and keep the roads clear. To do this he used our horse. They made him work from early in the morning until sunset. However, in doing this work he was able to still do what he did best, work with animals. And for my family this meant a lifeline to his horse and travel by me at night. Having access to the horse became a key part of our near term survival.

Within a few months the Gestapo established an open ghetto. This meant that the Jewish townspeople were cordoned off to a limited area. It was against the law to venture 1 kilometer beyond this border. Even though there were no walls or fences to enforce these policies I saw posters warning that Jews were under the threat of death if they went beyond the perimeter. In fact, at this time, you would never want to be on your own because the Nazis or their collaborators were always lurking in the shadows. You would never know who might inform upon you and tell the Nazis or worse, if you were caught alone, even within the ghetto, humiliation, beatings or death were not uncommon. Since most of the Jewish homes in the town were bunched together this became the perimeter of the ghetto. My home was inside of this boundary. The place I grew up became a prison, and all my family and the entire Jewish community its prisoners. None of us could escape. We spoke about this but had little choice. We had nowhere to go that we were sure we would be safe.

Every time the Gestapo came to town they would terrorize our neighborhood and demanded hostages, goods or money. One time they came unannounced and parked their Mercedes car by the brewery. It was about 1 kilometer from my home. They walked from

Star of David Armband
fig 42

there into the ghetto. This day was different because one of them hid a sub-machine gun under his civilian clothing. Later that same day I heard about a man who was just standing in his yard, minding his own business, when he was gunned down for no reason.

In another gruesome event the Gestapo walked into a house at the edge of the ghetto and without warning, started shooting. This was the home of the Hirsch family and everyone was inside including my friend, David. When they entered he ran, flushed out of his home, he ran for his life. It was to no avail, He was chased and caught near the railroad track and killed.

I don't know of any reason they raided this house other than blood sport, because they did not need a reason to torment the Jewish population. David's blood spilled on the tracks that day and they left him for dead. Here he remained with no burial. Eventually, nature ran its course. His entire family, perished on that day. This would not be the first or the last time the Gestapo acted with sadistic impunity.

My world did not change overnight. The rules were added one at a time like logs loaded on the back of a horse. My family and I felt abandoned as their hold tightened. Another poster notified everyone, *It is forbidden to help the Jews under penalty of death.* This made the impossible situation even more impossible. Ostracized from most of our Polish friends and the community, it did not take long before we were reduced to paupers. The only thing left we could do was to steal.

Photos of me at the time show a boy who looks Germanic with Nordic features and close-cropped blondish hair. These provided a kind of protective coloration. In fact, I looked more Aryan than most of the Germans. One month after the occupation began I turned 13, October 30th, 1939. I initially avoided getting an armband, and wasn't about to look for one even though I was required. Instead, I choose to ignore it. I knew that an armband would mark me for easy abuse. But if I was caught not wearing it, I could also have been severely punished. Weighing my options, I decided to take my chances with my combined natural Aryan looks and knowledge of the German language. Soon, it would be tested and my life would depend on it. So, I took my chances and found that I was able to move about relatively freely, more so than most of the other Jews, including my father. This limited extra measure of freedom enabled me to both gather items for my family to eat as well as gain critical access to current news and information.

I knew my community was being harmed daily, but there was not much I could do about it. It would have been suicide to fight back. However, the little I did do for my family to survive made a big difference, even though looking back it was so very little. If you

116

have ever felt the pangs of extended hunger, you may understand just how little. We needed outside intervention to help us and needed it quickly. The war seemed to stall on our doorsteps.

As the occupation ground on, the community did rally against the Nazis in a limited way. What they were able to do was set up a warning system, to alert the Jews when the Nazis were coming to town. It was a simple system. Somebody would whistle in the hills above our town at Przedmieście and when we heard this it meant, The Nazis are coming! Over time this alert drove the local police crazy. They could not figure out where it was coming from. Most probably it came from a few different people who were doing it, and if they were caught surely there would be hell to pay. When we heard this makeshift alarm we scattered to hide.

Jews could not go to the market; Jewish farmers couldn't farm and Jewish businesses and livelihoods were taken away. The only way left for us to get some food was to smuggle it at the risk of getting caught.

The biggest exception to our misery and our most important lifeline was the mercy of a few very brave Poles. Some of the local people acted with the greatest of courage and humanity by giving life-sustaining food and/or shelter to Jews. These folks and others like them risked their lives. They have become known to history as The Righteous. For all time they deserve to be honored. My family was blessed by one of these good souls too. Our savior lifeline was our neighbor, Tadeusz Skrabski and his family. He would bring greatly appreciated food to our home every week late in the evening, or he would send one of his daughters, Janka or Jadwiga. I don't know if my family could have lived through these tough times without their support. That is how desperate our situation was.

I know of only one Jew who was hidden in my area by the Poles. It was in the Przedmiescie area. He was a converted Jew who was married to a Polish girl. I remember him well because his last

117

name was the same as the one taken by Hitler, "Fuhrer." He was a teacher but not at my school. The family was well-known. They had a big house and a hotel in the downtown market square.

All the time I spent in the backwoods as a child paid off during the occupation by expanding my world beyond the ghetto. I carried no papers, wore no armband and looked and spoke perfect German. It wasn't getting caught that I worried about but getting caught and also being discovered as a Jew.

I would take my sack with me and fill it with whatever I could get. In the beginning of the occupation I could visit my relatives outside of the ghetto and family friends who lived outside of town. One of those cousins was Chaim Schagrin who lived in Stroze and had a small farm.

Once they were also brought into the ghetto this valuable source of nutrition dried up so the only other people I could rely upon were the non-Jews still living in the countryside. I am glad that my father did so many good deeds before the war making it possible to ask these people to help. It was all Underground and surreptitious so I was always alert and on the edge. Somehow, I always found something to bring home. But, I had no time to gloat; the situation was far too serious. So, as my father continued to do forced labor, I planned what might be possible to bring back that night. It was a good thing we still had our horse, wagon and sled. As long as my dad used the horse during the day to help the Germans, hopefully, they would not realize I used it at night.

Unexpectedly our home was searched by the police. It was as if a wolf entered the hen house. Armed men were tossing things around looking for contraband. We collectively cringed when they showed us what they were looking for, a bar of soap. Kubala held it tightly while yelling with his veins popping out of his head. "This is forbidden. You know the law. Jews are filthy swine not allowed to own soap."

118

What could we say? I'm sure he saw my mom holding a baby. Even if we didn't wash, a baby is endless work, and soap is the most basic of needs to do it.

He continued to berate us, "Where did you get this?" Silence followed his barrage. He put the soap in each of our faces to see if by moving closer he could intimidate us into figuring out whom to punish.

The next thing he did was really alarming. Our neighbor and my dad's best friend was arrested and charged with helping the Jews, a crime punishable by death. Because of a single bar of soap, Tadeusz Skrabski was forcefully taken away from his family, and his home. We all stood aghast, while they took him away.

My baby brother was crying and everyone was frantic. We were deeply concerned, but the fear in my family had another dimension. If he were forced to tell the authorities something about my actions gathering food each night, then I would be arrested too, or worse. We felt hopeless. There was nothing we could do.

As the days wore on, his chances of ever returning were slim. At the time, I did not know of a single instance where anyone taken would ever return. Many dreary days elapsed not knowing what was happening to him or going to happen to us. I felt abandoned.

About ten days later, Tadeusz walked home. It was like a dream, to see him return. It was nothing less than a miracle during these times. He was alive and well, except for a large bandage on his hand. He looked stoic, but his eyes were smiling. Then he spoke to us and we felt at ease, I told them nothing. The Nazi interrogators had broken all the fingers of one hand, one at a time. That night I thanked God for bringing him home safely and slept as well as I could, knowing we were safe, if at least for one more day.

Another time my father directed me to visit a peasant he knew so I could pick up a calf. I did as I was told. It was a long journey through the mountains, but I got the calf. The way back was difficult because the calf was so ornery I had to fight the beast the whole journey home. Other peasants helped us as well. I am glad my father treated them well in the good times. My daily life was reduced to finding a little food for my family to eat each night. We did whatever we had to do to survive including trading our clothing for food. We were not alone. All of the Jews were becoming paupers in their own homes by this time. Everything we did to survive was illegal. But given the choice between punishment or starvation. It wasn't much of a choice.

Our livelihoods and freedoms were taken away. The situation was becoming hopeless and the restrictions were wearing us all down. My poor brother and sisters were wasting away, and my mom was becoming despondent. Worse, I was beginning to realize our suffering was just beginning. I tried my best to bring things for

Barefoot Gypsies
Circa 1939 from Bagnowka website
fig 31

my family, and even though they were thankful we all knew it was never enough.

1941

The greater war beyond my community raged on. In June 1941, Germany broke the Non-Aggression Pact with Russia and began to invade in force. As the war was raging it created a perfect smoke screen for the Gestapo to begin the systematic destruction of the Jewish community and all of its inhabitants. This is when mass deportations and large-scale killings started.

The first murders I saw were simply by looking through the window of my own home. It was my neighbors, Mr. and Mrs. Bransteter. Soldiers came to their door demanding, "We are here to take your furs." Being from Newark, New Jersey, USA, Mrs. Bransteter did not feel she was under the same rules as the local Jews after all she was an American. When confronted she waved her passport at the soldiers and pleaded, "Ich bin American." In response, they dragged her and her husband out and shot them both. The sound still rings in my head. They fell lifeless as my heart sank.

One night I went to the Dominican monastery in Biała Niżna. It is located near the river about 2 kilometers from my home. It was run by an ancient order of nuns who were given this property in the 19th century by its last rich land owner. I'm sure it is still there. Because of their riverside location they had set up a water wheel and used it to grind flour. I reached the monastery in the dead of night and, cautiously, knocked on the door. It was very late so there was a long pause. The Mother Superior creaked open the door. She was equally cautious as she opened it. That is when she must have seen the desperation in my face. Without talking she took mercy on me and gave me both flour and oatmeal. Then in parting she warned, "Be careful, they are watching us too." My family was eternally grateful for the kindness of these courageous nuns.

The war to the east seemed to stall at our doorstep. The Germans were waging a full attack on Russia. Huge numbers of soldiers with their related war materials were engaged in the battle. Many of them passed through our town on their way to the Russian front. I remember one group of Italian troops, Nazis non-the-less, whose uniforms were clean and fancy. I distinctly remember their polished boots. A few months later I saw these same fellows again, back from the front, but this time they were demoralized and disarmed. They were now building roads, a mere shadow of their former glory.

And around the same time, in December, I saw a newspaper from Krakow. It reported, *The Germans were winning in the war with Russia.* This was in contrast to what I saw. Instead, they had retreated about 500 kilometers, and I'm sorry to say, we were still well within the German occupation zone. One thing was for sure, the war was unmistakably very close to home, because I could hear the big guns in the distance day and night. The local resort nearby in Krynica, became a hospital. Every day trains arrived in Grybow full of wounded soldiers. I saw other men, as well, who must have gone to war with a smile and returned broken and bandaged. Many were taken to Krynica for recovery.

Soon all Jews and Gypsies from the surrounding countryside were forced into the Grybow ghetto. The Gestapo was no longer satisfied with just putting all the townspeople in the ghetto. Now they wanted all the outcasts of the new regime. Since my home was within the restricted zone, we took on some of these new hapless people. We had so little but still we were willing and able to share. People were sleeping in every nook and cranny of our humble home. The attic up the stairs made room for two or three families, the bedrooms were overfilled, and the main family room was crowded. You could hardly walk around. We had at least eight extra people not just to give a place to sleep but also to feed. But, no matter what, we could not let them sleep outside or starve to death.

In spite of our own miserable condition, I was sent by foot to gather a few more people and bring them to our home. I was looking for my grandfather's youngest brother, Bernard and his family. They lived in a very remote area about 20 kilometers away, and like all the other country people they were given an order to leave their house and move to our ghetto. To do this, I made my way through the backwoods. It took me about four hours to get close. Along the way I had no fear of the Gestapo but I was on high alert for wild animals, especially wolves. I heard their howling the whole time I was walking and I knew if they found me I would not be able to do very much; I was defenseless against these organized marauders. The only thing I could do was keep up the pace while trying to concentrate on anything but wolves. As well as I knew the backwoods, this was a new area for me and I became lost. It is easy to get disoriented in the woods. I knew I was going in the correct general direction, but that was about it. I also knew that, no matter what, I could not allow myself to get caught out here alone at night. It would be dangerous. So I kept moving and luckily stumbled upon a peasant. He knew about where I needed to go and pointed for me to go over the next mountain ridge to the small town of Piorunka. It was directly on the border of Slovakia. I knew I had arrived when I saw a store with a sign that read proudly in Ukrainian lettering, 'Cooperativa Schagrin.' It was my grand uncle's general store and also his home.

By the time I reached him, his carriage was packed with all of his belongings and his horse was ready to go. I took a few minutes to see the place and help make sure everyone was ready. He gathered his children and his wife, and we all rode home on the rural unpaved road. I no longer worried about wolves because they wouldn't bother our noisy wagon. Towards the end of the day we arrived, and my family welcomed us with open arms. It was a stressful reunion because of our circumstances. However, we tried to make everyone comfortable.

It was now the depth of winter, December, and we were all in danger of freezing to death. There was plenty of coal in the area, but we were not allowed to buy any nor did we have any money. Nevertheless, the cold was turning deadly. The small children could hardly handle it at all. My mother was beside herself nursing my baby brother. She was rocking back and forth nervously in silent desperation. Temperatures relentlessly dropped. In total desperation we had to come up with a plan. We needed to do something before there would be a catastrophe. My father and I discussed how I could go to the railroad center 3 kilometers away and get coal from the huge pile used by the train. The trouble is I would have to do this late at night and probably I wouldn't be the only one desperate or foolhardy enough to do it.

We knew about this cache of coal because Chaim Kant, one of my relatives worked at the station. Chaim also had a brother, Norbert. He was a lawyer that also lived in our town and someone we could trust. So we hoped he would be there to help us. I did not know it then but Norbert, his youngest brother, would become crucial to me one day. To prepare to get the coal my father helped to take the bells off the horse. We both knew this must be done stealthily. Before I left he told me how sorry he was to have to send me on this dangerous mission. I nodded my head in agreement. We both knew that if I had been caught I would most likely been killed on the spot. But if we did nothing, we all would have frozen to death. So we continued to prepare the horse for the silent run.

As the darkness of the night enveloped everything I took the horse and sled out in the bitter cold and picked my way carefully through the local streets into back roads. Once I felt safe I quickened the pace and hurried to the station. I didn't see anyone along the way, and more importantly they didn't see me. When I finally arrived I realized this was not going to be easy. A new fence surrounded the coal and I could not get to it. Luckily, some good people on the other side tossed some of the coal over the fence, and I began to load the sled.

It was only a few minutes before I was discovered. At first I heard indecipherable shouting mixed with the wind. This was immediately followed by the sounds of a machine gun being fired towards me. I knew I was in immediate and dire danger. Without thinking, I raced away with my horse and sled. This was crazy because the roads were slick with ice and the sled became unstable. I was in a race for my life, sliding around dangerously. I almost got tossed off the road. As I was running away, I heard motorcycles coming toward me. The only thing I could do was continue my reckless driving. I did this until I found a small side trail and got off the road. I stopped for a moment and quickly covered my tracks. The motorcycles zoomed by, and I found myself safe in the white covered woods.

Slowly, I made my way through the thicket to a village where I knew I had friends. I went directly to the home of the Mol family who I knew were friends of my father. It was very late at night. I knocked on the door. I heard people stirring from the inside. A woman answered the door holding a kerosene lamp. It was dark, so it took her a moment to recognize me. I said, Please help me. The Gestapo are chasing me. Without words she directed her two boys to take my horse and sled. They moved the rig to the side, covered it with straw and unhooked the horse to put him in the barn. Then they took me into their house where it was thankfully, warm and safe. Mrs. Mol handed me a little soup. As I relaxed, I remember seeing some small children. This reminded me of my siblings, and the urgency of my mission.

I stayed there for a little while until I thought it was safe. Then before dawn I started again under the cover of darkness and bitter cold. I had to get back before daybreak. Thoughts were racing in my head. I looked for the enemy lurking behind every tree. But my family depended upon me, so I put these thoughts out of my head, gathered my senses and made my way home. When I arrived I was cold and tired but alert as if I was still being chased. It took awhile for me to calm down. My father knew that something must have happened but said nothing. He looked cold and tired. It was early in the morning but looking carefully I noticed our conditions were taking a toll on him too. My whole family and our guests looked blue with cold. We put a few of the bits of coals that I risked my life collecting in the stove and basked in its lifesaving warmth. About 16 of us huddled around that pathetic little stove.

All of the Nazis acted with impunity against the Jews but a few insidious characters still managed to stand out for their disdain of humanity. My own school acquaintance's father, Kubala, weighs heavily, and along with him was a hired killer who came from

126

Poznan. He was the Devil incarnate, earning the nickname *Zimny Mroz,* or Cold Frost. This nickname foretold his behavior. He was a killer, without conscience or remorse. He became a member of the Blue police. He reveled in walking side-by-side with the Gestapo. He was the one who arrested the teachers and intelligentsia, participating in their interrogations, beatings, deportations and indiscriminate murder.

Headmaster Korzen, of my old public school was arrested, I have no idea where he was taken and we never saw him again. I don't know what happened to him, such was the time in which I lived.

The change in attitude within my own town towards my race was like an hourglass had been turned over. Another world, far more sinister and deadly, replaced ours. Those who were slow to react to the change, or who resisted it openly were killed immediately or deported. Some, however, tried to assimilate into the new social order. These people became tools of the Nazis, who used them until their usefulness ended, and then they disposed of them as readily as they did anyone else. Others, mostly young men, took to the hills to organize an armed resistance. It was times like this that brought out the best and worst in people, sometimes both. At each location to which I was involuntarily taken, I was both victim and witness to what would happen. The word 'Holocaust' was never even used until years later. My life story was filled with dramatic instances of degradation contrasted by the humanity and the kindness of friends and strangers who kept me alive, all the while my life hung precariously by a thread.

The Polish Underground executed Zimmy Mroz in 1944. And the head of the local Grybow Underground was none other than the son of Mrs. Paszek. It was the same fellow who once in awhile would give me some change to buy a treat in the bakery for holding his horse, Franciszek Paszek Kmicic. And although I readily

Franciszek Paszek Kmicic
Head of Grybow Underground.
Family owned the local brewery
fig 46

give him credit for removing this scourge from the earth, I knew the Underground made it a point not to befriend Jews either. His mother, on the other hand, survived Auschwitz.

I made another trip that caused a temporary conflict with my father. He arranged for me to take a night trip to Tarnow to pick up a wagonload of flour. Somehow my cousins who lived in Tarnow had accumulated contraband flour. The danger was extreme. I traveled the 60 kilometers at night; my horse without his bells and my sled wagon without a lamp. Both forbidden actions.

The ride to Tarnow was uneventful but very cold. I reached the three story house that was my destination in six or seven hours. I even remember the address, Lwowska 3. My cousins greeted me warmly and while they loaded my wagon I slept the day away. That night it snowed as I began my trip home.

Again the lonely ride was quiet and uneventful with only my horse's steaming breath, the drifting snow and the starry sky to capture my attention. Along the road there were places to rest occasionally. The atmosphere was deceptively serene.

Suddenly I heard the order to halt and saw the lamp of two policemen - one Polish, the other German. My worst nightmare.

"What do you have there, boy?"

"Flour, sir," I answered.

The two policemen began to probe the bags of flour.

"Where are you taking it?"

128

"To the bakery, sir." We were close enough to Grybow
   for this to be a plausible story.
"Where are your horse's bells?"
"They must have fallen off, sir."
"And where is your lamp?"
I must have looked and sounded as if I had been sleeping
   on the job.
"I don't know, sir."
"You must have bells and a lamp," the policeman growled.
"I know, sir. I'm sorry."
"This is very serious, boy."
"Yes sir."

Satisfied that my load was indeed flour the Polish officer finally said, "Next time you will be arrested, boy."

I couldn't believe my luck. I had passed a test more important than any I had ever taken at school.

When I reached home it was still dark. My father was obviously relieved to see me safe and sound. Then the unloading began
and there, beneath the flour, were large bars of brown soap, pepper
and other forbidden items.

I felt betrayed. It was not the presence of these important
items that bothered me but the fact that my father and my cousins
had not told me of them. I angrily told my father that I would make
no more such trips. He simply shook his head and said something I
would find to be very true, "Leon," he said, "Life will show you that
sometimes you will have to cover up things."

1942

The Judenrat was the committee designated to disseminate
the German orders to the Jewish population as well as enforce the
laws with the Jewish police. This was a tortured organization be-

cause all the news and tasks were bad. The committee would meet in the now empty home of Dr. Kohn, next to the beautiful Grybow Park. This was a good location because it was spacious and conveniently located near the train station. Being near the station would make it easy for the Germans to visit the members of the committee. It was made up of senior community members but to the Germans they were a powerless pathetic organization, something to be viewed with derision.

One day an insidious request was issued by the Gestapo. They said, that by the end of the day, they wanted the Judenrat to produce one hundred people to be deported to work camps; in other words they wanted hostages. This request left the committee in disarray. They had no mechanism to choose one hundred individuals, let alone one person. The way they saw it, there was only one choice; they had to tell the Gestapo it was an impossible request or stall for time. So, when the Gestapo returned later that day, and asked, Where are the people we requested? A committeeman replied, I'm sorry but no one will volunteer. The Gestapo became incensed with an outburst of shouting, and violent scorn. Shaken, one committeeman made a brave but futile gesture, knowing it might be his last, by saying, If you want volunteers you will have to go house-to-house and get them yourselves.

What the Nazis did next sent shivers through the entire community. Outraged, they took the entire Jewish Committee to the park next to the house and summarily executed all of them. I heard a series of shots, from my home, knowing only that they were close by. Shortly, after the shots were fired, the Jewish police, represented by my old friends Eisen and Reinkraut, knocked on our door and approached my father. They were obviously shaken when they said, Mr. Schagrin, there has been a tragedy. We need your help to bring the bodies of our committeemen to the cemetery. They are all dead.

The news landed on our family like a bag of bricks would hit

The home of Dr. Kohn
Later the office of the Grybow Judenrat.
fig. 47

you in the face. This was horrific news that would almost certainly lead to the death of my father as well. Besides the stunning news we feared that once my father brought the bodies to the cemetery he would be killed as a cover-up for the event, a common practice. The Jewish police left. I heard this too and without discussion turned to my father, "Father, I will go with you." But I actually had a different plan; I could not let him go at all. I thought I had a better chance to survive. I was betting they would be less likely to kill a child. Together, we silently prepared the horse. Each step was slow and deliberate. Somehow he knew what I was thinking and was reluctant to allow me to go alone. I had to plead with him, Father you must not go. You must take care of mom and my brother and sisters. You have to let me do this. It is the only way.

Reluctantly he acquiesced. We both knew the risk I was taking, but we also both knew his risk was far greater. I ended up taking my friend, Roman Blauner to help me. He was only a couple of years older than me. We rode in the wagon the few blocks to the park in silence. It felt like the whole world was still except for the wheels creaking on the brick pavers. Here we were, two boys riding a wagon on the beginning of another cold March late afternoon. It was still winter but no snow had fallen that day. The park was green. When we arrived, we were both sickened by what we saw. This was the first time either of us had seen a dead body up close, or touched a dead body. By the time the occupation was over, I am sorry to say I would see thousands. Due to starvation, and our general conditions, I lost the ability to cry. Nor would the overseers of this disaster, the Nazis, give any of them a proper and decent burial.

The councilmen were heavy. It took both of us, Roman and me, to lift each body onto the wagon. We were lifting the bodies of the town's most prominent citizens. Red stained their fine clothing. It made an indelible impression on me. I will never be able to get this scene out of my mind. My boyhood had effectively ended the moment I touched the first body. I even had to shut the eyes of some of them. When the wagon was loaded the horse pulled hard on the heavy load and we started for the cemetery. Each step of my horse working pounded on my head like a hammer striking nails on a coffin. When we arrived at the cemetery, we met Mr. Romanek, the keeper, and his son Adam. They helped us unload the bodies in silence. No prayers were said, just silence. By this time, my wagon was filled with red pools spilling onto the ground. As we left late in the afternoon the blood continued to drip slowly upon the road.

Roman and I were understandably numb. I came home shaking and unable to speak. You might say this was my Bar Mitzvah,

132

how I became a man. My father snapped me out of it by forcing me to answer a few questions bereft of emotion, "Who did they get?"

I told him, "Goldman and his 2 sons, the fellow that was missing one hand from the First World War, Baldinger, Getz, and..." The rest I could not name. We sat for awhile until I calmed down.

There was little time for grieving. There was a general sense of disbelief and malaise about our whole existence. From this time forward the Judenrat was never re-established, and in its place the Nazis appointed a single secretary from Krynica. Also their lives were sacrificed in vain because, soon after, a hundred hostages were collected anyway. The hostages vanished, including my friend Mendel Scher, who was among them. Eventually, Mendel ended up in Birkenau with me. They got what they wanted, for now. Meanwhile, 1942 was another terrible winter especially for the Jews. It was bone-chilling cold with not even a fur to crawl under. You can imagine my parents, caring for 6 kids, mom nursing a baby, and the house full of guests from the countryside. None of us knew what would happen next. But no matter how bad it was none of us thought that the Nazis were planning the extermination of our entire race, from every corner of Europe and then the world. This was a war upon the Jews within the greater worldwide conflict.

Death became a familiar visitor. On one occasion I was sent to collect the body of a prominent citizen. I found him on the pathway by the Biała River. He was just under the bridge. When I discovered him he was wearing very fine mahogany leather shoes and beautiful clothing. The disparity between having nice shoes and being shot dead struck me as horribly incongruous. Worse, I knew the man. It was Dr. Ameisen, the judge of the local court. At the time, I didn't know why but this was his final judgment, and I was the unwitting bailiff. Later, I learn from my neighbors that Dr. Ameisen was Jewish but when he married a Catholic he renounced his faith in Judaism.

While my family suffered its misery, up the hill the Blauner family was doing no better. Max Blauner, the eldest child, told me what happened to him.

Max Blauner's Tale

Max was home feverishly working on his Singer Sewing Machine. Because all the fur coats were taken away, he was making a coat for his sister so she could go through the winter without freezing. But, on that day, he was supposed to report to the Gestapo in the morning where he would be assigned some menial laborer's job, like his father and the rest of the adult Jews in the town. You see Max was about 23 years old so he was required to assemble daily. On this morning he decided not to go, instead he thought it was much more important to make the jacket. While he was doing this a German soldier entered his home, unannounced, and saw him working.

The soldier demanded, "*Why did you not* you come to clean the garbage in the streets like the rest of the Jews?"

Max replied, "It's better that for me I make a warm jacket for my sister before the cold comes."

The soldier asked, "Are you a tailor?"

Max replied that he was, indeed, a tailor.

The soldier looked around the room and saw the tools and materials of a tailor, "Can you fix my two buttons?"

Max nodded, "Why not?"

The soldier took his jacket off and showed Max it was missing two buttons. Max proceeded deftly to replace them. When he was finished, he returned the jacket to his abhorred customer. Satisfied with the work the soldier said, "Continue what you are doing until you are finished."

At this time, Yom Kippur arrived. It is one of the most important holidays for the Jews, and Max's father decided to gather a minyan (ten men) at the synagogue and told Max he would need his help keeping an eye out for the Germans. When the time arrived, Max did as he was told. Most probably it was the last minyan at the Grybow Orthodox Temple. As the men prayed to God that the war should be over soon, Max waited and watched outside obedient to the wishes of his father. Thankfully, the night was quiet, and no one came.

After this, Max started to plan his escape. As part of the plan he went to Nowy-Sacz and found some small flint stones that he wanted to take with him and purchased 100 Zloty worth. Since they were small he could carry them easily in his pocket. He thought, wherever he went maybe he could sell them. This money would be a big help. Once the purchase was completed he returned to German occupied Grybow. Four days later on the Jewish holiday of Sukkot he said to his father, "Papa, I'm leaving; I can't live here anymore." His mother started to cry. "Papa, I want you should sell me a horse and a buggy." With this buggy and the flint stones rattling in his pocket he took three friends, Isaac Goldman, and 2 others, and they all left. Isaac survived the war. They all said goodbye to their families and traveled southeast down to the river that divided Poland and Russia. They followed the river until they could find a spot low enough to cross and entered Russia. Before long they ended up in Lwów. Max, loved this city. He said, ..."it had everything I could have wanted."

Max started to trade on the Black Market. It worked out brilliantly. The flint stones he brought turned out to be worth a great deal. He sold them to a few people, earning 500 Zloty on his 100 Zloty investment. This money made it possible to live well, at least for a little while. Then a combination of concern for his family and the need to replenish his supply of stones led him to think about going back for more. Which is exactly what he did.

On his second trip, Max went to the river again and crossed it. It was now early fall, but there was still no snow or ice on the ground. It was just chilly. As he was crossing the river a Russian shot at him. Since, he was already half way across the shooter must not have been so accurate because he missed.

After brazenly crossing Max was full of nerve and went directly to the Gestapo. At the office he casually said, I need a permit to go to Grybow and Nowy-Sacz. The Gestapo did not ask many questions and certainly things would have been different had they known he was Jewish. It would be unthinkable that a Jew would ask for a permit, so the man behind the desk did as requested and gave the permit to him.

Max meandered his way back into Grybow being careful to avoid the authorities. Even though he had a permit there was no reason to flaunt it. When he saw his father, his father's eyes lit up with joy. Then Max pleaded, "Papa I found the City of Lwów. It is a good place in the hands of the Russians. Our family will be safe there until after the war. I want to move you and the rest of the family there as soon as possible." His papa forever the optimist refused saying the war will be over soon and things will return to normal. He would not budge. Then he said with a serious look of concern, "Max, they are looking for you already."

"Who?" Max asked.

"The Gestapo," his father replied.

Max wondered out loud, "Why, why are they looking?"

His father said, "Because they are saying you are with the partisans." The very last thing he said to Max was, "You better leave right away!"

Again, Max said goodbye to his family and left, carefully picking his way through the town.

But before he would go back to Russia, he wanted more stones back in Nowy-Sacz. These stones had a Yiddish name. 'Szteindlech,' It's a slang term. It comes from the combination of Sztein or big rock and Lech or small. But their value had nothing to do with their size. Their value had to do with the spark they could create when you scratched them. And their size made them perfect for cigarette lighters. These stones were flint, and they were valuable because self-contained lighters with lighter fluid and a wick were the fashion. And Max knew there was a shortage of flint in Russia. With his refreshed pocketful of flint, he left and went back to Russia again. This time he took his sister and her boyfriend.

But things were different. This time they all left by train. Their destination was Krosno on the border. Max knew that there was an exchange between Russia and Poland by the bridge. There, the Germans were letting Jews and others go to Russia, and accepting from Russia anyone who wanted to come to Germany. But, by the time they arrived, no one was allowed to cross the bridge. This border was sealed. So, instead they tried to cross the river. Gunshots told them not to take another step so they turned back. Max had to do a little planning. The way he saw it, the bridge was being guarded and no one was allowed to leave during the day. But that would also mean the guards would be thin outside of this area, and he would try to cross at night, away from the bridge. So he went about 200 meters beyond the bridge and passed through with two of his friends. Immediately, the Russian police stopped them and without hesitation Max reached into his pocket and pulled out a few of the small stones offering the policeman a bribe. He took it and said, Go. Get the hell out of here.

Again Max was safely in Russia. Sadly, his sister never got to cross with her boyfriend, and therefore did not survive. Max went right back to Lwów. This time he made even more money selling the small but valuable stones, maybe 700 or 800 Zloty. No one asked questions; they just wanted the stones.

A few months later Max was preparing to come back to Gry-

Russian Gulag building roads by hand fig 48

bow again. He was running out of money and was beginning to get very concerned with his own family's safety. He wanted to try one more time to take them to Russia before it was too late. So again, he readied himself for the trip back. This time he would be traveling in freezing cold weather. He wrapped himself up tightly and found a spot by the river where he would cross. He looked around to make sure he wasn't being watched and began to cross the border. As he started he heard shouts, Stop, don't move.

Max was arrested by the Russians. He knew this was not going to be good. He had no more stones to try and bribe the guards. They took him to jail, where he was convicted in a *kangaroo court* run by the Soviet Russian Police. The proceeding took all of five minutes. As the judge delivered the sentence it hung heavy upon his

Roadwork in Poland during 1942 note bare feet fig 49

shoulders, Five years hard labor in the Gulag, the Russian prison system in Siberia. It was a frozen frontier wasteland that might as well be the moon. Within a few days he was placed on a train, and whisked off to Siberia.

The train ride was very long but finally it stopped. It could not go any further. It was the end of the tracks. When he got out of the car there was nothing, no train station, no buildings, nothing. The prisoners were formed into a line and they started to walk, and walk.

Days later they reached their destination. It was an area marked with red flags around a field, no barracks, no tents, nothing, just a field. Once they arrived they were assembled and told to dig a hole. Eventually this would become a cave and all the men would fit inside for a little shelter from the elements, "This is where you will sleep." So using shovels they dug holes as instructed to get a little protection from the weather, and in the morning they began to build a road with nothing but hand tools.

This is what he did every day, the same thing over and over. It would be five long years of backbreaking work. But, by the time his sentence was over, the war would also be over. And as unbelievable as it might sound, prison may have saved his life.

Since Russia and the Allies won the war, as soon as Max returned to Lwów he decided to join the Russian Army. Being a soldier would provide him with a weapon and safe passage back to pick up the pieces in Grybow. With weapons, and home as his destination, he left Russia and crossed the border without incident.

The Long Journey Begins

While Max was selling flint in Lwow, back in Grybow I was preparing to leave home with my parents' blessing. Other kids were doing the same but I was one of the first. I said goodbye and started to walk with all my belongings. It wasn't much, a small rucksack. I wasn't sure where to go. Without too much deliberation, I choose north. About 25 miles away I found what I was looking for - a series of work camps. There were hundreds of people in different work camps. They were all building a road. It looked like hard labor, but there was some heavy equipment to make it easier.

I approached a foreman and said only, "I want to work."
Without questioning me he said, "Grab a shovel."
He didn't ask if I was Jewish, and I did not volunteer this information. Soon, others would follow. Many people from Grybow ended up working here. There were three in my camp that I knew well, the Lipczer kids, or at least three of them. Usher, Joshua and a third I can't remember. Since our camp was open people could eas-

ily come and go. But the Lipczers and many others wore the telltale armbands, making them easy targets for abuse, while I still did not wear one.

As expected, the work was back breaking, but I was paid biweekly, and they fed me. In my position, this was as comfortable as I could be. One small comfort was that I knew many of the other young men who were working with me. I found myself living in an open work camp for Poles. Any one of my mates could have turned me in, but they didn't bother, nor was I harassed by them in any way. On the contrary, we all needed each other and felt more trust among ourselves than with the occupying force. However, this did not change the fact that I lived in constant fear that at any moment I could be singled out and arrested for being Jewish. I pushed all of this out of my mind and worked diligently building the road. Eventually, the foreman took notice of my effort. Approvingly, he assigned me to the quarry to load stones on trucks. This was harder work but I was up for it. Looking back work would be my salvation over and over again.

We were not the only road camp. This was a massive concerted effort. There were many other camps up and down the road for about a twenty-mile stretch. The farthest was building a dam on the Dunajec River. This river flowed forcibly from the mountains into the mighty Vistula River making for a good supply of free power and saving time to go East via car. One day, I took a walk to see all the camps along the road. Each had its own character depending on the race, age of people it engaged and disposition of the leader. Some of the camps where manned solely by Jews. I watched how these men toiled under harsher conditions than the rest and felt bad for them.

Because I was living with the non-Jews, I was free to come and go as I pleased. This is how I heard that one of my cousins was executed because he got sick with typhoid fever. When I heard this news, I could not even flinch in fear of giving up my own identity. Up to this point, I think the main reason for my safety was that the foreman of my camp, even though he was a German, was focused on completing the road and needed all the labor he could get. He didn't care about anything else. I had no idea how long it might last, but being out of immediate danger I just did my job and said nothing.

One day, a fellow laborer and Catholic friend of mine, Adam Kmak, came up to me and said, "Leon, I think your family is in trouble. I heard that the Jews from Grybow will be deported to the ghetto in Nowy-Sacz tomorrow." I quickly gathered what little I had and left. If he was right I did not have much time to get back. Even though this affected many of the other boys like the Lipczers, I slipped away from camp by myself and walked through the back roads by the compass in my head. I knew those backwoods well. I think my friends were restricted by their arm bands. At the time I was fearless. I would frequently go off into the hills and trade for food or even ask the Germans for things I wanted. They never suspected my race. I was just a kid to them.

When I arrived at my home my mother and sisters were crying hysterically, the baby too. My father was breaking the kitchen furniture. He saw me as he smashed a chair and said angrily, "We are not leaving them anything." Without pause he gathered the next chair to smash it while he spoke. Then catching his composure he put the chair down and turned towards me, "Why did you come back here?" I told him the truth, "I wanted to help you. I heard the town will soon be deported, and I was scared for you." In a cold voice, he said, *"We will help ourselves. Go back. It is enough that they will kill seven people. You must leave."*

My father spoke in this manner to help me break the emotional bonds to my family. Then he confirmed what I was told, tomorrow they would be leaving our home for good. That is when he also mentioned a worrisome thing, *Leon, what they are doing with us I can't be sure. But I don't trust them. Yesterday I met with the Mol boys, Ludwik and Jasiek,* These were the same ones who helped me when I was chased by the Gestapo for stealing coal. Leon, what they told me about was *some strange digging near their home. Because of the timing on the deportation they are afraid it's going to be the site of a mass killing. There was no other reason they could figure why a ditch would be dug, near there home, in this remote location.*

Our conversation was interrupted by a knock upon the door. At first we were frightened. Did someone see me coming home? Did someone report the noise my father was making? My father opened the door cautiously, as I got out of sight. Thankfully, it was our next-door neighbor Tadeusz Skrabski.

His hand was still bandaged and in a homemade sling. "I heard Leon is home, so I came right over," he said. I stepped out of the shadow feeling safe. I was practically raised at his house. All the memories flooded back to me when I saw him; picking vegetables when I was very young, playing with his kids, dinners at his house. Tadeusz, like my father was agitated and speaking anxiously, he said to my father while pointing at me, "This boy should immediately escape to Hungary."

My father shook his head, his eyes full of emotion. After a long pause he said, *Tadeusz, I have known you a long time. You will see that none of us will come back, except Leon.* Then he looked at him intently, *I am asking you, dear friend, that when Leon does return you must help him. My sisters in the United States will pay you.* This conversation was taking place with the three of us now outside my family home so as not to upset my mother more than she already was. I told them both I didn't want to leave my family alone. My dad paused and with great sincerity said, *Son, if you survive, tell the story of everything that happened to us. They must know.*

That was the day I learned my father was 42 years old and my mother was 38. I had never known how old they were before. There was no reason to know. Obviously, under duress, my father tried to explain, *Son for some time I was very tough with you ...* This was his goodbye speech. I have played it over and over in my head thousands of times. I will never forget.

You were not such a good boy. You didn't want to go to school or help me with my work. I know you are not a soft child, but as a child you were deathly ill with pneumonia, and we were scared to death you would pass away. It's a miracle that you are even standing here. Your mother and I lost two young children before you. They were very young, but old enough for us to fall in love with each of them and when each died, it was like the end of the world for us. So when you got sick, we thought we might be cursed, hopelessly repeating the past. The whole community rallied in your behalf, praying and doing whatever they could to help. They even held a constant vigil, day and night, just for you. And miraculously, you got better.

My father continued, *Once you were strong enough, your mother and I took you to the famous Tsadik in Tyczyn who gave you a special blessing. He told us, 'This boy will outlive your whole fam-ily.' Leon, I think he was right - you will live longer than any of us.*

Silently, my father turned away, a proud man reduced to tears. He did not want to show me his grief. But he found his composure, and with conviction in his tone said one more thing; *Leon, if you should survive, you should know where our bones rest.* He pointed to me and to our neighbor, *Tadeusz, take him like your own child.*

The last thing my father said to me was, Go back. You have a chance. Go back. He turned, defeated and went back into the house. Soon, I heard another piece of furniture break into pieces. I was

144

deeply distraught but I didn't cry, I just walked with Tadeusz. We both sensed our world was changing forever. I did not stay long, but before I left my mother gave me her wedding ring. At the time she seemed disoriented. She was crying and completely speechless. I said goodbye to my baby brother and sisters. Without looking back I left.

But I did not leave empty handed. With all the tumult going on around my community, another one of my father's friends, Mr. Romanek, the superintendent of the Jewish cemetery, loaded up a horse and buggy with packages to give to the boys from the town who were working with me at the road camp. To deliver these I made a plan to meet his son Adam outside the town. I could not walk with him through the town or I might have been discovered. I left on my own. Soon, I met up with Adam, as we agreed outside the town, and together we took the horse following the back roads I had taken earlier.

At about one quarter mile from the camp we unloaded the packages on the side of the road just out of sight. I said goodbye to Adam and he turned the horse around, back to Grybow. Most likely this was his last act of good will for all of the Jewish citizens, before they were deported. Mr. Romanek and his son stayed behind, they were Catholic. On my own, I walked towards my camp and re-entered without fanfare. I was only gone a single day. As soon as I could, I told my friends Usher and the rest, about the gifts from home, how each one has their name on it and where I left them on the side of the road, out of sight, not far away. They scrambled to collect their packages. For the next few days everyone was appreciative savoring the last gifts of their families. I saw Adam after the war. He had become a local policeman.

146

Chapter Five

Poor Tarnow
August 20th, 1942

Like clockwork, the deportation from Grybow began on Thursday the 20th just as my friend foretold. The Jews were assembled downtown next to the bathhouse, not far from the slaughterhouse.... the young and old, husbands and wives, everyone assembled was present including the Gestapo who were out in force that day. Once assembled the crowd was addressed, "Anyone who cannot walk will be taken by trucks. Anyone capable of walking will begin to head to Nowy-Sacz."

I should have said almost everyone assembled because there was at least one person who did not - the mentally disturbed Rachel Grubel, who lived in my house. When she was called to assemble with the rest, she remained holding her four cats. Two troopers doing a security sweep entered my home and tried to pull the cats away from her, but the cats attacked with claws and hissing. With little hesitation the troopers brought her outside with the cats and shot them all on the spot,

About 365 of the Jews who could not make the walk were instead loaded on trucks. My heart sinks when I tell you they were not taken to Nowy-Sacz, but only about 3 kilometers to Biała Niżna. This was near the road to Grodek, next to an ancient monastery that also made the flour, and just as the Mol brothers feared, to the large ditch that was dug the day before by the Hitler Youth.

After the war I was able to spend some time with the Mol brothers. They witnessed the grotesque episode that followed the arrival of the trucks. At 9 AM, Zimny Mroz and the Gestapo arrived with a few trucks full of the feeblest Jewish townspeople. Shouting began to get the people out of the trucks. Then we heard the Nazis

147

The place of Deportation. In front of the technical school.
fig 53

order to the people, "Take your clothes off." Since these were decent people, an order like this could only mean one thing. The scene soon turned horrific. Some had to be dragged. One ran but was caught and brought back.

Children would not let go of parents. People were screaming and resisting in whatever way they could. The Gestapo shot every one of these defenseless people. Most were placed at the edge of the ditch before the lethal weapons were unleashed. Then afterwards, your father's brother, Izrael with the fellow that was staying at your home, Mr. Goldfinger, was selected to complete the burial. They worked for a long while covering the remains as best they could.

When they were done, they were added to the pile. Throughout the day there was lots of shooting followed by silence and some talk of celebration. Towards the end of the day the Germans and Zimney Mroz were congratulating themselves. When I heard this story, my heart sank and I was dumbfounded. In questioning the brothers I learned this is also where the Blauners lost their father.

The Blauner's Father fig 54

The rest of the town's Jews, about 1,500 people of all ages, walked to Nowy-Sacz oblivious to the plight of others and entered the ghetto. Among them were my father and mother with five young children. My father, ever the horseman, put them on the cart for the horse to pull. Also among the shunned and unwanted were the despised Jewish policeman, Reinkraut and the Eisen's son.

None of the people from Grybow remained in Nowy-Sacz for long. Soon after their arrival most of them, my family included, were deported to Belzec where they perished in the gas chambers. I would, however, see my father one more time, but by then all hope was lost. I learned what happened to my mother and young brothers and sisters from a locomotive engineer. He said, All the Jews from Grybow who were deported went to Nowy-Sacz and were divided into three transports soon after their arrival. They became part of 12,000 - 15,000 people who were sent to Belzec." Once there six gas chambers worked 24 hours a day to destroy all of them.

We know they were exterminated because there was no barracks at Belzec. Belzec was not a concentration camp at all, it was strictly an extermination center. The victims sat in a field where they were forced to wait their turns in the gas chamber, and then the bodies were thrown into mass graves. Belzec was a killing factory.

I went back to work with the road crew in Zbyszyce, and the foreman, again, sent me back to the quarry. I was still free. While I was at the camp I heard about my deported community and worried over my family's hardships. This is where I also learned that after Reinkraut was deported with the others, he told the SS that he hid valuables back at Grybow, and if they would let him return, he would show them where to find the loot. It did not take too much cajoling to have them bring him back. 'Cold Frost' himself, escorted this young man around the town and down by the River Biała. Eventually, they realized it was a ruse and he was lying. For the crime of wasting their time, he was beaten, shot and killed right by the river. This was strange justice for a Jewish boy who became a policeman who turned on his own people.

It wasn't long after this that things turned nightmarish for me too. Less than ten days after my return, August 28, 1942, my name was called as I worked, Leon Schagrin, followed by terse orders, Step away from the rocks, Under guard they took me to a large gathering of other workers they detained that day, all Jews. Together, over 1,000 of us, were walked to a secure campsite. Upon arrival the men were separated from the women and children. I got into the appropriate line and waited.

I remember clearly we were being detained between two bridges in Sacz. Accidentally, while I was in line, I saw my father and instinctively tried to step into his group. A guard prevented it. This freak happenstance was the last time I ever saw my father. From here I walked away from him towards my own fate. The next thing they did to me was a shake down. I heard, "Empty your pockets. If anything is found in your pockets, we will hang you from those hooks." I reached into my pocket and put my mother's wedding ring in a basket where it was lost for the ages. I saw many other rings in that basket. Their mothers must have done the same thing for them that mine did for me. Stripped of the one last shred of connection I had to my family I waited as required until everyone was processed. Then we walked under guard to the local jail where we lingered for three or four days.

As we waited, the rest of the Jews from Grybow, my father among them, were loaded onto cattle cars destined for Belzec. While I sat in prison for the crime of being a Jew, he was killed along with the rest who left for the same crime. Everything was a mystery. I had no idea if they were being relocated nor did I know what Belzec was at the time. So, I still held unto hope, as I pondered my own destiny.

The local prison they put me in was a harrowing experience. I heard beatings, senseless shouting and shooting at all times of the day and night. I could not sleep. The commander in charge of us was the notorious Obersturmfuhrer or First Lieutenant, Henriek Hamann. He was characterized after the war as the mastermind of extermination details, and the operations manager for the murder of hundreds of thousands of innocent people. I heard he once said, I am Hamann, your worst nightmare, just like in the Old Testament. He knew the significance of his name to the Jews as the dreaded Hamann from the story of Purim.

This young, up and coming, Nazi did not act alone, he also had two notorious assistants, Gorka and Johann Bornholt. The first of his assistants made it his mission to mistreat the Jews directly while the other, Bornholt, had direct charge of the prison where I happened to find myself. After the war Gorka was caught by the Russians and placed in a large cage on the back of a jeep. Then he was paraded around the town in mockery and killed, but while I was there, he was in charge and terror ruled the day and never subsided in the night.

Well before my arrival in Tarnow, my friend, Moshe Katz, was working in the local stables. Like Grybow, his small town of Nowy Sacz was kicked like an anthill and all of the Jews were de-

A stable in Tarnow Ghetto fig 55

ported to Tarnow, Belzec or Auschwitz. Moshe, being only 17 at the time, went on a similar trek as me working on the roads in Rożnów. It was 1942, at the time I was one year younger, 16.

Today, as a Survivor, in speaking with him you can quickly see a great personality with an uncanny and infectious way of making friends. I think he picked up a part of his sensibilities the way I did, at the Jarmark. In his old town, just like Grybow, a Jarmark was also held each week, and like me, he thrived in this environment. Well, maybe thrived is too big a word since his family was poor. He was more like a small time *hondeler* buying at one price to sell at another to make a small profit, but to do this takes skill and finesse. The funny thing is, that also like me, he did not enjoy school. Still Max attended both public and the Jewish *hadar*, or Hebrew school

The type of carriage Moshe & Leon Drove in Tarnow.
Two soft seats across from two hard seats. fig 56

for many years.

I spoke with Moshe and this is what he told me about his experience.

Moshe Katz

I was working on the roads when I was rounded up with 400 others and deported to Tarnow. On the day I arrived in Tarnow, the ghetto was already fully established. Being new and not knowing where to go, the local Jewish Ordnungsdienst, (Jewish Police) wearing his signature cap and armband escorted me and 10-12 other guys to the home of a mother and child. It was odd at first. The woman clearly did not want a parade of homeless men into her home. The

153

Ordnungdienst Cap- Jewish Police Cap fig 57

policeman did not speak much. All he said is that you will stay here. As soon as he left, I learned the woman's husband was deported the day before. It was very crowded in her small apartment and she was not at all welcoming. She did not want us there and made this clear. She yelled at all of us, 'Leave, go away, what are you doing here,' but none of us had anyplace to go and it was very cold outside, especially at night. But, rather than stay, I left with my hat in my hand and nothing else. The night air was cold but I was used to poor living conditions. I did the best I could and found a stairway with a little protection from the wind and cold. That night, I held onto my jacket and tried not to freeze. The temperature must have dipped well below freezing. Needless to say, it took all my strength to just stay alive let alone capture a wink of sleep. While sitting there freezing I thought of how am I going to survive here? What am I going to do to get food? I knew I was in a very desperate situation, surrounded by thousands of people just like me, making it that much harder to find food or work but I had to do something. I had no money but knew in the morning I would figure something out. I bundled up tightly and

Ordnungdienst Line Up- Jewish Police Line Up fig 58

let the wind blow. The ghetto slept, if you can call it that.

The next morning I took a walk and came upon a large horse and carriage. While admiring the horse a guy comes over to me and says, "What are you doing?" I must have been staring at the beautiful animal for too long, but being displaced I had nothing else to do. Hunger was really on my mind when I answered him. "If you will give me some water, I will wash the carriage."

The fellow said, "You know how to wash?"

It seemed easy enough. So I said with confidence and a wide smile, "Of course."

This is how I was given the chance to wash the fellow's carriage, and because I was in dire straits I washed the carriage as if there was nothing else of importance in the entire world. Eventually, seeing what a good job I was doing, the man said, "Have you had any breakfast?"

I gazed down and said meekly, 'No.'

Upon hearing this, the good fellow brought me to the back of his carriage and showed me a little bread and a little butter. Sharing this bread with me at the time was one of the kindest acts a man could do for another, and we became friends or rather ghetto employee and employer.

Sol Westreich, the owner of the horse and carriage, was a tailor before the war. His father had owned the horses and carriages near the mikvah (bath house) but now his father was gone, deported. In fact Sol's whole family was deported and I don't think any survived including Sol. But at that moment Sol, age 27, was the head of his family with a brother and sister, and horses and carriages to care for. When I came to Tarnow, the three of them were still living at the family house and still trying to care for each other as well as the horses. But this was a big stable and they needed help. The timing was perfect.

Sol asked me where I slept last night. I told him that I was working at a road camp not far from here when I was arrested for being Jewish and herded with about 400 other Jews onto a train that took us to Tarnow. When I got here the Ordnungsdienst[6] took me to a home of a widow and her child with over ten other displaced men and even though the home offered a little protection from the elements it was so overcrowded the woman tried to chase us all out and that last night I slept on the stairs.

Sol could see right through me as I added with a smile that I preferred to see the stars. Sol was not shocked by anything I was saying. Living in Tarnow, he must have seen so many bad things happen in the ghetto that this was just another one. For me, it was more important that he asked anything. Luckily, when I was done, Sol said, "You can sleep in the stables if you want to."

Upon hearing this, my eyes brightened and I readily agreed. That night I slept in luxury. The horse stable was like a hotel to me. There was plenty of room, and straw for a blanket, plus the horses were good company, and the rich odor of the manure did not bother me in the least. Before long, I was driving the carriage I cleaned, and

156

my *customers* would be the feared Gestapo or the local Judenrat. No one paid for my services but now I had a little freedom and a way to get around.

When the Gestapo wanted service, The Jewish Police would come to the stable and give the order to the next driver in line. I remember one morning a policeman stood in front of me and said, "You need to go to Urszulanka 22," Gestapo headquarters. It was located outside of the ghetto in the town of Tarnow. This is the first time I met two characters in fancy black jackboots, Kastura and Grunov, and took them to a local restaurant and bar as they instructed. I was always subservient to their requests. I expected no payment and they expected little discussion, other than, "Yes, Sir." Most times I did not know where I was going. They preferred to direct me, right here or left there, until we reached the destination. Once I followed these a few times I began to know where they wanted to go without further assistance.

I can still see them dressed in their uniforms. They wore fine clothing with official looking badges while I was wearing my Star of David armband. When they gave me orders I did not have to answer. If you stood on the side of the road as we trotted by and looked toward us as we passed you would see two Nazis with their tight haircuts and flat hats with the black leather circling the brim and a Star of David on the back of the carriage.

I was summoned on multiple occasions to drive Kastura and Grunov and after I dropped them off sometimes I would wait as instructed, and other times I would return to the ghetto. But, at all times, I was a careful observer, and the thing I was most interested in was the marketplace. First, I bought potatoes. I don't know where I got a little money to make the first purchase, but I traded the little I had for spuds and hid them in the back of the wagon. Doing this frequently, I became a valuable lifeline to the most valuable thing in the ghetto, food.

On my first purchase the woman was selling a pakiet ziemniaka, a bundle of potatoes, for 100 zloty, but I only had 80. So, she took a few out and gave me most of the bag. This made it possible to make the first purchase. On the way back into the ghetto I had to be recognized by the Jewish police. They were in charge of the gate. They let me through without too much trouble. I sold the potatoes for three times what I paid, and quickly made a reasonable profit. This I parlayed into other purchases, always following the same basic plan, driving the Gestapo and ending up at the market. It took some courage for me to do this. I am not sure what would have happened if I had been searched, but I'm sure it wouldn't have been good.

The following trip I started to get a little more bold. I purchased a chicken, and some vodka. Gold would be less valuable than this in the ghetto. With the money I earned I purchased clothing and boots. Taking care of the horses and equipment, staying warm, and keeping my stomach from being empty was my whole life. All I had to do was to drive the bastard Gestapo wherever they wanted to go.

Over time I did not want any more potatoes. Instead I preferred things that I could hide in smaller packages, like vodka. Soon, Sol learned about my dealings. He waited by the gate for me to return. When I crossed into the ghetto and past the Jewish police, Sol stopped me and said, "You're not going to sell this." He didn't even know what I had on that trip before he spoke. He continued, "I need it for my sister and brother." I owed Sol my life and would gladly do anything for him, so of course I gave him the items. Sol, however, did not want me to be empty handed and agreed he would pay the cost of the items. On that day I was very pleased to pay Sol back in this small way.

There was plenty of downtime in the small ghetto. It was only 3 blocks long by 4 blocks wide. And even though the ghetto was filled with thousands of people it was easy to meet some of

158

same people on the street over and over. One day I met a young man named Chaim. He was friendly and we shared a little bread. It wasn't hard to figure out that Chaim was a little more religious than I was but this didn't matter. Chaim needed work, but I was not in a position at the time to help him other than to share stories and a little food. While eating we commiserated about our situation; both of us being displaced in the ghetto and without parents. Chaim told me he was from Bochnia. One day, a random selection descended upon the ghetto and Chaim was gone, reportedly to Auschwitz. I had heard the name of this place more than once. It was associated with strange rumors of systematically killing people.

The Jewish police eventually found out what I was doing, and they were not happy. If the Gestapo found out I was smuggling food and other things into the ghetto there would be serious trouble. Both the police and I would have been held responsible. Plus the action could result in punishing the whole community in the form of deportations, including many of the Jewish Police themselves. Because of their Nazi overseers the Jewish Police decided to get rid of me, a strange twist on the expression, "Don't bite the hand that feeds you." But these were backwards times when even starvation was better than the wrath of the Gestapo. Anyway, apparently there was no rush. Months went by while I continued to bring the little I could into the ghetto on each successive trip to the town.

One day I saw a young boy standing by the stables looking at the horses, just like I had a few weeks before and I startled the boy by asking, "What are you looking at?" The boy was at first shy and speechless. He had just arrived from the road works as well, via a short stop in the local prison of Tarnow. I knew exactly how he must have felt, the memory was fresh in my mind when I did the same thing. I prodded the boy, "What do you want?"

The boy, all of 16, said, "I am good at taking care of horses, do you need any help? Well, really his father and his grandfather were skilled in taking care of horses, but he must have learned something, because he was able to point things out to me that made sense. Before long the boy, Leon, had a place to sleep in the stable using the hay as a blanket too, and with the horses as companions.

Leon Continues

The difference between Moshe and me is that I had a way with horses, and the large gelding, Maciek, quickly bonded to me, this was reinforced by sleeping at the stables. If you can get a horse to bond with you, they will follow all of your actions during the entire day. In this way, Moshe made it possible for me to have a coveted job at the Tarnow stables.

Moshe made friends with everyone, or at least he did not make enemies. His only friction came from the Jewish police and they were hungry too. In a short period of time he would get to know the people at the market place, and they expected him. He would buy from them every chance he got. To get past the guards he cut them in on some of the bounty. As much as it sounds like a lot, so many years later, he realized it wasn't much. The risk of getting caught was always high. And even if he wanted to, he was not driving the carriage all the time. There was much downtime, waiting for jobs. Long periods of time were spent at the stables just taking care of the animals, and now with me doing much of the cleaning, Moshe could stretch his legs.

Sol was the owner of the stable and a young man himself. The ghetto, his home, was overpopulated. People were starving, and being deported by surprise. But, whenever anyone came to him and asked for something he always gave a little. On many occasions he would reach into his pocket and take out some money to give it to anyone who asked. Moshe and Sol became good friends. They both helped each other. With the risks Moshe was taking to bring things into the ghetto and Sol's natural love of people they made a fine team and even a little money. But still, Moshe felt like a beggar, living on the street in comparison. Once, when he asked Sol for some food outside of his home, he said, "If you will give me something to eat, I will bring it to the stable."

Sol could read between the lines of what he was saying and responded, "You're too embarrassed to come into my house and eat, but you're not ashamed to take the food to the stables and eat it there; that is a good combination."

Just a few days before I met Moshe, I was taken from the road works and became a citizen non-grata with the rest of the Jews. I'm not sure how they got my name as I still had no armband. The Germans did not want either of us in their vision of a perfect racially pure state. I was rounded up with the other Jewish boys working on the road works and languished for a few days until the Gestapo loaded us onto a train. We were expecting to go to Tarnow ghetto, but instead we went to the local Tarnow prison. I later heard that the reason we were in that prison instead of going directly to Tarnow ghetto was that the Nazis were trying to use us as hostages for money. So, as we waited, our fate was parlayed by the Nazis and must have been pondered anxiously by the Judenrat of Tarnow. With so little cash and other resources to draw from, I'm sure this must have been another torture for the Judenrat. Later, I met the leaders of the Judenrat.

I learned the Judenrat was told, "If we do not get what we want, (referring to money) we will execute the prisoners. Our lives hung in the balance. We were turned into hostages for ransom before we were even allowed the privilege to enter the ghetto. I don't know how this was resolved, but eventually we were released and finally brought under guard to Tarnow.

From my perspective, my ordeal was just beginning. Standing in front of the ghetto we were formed into lines. Ahead of me was a selection committee. When I reached the front of the line, I was asked, "What is your profession?"

I told them, "I was helping to build a road."

They sent me to ghetto *A* or *Arbeit Loss* meaning, the unemployed ghetto. I guess there were no roads to build in Tarnow ghetto. Once inside, I learned my cousins were also in the ghetto with their kids. But not before I spent a couple of cold nights on the stairs. A few days later, I found them and they took me in. One was on her way to work in ghetto *B* or *Besheftig*; The Workers ghetto.

It took a few months for the Jewish police to finally remove Moshe from Tarnow. On April 30th, 1943, there was a selection to send people to a camp nearby called, Szebnie. Tarnow was becoming overcrowded again, and they wanted to make room by taking some people to other camps. When the Jewish police were given the order to round up people they could not find Moshe. Sol was hiding him in his apartment. Eventually, when the coast was clear Moshe went back to work and of course started doing exactly the same thing, driving the Gestapo, and going to the market. Again, the Jewish police were frustrated, forced to accept the situation. Meanwhile, Moshe was a godsend to the ghetto. So little was coming in, and so many people were starving.

Three weeks later, more people were needed for another work camp called Rymanow. This time the Jewish police went directly to Sol and said, "If you don't give up Moshe, we will take you instead." Moshe heard this, and voluntarily turned himself in. He couldn't let anything happen to Sol. I saw Moshe that morning. He was gone by the afternoon. There was nothing to take with him and little reason to say goodbye. We were all in dire straits. That day I became the driver of my own rig, Moshe's Carriage Number 7 with the majestic gelding Maciek as my steed.

Within a few days of my arrival, I had found my relatives and first cousins, Roman and Usher Flink. Tarnow was their home prior to the occupation so they were able to give me shelter. I was glad to see them, especially in these circumstances, and thankful to still have some family I could rely upon. I was in a terrible state of mind. By this time I thought my family was gone forever and I was now alone in the world. I was despondent, but I had little time for pity if I was going to survive. My stomach growled, and I still needed some kind of work to do. I had not yet found the stables, Moshe, Sol or Maciek.

At first I walked around aimlessly. As I did this I found myself looking into the faces of people who like me thought they were all condemned. It did not take long to realize we were all suffering badly. Unable to help them let alone help myself, I concentrated on finding some kind of work to do. Jobs were coveted. To find a job I needed to find a friend or make some friends quickly. No one wanted me. It was not going to be easy. I was sickened by the noises and the smells, tormented with images of my family and friends whenever I lay down to close my eyes. During the night, I tossed and turned as I heard the Nazis celebrating outside the ghetto walls. At some point I stopped wallowing in my misery, and found the words of my father, "You will live longer than all of us." With little hope for myself, and feeling my own time was short, I could not help thinking I would soon see my family in the afterlife. But, even though my subconscious was thinking these terrible thoughts, I planned on what to do in order to live. I never gave up hope. I did everything to plan on living. I knew my only *real* hope was rescue from the world outside, so I just had to hang on. The nearest saviors would be the Russians or possibly the English and the Americans combined, but neither force was close. I was sadly on my own. I said to myself, "If you are going to survive you will need to stay busy working."

That first month in Tarnow was very tough. I did not have a job and there was little food or anything else for that matter. In this squalid environment I became feverishly ill. I became so sick that my cousin brought me to the hospital. I was given treatment for 'belly' typhus. It would be the first time I had this potentially deadly disease but not the last. I stayed in the hospital for 3-4 days until I was strong enough to be released. Before I was released, my cousin brought me something I would not have expected in a million years, an orange. This is a tropical fruit, rare in this part of the world, but somehow he got one and gave it to me saying, "This will be good for what is ailing you." A few days later I was back on my feet and finally found that coveted job.

As you might imagine, I grew up very fast. Fear does that to you. No longer could I escape wearing the blue and white emblem of my race, 'The Star of David,' as an armband. It was required. Grief was my closest companion, hunger my obsession. I was a teenage prisoner. Everything was taken away, with no end in sight. Every day was a new atrocity.

One of the most heartbreaking things I ever saw while in Tarnow was a mother forcibly loaded into a truck, while her small child wept and called out to her. She just happened to be out looking for food when one of the surprise purges occurred. I will never forget her wailing nor her child's. What kind of people could separate a mother from her child like that? Sadly, I was in no position to help. None of us could. They would shoot you if you did. And if you died because of this they would let you rot in the street. The smells were atrocious. We were all starving and competing for the smallest shred of anything. When the trucks would appear, the whole community scattered trying to hide anywhere they could. Once the Nazis left, the ghetto daily activity resumed.

My cousin, knowing I came from a family of horsemen, told me he would ask his friend if they would give me a job working at the stable. It did not seem appropriate to me in my desperation to explain to him that I tried to avoid my father's work every chance I got. But, this is how I learned about the stables and was discovered by Moshe. So, I ended up working at the Tarnow ghetto stables with Sol Westreich. Sol was mismatched for this job as well. He was a tailor before the war. Now, he was in charge of the stables. From my perspective, I could not thank him enough for allowing me to work there, and I was eager to do anything. He showed me around. It didn't take much for me to be familiar with taking care of horses. Then he said, "The stables are relatively safe, plus, you can sleep here too. All I ask in return is that you and the horse are ready at all times."

I started to care for the horse I was assigned right away. Working with him took my mind off of everything. He was a giant beast. I kept him cleaner than a human. And because I also slept near him, he bonded with me. He soon became *my* horse. I also cared for the carriage as well. It was a modest but elegant coach emblazoned with the number 7. I loved this horse and I made sure he was always ready to move. His name was *Maciek*, and he was better fed than the rest of the ghetto, courtesy of the Nazis through the Judenrat. Little did I realize that taking care of the horse and carriage would be the easy part. The hard part was the reluctant willingness to drive the Gestapo on demand. Maybe my naivety is why I was chosen in the first place? To me this job was a godsend. I didn't have the luxury of even thinking about why I was hired at the time. My whole life became that of a *ghetto driver* and little did I expect that I would soon become the preferred driver for Commandant Blache, and some of his Gestapo as well as the Jewish president of the Judenrat.

Now, instead of hiding when the Gestapo would come randomly with their trucks I would instead collect my horse and carriage and fall into line, a kind of horse taxi, ready to serve. Around me, everyone would be scattering in fear, and the streets would soon empty except for eight young ghetto boys with their horses and carriages, all at the ready.

I believe I owe my life to Maciek, and that coach with the

Official Ordnungdienst Stamp fig 59

brass lamps. Sol trained me well. I remember my first meeting with SS Hauptsturmfuhrer Commandant Hermann Blache. The first thing he said, to me, as he inspected my horse and carriage was, "You don't look Jewish?"

I acknowledged without embellishment, "Yes Sir." It struck me how politely he spoke to me. He seemed sympathetic to my plight and was in a good mood. Right away he gave me a nickname, *Junge* or *The Young Boy*. Then he said, "If you need any rations for the horse they will be available through the Jewish Committee."

From that point forward I became the commandant's preferred driver and he would ask for me frequently by my nickname, Junge. I drove him many places in and out of the ghetto. By doing this I gained a small measure of freedom, as well. For one I got to see Tarnow not just the ghetto but the town, and while I waited between trips, I was able to sell things, like shoes and clothing, in exchange for food, I could bring this back into the ghetto, as if it were gold. My passengers, the Gestapo, did not try and stop these transgressions. I couldn't do it in front of them but there was always some extra time between trips.

I also became friendly with a woman outside the ghetto who worked at the market. She frequently gave me chicken, bread and butter, all of which were delicacies. She was a good soul. She never knew when I would come, but she was always ready with some food. I am sorry I don't remember her name. What I do remember however was that she was a large woman who always wore an apron as she worked in the market. Meanwhile, even though I was doing a little trading on the black market, I was also gaining trust with the Gestapo as a good driver.

When Blache would visit the ghetto, unlike the regular storm troops, no one had to run, so they didn't. He was polite and the Jewish ghetto dwellers returned the favor by tipping their hats. I know this sounds odd but it is the truth. Make no mistake, as harmless as he seemed he was completely caught up in the terrible events that would surround Tarnow, and in part, because of his efforts thousands of innocent people would be killed. Knowing this, it makes it harder for me to share with you that he was polite, on a day-to-day basis.

Years later, well after the war, I spoke with Eli Sommer. He was one of the Jewish policemen at the ghetto Tarnow and he agreed with me that Blache was a decent respectful person but then in a twisted story he recounted to me one tragedy at the hands of Blache that is inconsistent with both our opinions. I think this is also an example of how we were all coerced or somehow resigned to the realization that we were second-class citizens with no rights or privileges, sub-human.

Here is what Eli said, "The ghetto Tarnow was reduced to only 150 Jewish Policemen. I was one of them. I was being used to help clean up the mess after the deportations and mass killings. My job, along with 11 others was to take the confiscated property, furniture and such, and load it onto a truck that would be taken to a train nearby. One day while doing this all 12 of us were called to the security office and interrogated one at a time.

We were each asked, "Do you have any valuables in your pockets?" I knew this was a crime punishable by death. I had some valuables but I said. "No." When they reached my friend Goldman they checked his pockets and found something. He was immediately brought outside in front of us and was executed by Blache himself."

Even though most days were uneventful it didn't take more than a few such incidents to realize how dangerous this whole experience was. One day, I was directed to drive over to the Gestapo headquarters and pick up two officers. They introduced themselves, as Officers Grunow and Kastura.

The first thing they said to me was in the form of a command, "Take off the armband," after a pause he continued, "Whenever you take us anywhere, never wear that armband."

I asked him, "How can I do that? I might be stopped by other Gestapo."

He laughed, "We are the Gestapo. Only we will know you are Jewish."

I took off my armband as I was told. I was glad to take it off. At first driving them was not so bad. They seemed to like me too. Frequently they would ask me to take them to the nightclub on Crakauer Street. Sometimes they asked me to wait for them. Outside the club, I kept busy talking to people, grooming the horse and seeing if I could scrounge up a little food; usually, I could do all three.

I will never forget one trip with Grunow and Kastura. I arrived to pick them up on time. My horse was groomed and carriage polished. My armband was in my coat pocket. They got in the carriage as usual but their faces looked serious. Without speaking where to go we rolled away from Gestapo headquarters. Normally, they would give me a destination and expect I knew how to get there, but this time it was different. I was only given specific directions. *Turn Left, go to the end, and turn right.*

Eventually, we ended up in front of a building. The sign read, 'Leather Goods.' I waited, as they both went inside with a deliberate stride. Within a few moments they came out with two young girls. The girls were well dressed, but their faces looked like they were sent to the principal of my old school. I could not imagine what they may have done to deserve the involvement of Gestapo nor would I be so bold as to ask. Still speaking with as few words as possible they gestured to the girls to sit on the two hard seats of the carriage across from theirs. The girls did as they were told. I was right behind them.

I felt uneasiness from everyone. I still didn't know why, but something serious must have happened. I started my horse, and again, without giving me a destination they just gave me directions, "Right here...Left there..." I was puzzled where they wanted to go, until I found myself on the street that led to the Jewish cemetery. I had a feeling this was going to be tragic. But if I were to do anything to reveal my personal abhorrence they wouldn't hesitate to include me in whatever they were up to. I let my horse do the work and kept my wits clear even though my heart was racing. The girls said nothing. The gate was open as if they were expecting us.

We rode inside the entrance, and in what seems today to feel like slow motion, the two Gestapo soldiers gestured abruptly for the girls to get out. Continuing with hand motions, they pointed to them to go over there. It hardly mattered where. In silence, they both pointed their guns and shots ripped the early evening. The girls fell. Still silent, the men gestured for me to come down from the coach and go with them. I thought, I would be killed at that very moment. Instead, one broke the silence, and said only, "Take the boots."

Regretfully, I took the boots off their now limp bodies, and returned to the coach. I carefully put both pairs in a box next to my driver's seat. With the deadly act completed both of their moods changed. Speaking with a sense of relief they told me, "Take us to the Krakowska Street nightclub."

As we drove, their conversation returned to regular banter. They did not speak about what they had done only about whom they might meet tonight at the nightclub. When we arrived they got out of the carriage. It was as if nothing happened.

I asked them as innocently as possible, "What should I do

with the boots?"

Kastura said, "Sell them." He knew I was making small deals on the street while I waited and did not care.

They left to go inside the nightclub as I stood there dazed, a witness to murder, helpless in my situation. Later that night, I returned to the ghetto and shared my experience with Sol and the other stable boys. They already knew about it. They said, the reason those girls were killed, was that they were Jewish, but had non-Jewish papers, and someone tipped off the Gestapo.

On another night, I got another job from Kastura. I learned of this job via the Jewish police. The Jewish police found me at the stable and told me to pick up a bread wagon and go to a certain place. Since the bread wagon in the ghetto was used for picking up dead bodies, I knew this could not be good. I arrived around midnight and alerted the guard that I was there to pick up the bread wagon. Then I backed up the horse and connected the wagon. As I did this, out of the shadows came two prisoners carrying a box on poles. They placed the box into the back of the wagon, and left. Within the box, I saw a person and thought he was dead. Then Kastura appeared as if from nowhere and sat next to me. "Junge, go to the cemetery," he said. When we arrived, I parked next to an open grave. I had no idea who the man was in the box and would not dare to ask.

Within a few moments a few more Gestapo arrived. They parked their Mercedes and got out of the car. As I held my horse still, workers from the cemetery took the box from the wagon. That is when I realized the person was still alive, badly beaten. I heard sharp interrogation and additional beatings. Then they dropped him into an open grave and a single shot put him to sleep forever. To this day I have no idea who he was, but as before, with the evening's work completed, Kastura's mood changed as he directed me to take him to the nightclub.

Most of my trips did not result in murder. Being a driver, I took many trips all over the City of Tarnow, inside and outside of the ghetto. Because of this, when I was outside, I noticed, life went on as before. I saw people laughing and going to church, even the SS were going to church. Knowing all too well the wretchedness of my people, I found this incongruous. What could the preacher be saying to the good townspeople while my people were being subjected to abject misery? I also noticed the town was rife with black market activity making it easy for me, or anybody, to buy whatever I wanted.

One day, I found myself driving Mr. Volkman and Mr. Lerhaupt, both the leaders of the Judenrat, and Commandant Blache, all three together. I was taking Blache to his home and the others were along for the ride. As the driver, I was only able to understand a little bit of what they were talking about. What I heard was the committeemen trying to make a deal by pleading with Blache. They were emphatically asking to allow more Jews to work (so as to save their lives). In response, I heard Blache say, "The Gestapo want numbers." I knew he was referring to their deadly quotas, that is what the random truck deportations were all about.

The ride was about a half an hour long. When I finished dropping Blache off, I brought Volkman and Lerhaupt back to the ghetto. On the drive back the two men were commiserating, "We can not do anything with them. The Germans are very stubborn." Followed by, "But we can not give up. We must figure a way to put more people to work."

They were referring to some of the local ghetto work places. One of these companies was Madricz. It made uniforms for soldiers. Since a German owned it, and it was located in the Jewish ghetto, they were allowed to operate using Jewish labor at little or no cost. The Jews were begging to work. I understood this implicitly. I don't know how anyone could survive without work.

Luckily, both my cousins worked there. I remember that to get to work they had to cross from ghetto *A* to ghetto *B*. My own

The Sternlicht Sisters
Bronislawa - Betty, Sydonia, Helena

Oscar Schindler's List

L.	Ln.	Rel.	Natn.	H. No	Surname	Forename	Birth	Occupation
1	260	Ju.	Po.	76463	STERNLICHT	Bronislawa	3.5.22	Metallarbeiterin
1	261	Ju.	Po.	76464	STERNLICHT	Helena	25.4.25	Metallarbeiterin
1	262	Ju.	Po.	76465	STERNLICHT	Sydonia	24.2.20	Metallarbeiterin

fig 61

wife to be, Betty (Bronislawa), also worked for a division of this same company in Krakow. She worked at this factory until she was selected along with her sisters to join Oscar Schindler's famous list.[9] In the movie, *Schindler's List* you can see vignettes of her sister, Helen, being mistreated while working for Commandant Goth. Helen, was also featured in an award winning documentary called, *Inheritance*, in which she meets the sheltered daughter of Commandant Goth, well after the war.

Madricz was not the only business Jews could work at. There were others as well. For instance, Gross Schneideraj made coats for ladies. These jobs would save lives. The Tarnow Judenrat only wanted permission to give more people a chance.

In this way, I lived from August 1942 to August 1943 until the liquidation of the Tarnow ghetto.

The End of the Tarnow Ghetto

On Thursday, the last week in August 1943, the Gestapo surrounded the Tarnow ghetto. In the distance, I saw machine guns mounted on trucks, and troops on roofs of the apartments outside the ghetto. At 5.00 - 6:00 AM the Jewish police gave orders to all the people to assemble in the Appelplatz (Market Square). Meanwhile, the ghetto drivers, myself included, prepared our horses and carriages and stood ready for orders. Once the rigs were ready we waited about an hour before the Gestapo entered the ghetto. I saw new faces dressed sharply and with stern condescending looks. Standing directly before me was the feared Hauptsturmfuhrer of Krakow, Amon Leopold Goth. Near him I saw Roman Blauner and his flatbed carriage designed to move furniture,

Goth was with his elite team. Eight carriages were lined up across from them with their drivers. I was among them. The streets were mostly cleared by the time they entered. Commandant Blache walked towards us taking Goth and his staff to show him the fine horses. As they approached he said, "These are our ghetto drivers, they have been individually selected." First he pointed to Sol and with slight derision said, "They are owned by this Jew but we use them as we wish." Goth pointed to Sol Westreich and said with indignation, "You must go to the Appellplatz. Leave now." Sol skulked away. This was the last time I ever saw him.

Goth then looked at the first driver and said, "Take me to the Appellplatz." Before they left, Commandant Blache identified me to Goth saying, "This is Junge, my personal driver." Goth directed his staff, "Leave him." I remained unflinching until they moved. It seemed like an eternity before they took their attention from me, finally I breathed.

The remainder of the drivers including me were taken to a holding area by what I thought was the wood mill. Then they locked the gates and posted Special Police guards. I remember their blue uniforms, hats with brass eagles, and the insignia, *S. P.* We were being held to clean up the ghetto once the deportation was completed. But the police were posted not to keep us in, but to make sure that no others would join us or try to avoid the deportation. It did not take much imagination that this would be the setting for a heart-wrenching tragedy. I am haunted by this event to this day, over sixty years later. From my position I heard fear and panic spread everywhere, while the Jewish police were scurrying around trying to move all the people to the market place.

It was chaos. Nobody knew what was going to happen, but everyone feared whatever would happen next. They all thought, as bad as the ghetto was, being deported must be worse. Since, the death camps were no secret by then they had every right to be frantic.

While this tragedy played out, I had plenty of time to realize I was not really in a wood mill but the Singer crate factory. As

174

I watched and waited those assembled were loaded on trucks and slowly the ghetto was being completely emptied. This was perhaps the worst thing I have ever witnessed.

I do know one family that escaped, The Volkman family. Somehow they were spared and sent with an officer named Kellerman who took them across the border to Hungary. I can only imagine there must have been some kind of payment or favor to do this. It took awhile but with most of the people gone the market place was empty and the town was essentially without Jews. At this point a big truck came into the square and parked. A Ukrainian driver exited the vehicle and stood nearby. In front of the truck was a sparkling black Mercedes car. The truck driver was ordered to collect any valuables still left in the ghetto.

Just before we were released to begin the clean up about fifty people were flushed out of hiding places still in the ghetto, most were women with small children. With little fanfare they were promptly lined up and executed, some while holding their babies. As this was done, Blache and Goth stoically looked on. I too watched this, but for me, I watched in abject horror. I could see the whole thing from my location. By this time of my young life, I had seen many deaths, but this was one of the most callous events I ever witnessed. Children in the arms of their parents dropped after loud sounds cracked the air. A single bullet would shoot through both their bodies. Pools of blood formed around them as they wilted to the ground.

At one point Goth became annoyed. His boots had become bloody with the gore from the executions. Calling over to the Special Police guarding us, he gestured towards his boots, "Send me someone to clean my boots." We stood frozen; none of us wanted to be picked. This could easily be the last thing any of us ever would do. The guard turned to me and using only his finger directed me to go and help the dreaded Hauptsturmfuhrer. I couldn't hide. I was selected. Reluctantly, I walked over and bent down to clean the boots of Amon Goth with my cap while the shooting continued around us. As he stood arrogantly in his boots I was shaking in mine. After I cleaned them, he looked at me and asked Commandant Blache, "Who is this boy?" At that moment I realized I did not have an armband. Again, I froze in the August heat. Blache responded in a way to distract and yet move the conversation forward, "Just leave him to clean up."

They walked away and I returned to the limited safety of my temporary horse pen. My friends looked at me as if I had touched the Devil. Nothing needed to be said. I put my bloodstained cap back on. We were all in a state of horror and shock. Finally, late in the morning, we were released to begin the clean up. Kastura and Grunov were assigned to direct about 200 of us. All-in-all about 600 Jews remained to clean up the ghetto. All they said as we started to leave was, "You will work in pairs." This terrible day was still just beginning.

People were still hiding any place they could. To finish the cleanup, four companies of SS kommandos entered the market place. One came with dogs, another with dynamite, a 3rd with a flamethrower, and a forth with machine guns. First they entered ghetto *A*. I heard lots of shooting but I could not see what was going on. Then, nearby, I caught a glimpse of my cousin's sweet wife, the one who worked at Madricz. She stepped out of the shadows with her two children. Then my other cousin also came forward with her child. Our eyes met for a moment, the image is fixed in my mind forever. I could not say or do anything to help. A guard took them to a wall where shots, once again, ended their suffering.

The liquidation of the Tarnow ghetto was started on Thursday, but it wasn't until three long and despicable days later, on Sunday, that it was over. After the main population was removed, the Gestapo methodically started a sweep building by building to make sure the ghetto was empty. If they found anyone alive, they

176

were instantly killed. They used every means at their disposal to eradicate the Jews from the ghetto. Dogs sniffed for people, while flamethrowers and dynamite did massive damage to buildings. It took dynamiting to bring down the majestic Jewish temple. All that stands today are the central columns. I learned later that they were still finding people hiding after one month.

I was directed to take my horse and wagon to ghetto A. As soon as I turned the corner I saw the bodies stacked in two areas. One of them was resting against the synagogue, blood marking the wall and the ground. Moshe Blauner and I looked at each other and this eerie site.

After a brief pause we both spoke, "This will be the end of us."

Kastura broke our fixation, "Pick up those bodies."

That is when I saw the remains of my dear cousin with her children. I told Moshe Blauner, "Let's pick them up first."

Grunov came over to us and with the slightest remorse said, "Take a sheet and cover the bodies."

He was drinking whiskey and the site must have sickened him too. He took a drink and said, "Come here fellows, I want you each to take a pull of this whiskey."

With the whiskey fortifying us we proceeded to go to work picking up the bodies, one at a time. But there is no amount of liquor that could make this situation better.

Once the wagon was filled we brought our grisly load about one kilometer to the cemetery. Here, we dropped the bodies into mass graves and then returned for more. On the way to the cemetery I saw some of the townspeople, in shame, peaking through the curtains of their homes. They were also powerless to help. Now the ghetto was Judenfrei. All the Jews were gone with the exception of the bodies and ourselves. And my chances of survival were fast approaching zero.

By the time we were finished we had filled up two mass graves about 20 x 20 meters square and 10-15 meters deep. It must have held many thousand people. The giant ditches were dug out by machine. As the day wore on Moshe Blauner and I were commanded to go into the pit to search the bodies for valuables. We entered the mass grave as instructed by descending down a ladder, certain this was the end. I reached the bottom and found myself standing in a pool of blood and surrounded by a stack of thousands of bodies. No one was alive. It was silent, except for the insects and noises from the guards above. I was forced to step on the bodies, slipping on them to check their threadbare clothing. This resulted in finding little if anything. I wasn't sure if we were actually doing something or just entertaining the sadistic guards above.

I wasn't alone. There were about twenty other prisoners with me doing the same thing. We were the only moving things in this ghastly pit. All of us were dealing with the dead bodies; some were stacking them as best they could and others like me were searching them. The whole experience was a nightmare. Lying haphazardly, I saw men, women and children all mangled together in a strange kind of mass with flies everywhere. Moshe and I looked at each other, both of us knowing the likelihood of our surviving as soon as we were done, was unlikely.

After rummaging in the pit for three or four hours, I happened to look up and saw Hauptsturmfuhrer Blache in the sun. My eyes burned. He had come by to inspect the work being done. Recognizing Moshe and me, he shouted, "Who put you down there?" I gestured to the guard standing over us holding a submachine gun. Without hesitation he waved for us to immediately come out, shouting, "Schnell." The guard shouted at the commandant, "This is forbidden."

Commandant Blache pointed his finger at the guard as he walked over to him. I heard a strong exchange of words. I don't know what he said. Except that he came back and commanded us again, "Come out of there right now, schnell." Without question we climbed the ladder, and stood together facing him with our lives hanging tenuously in the balance. He asked, "Where is your horse?"

I told him he had broken away and was probably eating grass. He told me to find the horse and meet him at the deportation place. I started to look for my horse and found a child, still alive. I put him at the side in the grass and kept looking for my horse. The boy started crying and Kastura's ears perked up. He heard the crying. Casually he walked over to the child, took out his gun and ended his life. Leaving him there, he walked away, as if nothing had happened. I could not stop to help the little boy. Nor was there anything I could have done. The only option was to find my horse and meet the Commandant. By this time I was soaked with the blood of the ghetto, underfed for months, and forced to watch all kinds of debased behaviors for an extended period of time. I could not cry. I could hardly think about anything other than finding the horse. Moshe was equally distraught and disheveled. Neither of us however was unnerved; we were instead numb in the deepest sense of the word.

As I looked for the horse, I saw other ghetto workers. Some were still picking up furniture house-to-house and placing it in a big truck. Eli Sommer, who I met after the war was among them. He confirmed that the truck was going to bring the Jewish property to Germany. Others, like me, were cleaning up bodies and debris. The ghetto was empty but for us, a few workers and the Gestapo. I saw old clothing strewn all over the place as well. It wasn't difficult to find some that fit me. I quickly changed clothing. Then, as directed, Moshe and I reported with the horse to the deportation area where Commandant Blache was waiting for us just as he said he would.

Looking back, I realize how hard it is for me to weigh the fact that by shipping us off he was saving our lives at least for the time being. As we prepared to leave Tarnow he said, "You cannot stay here because they will shoot you. Here is a letter of recommendation. You are to take this with these two Ukrainian guards and the horse. They will take you to a work camp. I know the commandant there. He will take care of you." Maciek stood, his long tail flowing in the breeze, as the commandant spoke. I don't know how animals process the misery that I saw that day but at that moment he was my ticket to another day of life. And leaving here I thought it could not get any worse. How wrong I was.

Before parting, Blache touched the nose of Maciek and wished him, Auf Wiedersehen. I know he was talking to the horse but I am sure he meant all of us. As he turned away we were quickly loaded on to a cattle car with Maciek. Once on board, we traveled about 60 miles to Szebnie (Sheb-Knee-ah), a combined horse stable and concentration camp.

This is how Moshe Blauner and I both got out of Tarnow alive. I have never returned to Tarnow nor did I ever see Blache again. I passed by years later but the thought of returning sickens me to this day. It is hard to think I may have to thank Blache for my life, knowing later after the war that according to the courts he was a cold-blooded murderer of mass proportions - at the time he was a savior, mine. For years I have tried to come to terms with why he would have put himself at risk to save Moshe and me.

Chapter Six

My Maciek

The train took us to Moderowka station on the last day of August, 1943. When the train stopped and the door opened to the cattle car, I carefully led Maciek out of this closed space. Standing for a moment, we waited for the two guards to direct us. They pointed us towards the camp and we walked about 3 kilometers to the hill next to the main east-west roads. They brought us directly to headquarters of Szebnie where we met the Commander of the Ukrainian guards Grzimek and his Commandant Kellerman (the same Kellerman that saved the Volkman family). Grzimek was pleased to see us. Maciek made for a stunning introduction. Grzimek was being handed a prize, this giant horse, and he knew it. He looked at him carefully and liked what he saw.

We were also there, of course, but mostly part of the scenery. He did greet us, but it was more to check our general state, he was more interested in checking the horse than anything else. He was able to quickly pick up on what everyone already knew, Maciek was bonded to me. I am sure to him, Moshe and I were just chattel, the horse's aides. A few minutes passed as he read the letter. Half starved with my well fed horse, Moshe Blauner and I stood awaiting our fate. The Commandant turned to Kellerman, obviously pleased with the handsome horse and then to us. He said something to Kellerman. After they spoke, Kellerman immediately summoned the Staff Sergeant.

Staff Sergeant Strybuc arrived smoking his pipe. He was about forty with a distinctive mustache. Grzimek ordered him to take the horse and its keepers to the stable. Once again, my horse saved us. The stable was a white brick building located on the opposite side of the road from the main camp. The camp held about 3,000

181

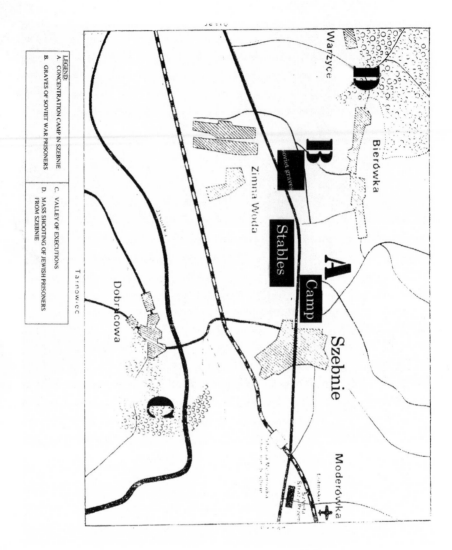

A. Prison camp 'Szebnie,' a sub camp of Plaskow
B. Soviet mass grave site
C. Valley of executions
D. Mass execution of Jewish prisoners

fig 69

Jewish prisoners. The stable, however, was nothing like a prison. It had about 20 people working there and only a few were Jews. As we arrived, I got my first impressions of this combined place. It was a concentration camp. I had heard about these but never seen one before. Within the confines I saw Jews from many different places and Jewish policemen who stood out from the general population but were also obviously prisoners. The camp was so close to the stable that once in awhile I heard a Russian style of music, and because of this, I knew that Ukrainians must be running it.

Sergeant Strybuc walked with us to the stable. On the way he was admiring Maciek. Upon arrival he released us into the hands of our new kapo, Leon Feigenbaum, the fellow in charge of the stable. We stood at attention while the kapo spoke to Strybuc. The kapo then directed me, while pointing, "Take the horse to that pen and stay with him." A little later he explained, "Your job is to prepare the horse that you brought into the camp for the Commandant to ride. You will sleep over there, near the horse." He then turned to Moshe B. and said, "For now go with Sergeant Strybuc, and we will find you a suitable job shortly." Soon Moshe B. would be given the job of taking care of the pigs. If there is one animal that Jews detest it is pigs.

The stable was busy and luckily, as if by a miracle, I realized my old friend Moshe Katz was already there. He wandered in while we were being processed and noticed Maciek. He asked one of the other boys, "What is this horse doing here? I know him." Then he noticed Moshe B. and me. Moshe K. had arrived one day before us. I don't know how he did it, but Moshe must have talked himself *in* with his uncanny ability to bargain. This ability would soon become valuable to us again. Moshe K.'s main job was to handle the garbage. At first it may seem like a menial job, and it is, except the collection site was outside the stables and that made it possible to smuggle goods on the black market. Moshe could go right back to his old habits of trading for vodka to bribe the guards and cheese to supplement our poor diets for us. I am sure it is easy to realize how important this was to us. For many survivors the difference in living and dying would be a few extra calories a day. I remember one incident where the kommando that cleaned the pillowcases for the camp stole one and put it into the garbage. Moshe K. understood that this was not trash and traded it for something of value. Moshe thrived on doing these meager deals as much as a prisoner could thrive on anything. And doing them made him the favorite of the guards and inmates alike. He told me he learned his trading skills before the war when he was growing up. Like me, he also hated school. Instead, he loved to hang around the local Jarmark in his town of Nowy-Sacz. Where he would try to make money however he could.

Moshe K. and I had plenty of time to talk at our new home. Once he had left Tarnow well ahead of the destruction of that ghetto he went to Rymanow as part of a work detail of 300 Jews. Prior to his arrival the Germans killed 10,000 Russian POW's at this location. I heard two reports about this, one was that they were all shot and the other was that they were locked in the barracks and left to rot. Either way, the camp at Rymanow was liquidated completely, erased from the earth, but materials were scarce and the Germans wanted to use them again.

By the time Moshe K. arrived the POW bodies had been removed. He did not see any of the bodies. His team went to work and collected the barbed wire while disassembling the barracks for transport to another location. It took months to do this, from the middle of May to the end of August. Moshe was there from the beginning to the end. This was the worst camp he was ever in because the amount of food given the prisoners was appallingly little and the ability to supplement this with food from the outside was non-existent. He is lucky he made it through this terrible period of his life. To give you an idea of what he went through - to feed 300 prisoners,

184

Leon with Maciek, Artist's Rendition

Leon and Maciek
Artist's Conception fig 70

3 pails of cabbages were made into soup and 1.5 pounds of bread was given to each prisoner every 10 days. There is no way to live on this restricted diet for very long. When the work was completed his entire group was shipped to Szebnie. By the time they arrived they were half-dead from starvation and in such bad shape that the Jewish police told the rest of the Jewish prisoners that even though we have little to eat to save something to give to these poor starving brothers. This was a gift of life for them, without this little extra they surely would have perished.

Compared to what Moshe K. had been through and the prisoners on the other side of the road, I was quite free. It didn't take long before I understood that the kapo makes all the individual assignments. He told me that when I arrived with my fine horse, he wanted to give him to his brother, but Strybuc warned him in that short conversation before I got my assignment, if you make any changes to the commandant's orders regarding this horse or his assistant you will be shot. Strybuc didn't talk much but whatever Blache wrote in that letter got translated to him that only I was to take care of Maciek. So, this is where I lived with no idea when it would change. I knew it could not last for long, but I hoped, maybe, the war would be over before I would have to leave. With only one thing keeping me alive I kept that horse cleaner than a person, certainly better than I could clean myself.

But I also had a vexing problem. Maciek had never been ridden before. He was a carriage horse. And now he was supposed to be saddled with the Commandant as his rider and I was to make sure this would happen. Yet, every time I put a saddle on him, he bolted. After he was spooked it took awhile to calm him down. I guess I learned something from my grandfather because I coaxed, and teased him with bricks of sugar. Eventually it worked and the horse allowed the Commandant to ride him and from this point forward Maciek became the personal horse of the Commandant. After the war I learned he took that horse to Krakow and then later to Plaszow. But, for me right then and there, I felt as long as I took care of that horse I was safe. It turned out to be only eight weeks.

One day I was walking Maciek when my old neighbor Tadeusz Skrabski happened to drive by in his carriage. He was on his way to the Jasło Jarmark to trade horses. Riding with him were some SS members who most likely wanted his expertise in choosing the best animals. His hand was still wrapped in bandages. When he saw me working that beautiful horse, he could not believe his eyes and had to stop to say hello. He got out of the carriage, and walked to an area on the road above me, as the place was on a hill.

Just by stopping he was under great danger. The guardhouse was watching us closely. The Ukrainian SS men were pointing their rifles at Tadeusz, and with their fingers itching. I wondered what his Nazi guests must have thought as they watched him stop to talk to a prisoner. I can only imagine the beauty and size of my horse must have mesmerized all of them. We spoke briefly. He was glad to see me and I was glad to see him too. By the end of our short conversation he gave me a small measure of hope promising to bring me food every week. Then, somehow, he slipped me some money. It was 500 Zoltys, a large number on a single bill. I was glad to see him, being someone so close to my family. And for the next few weeks, just as he promised, he brought me a basket of food every Thursday.

I don't know if you can understand my joy, getting a package with sausage and bread each week. Without asking he would toss it towards me and I would then pick it up. Luckily the guards either did not see this or they ignored it. For as long as I received these care packages I shared them with my friends. Later, when I needed help, it would be my friends who saved me.

One night when Moshe K. was about to take out the trash, the kapo stopped him, You are not going to take the garbage out today. He had decided Fritz would do it instead. I did not know Fritz very well. He must have bribed the kapo or more likely enticed Strybuc. Fritz lived in the area around the camp before the war so he knew it well. When the time came, Fritz left with Sergeant Strybuc and the garbage. Once outside the compound, Fritz took Strybuc to a flour mill and within a short period he had escaped. Strybuc was furious. He must have also been afraid of what his Commandant would say when he returned without the prisoner. Frantically, he looked everywhere. But the mill operator, a man who could pass for a hard-core Nazi with no trouble at all, assured him, Don't worry, I will find him and bring him back to you personally in the morning.

The Sergeant returned to the stable empty-handed and furious. As soon as he returned, he woke up all the stable boys and marched us up the hill to the front of the headquarters building, Moshe Blauner, Moshe Katz and me among them, barking orders along the way. Commander Grzimek himself conducted the interrogations. First, he took one fellow prisoner named Golb and hung him on a pole by his hands. I don't know why he was singled out. Then he interrogated the rest of us roughly, Do you know where Fritz went? Did Fritz tell you of his plans to escape? Then we were lined up against a wall and a guard covered each of our heads with a sack.

I was certain we were going to be executed one at a time. A series of gunshots rang out. Blinded by the hood each shot shook me to my bones. I thought my friends were being executed. I thought I would be next. Finally, Grzimek said to me as I was wearing the hood over my face, "I killed your friends and I will kill you too if you don't tell me where to find Fritz." But I had no idea where he was or even his intention to escape. I said, resigned to my fate fearing the worst, "I don't know."

Miraculously, the shots did not kill any of us. It was just a fear tactic to get us to talk. After some tense moments Strybuc returned us to the stable. Fritz never returned. He was one of the few who escaped successfully.

Days later another nightmare occurred on the Jewish holiday of Simchas Torah[7] It was done specifically on the Jewish holiday to add an extra measure of sadism. About 800 prisoners were gathered up, placed on trucks and executed about 2 kilometers from the prison in the nearby woods. Sergeant Strybuc participated in this. He chose my friend Goldberg to help clean up the mess. Goldberg never came back. Most likely he was killed after helping dispose of the bodies. This is how many executions were covered up. They would choose a Jew to help bury the rest then kill the one who helped to cover the trail. This was a callous execution of almost one third of the camp. I was given the details about it from a peasant who worked with me in our stable. He was not a prisoner, so he was free to come and go as he pleased. He told me once the prisoners were killed their bodies were piled up on railroad ties and set on fire. He did not have to tell me about the smoke or the smell. I will never forget the disgusting odor or the long trail of smoke in the sky. It went on for the whole night.

All of us from the stable were becoming very uncomfortable with our situation and considered escape. That is when I heard that nearby, in Jaslo, the Underground had attacked one of the prison camps and successfully locked up the German guards, releasing the prisoners. These prisoners were now partisans all over the area including the area surrounding my camp. It may be this incident and the related mayhem that made the Germans anxious at my camp. They wanted to reduce the numbers of prisoners to make the camp more controllable while also sending a message to the Resistance that attack would not be tolerated. But I could not think about *their* reasons for doing anything. What I could do instead was escape and join the Underground. It was risky to just talk about it, but I was desperate. So, I took a chance and asked my friend, Tony Anthony, if the Underground would accept me. A few days later I got my answer, no Jews. Resigned to my fate I realized even if I could escape I would have no place to go.

About eight weeks after my arrival at Szebnie, at the end of October, around the day of my birthday, Sergeant Strybuc announced he was taking us to the camp across the street for a special roll call. This was exactly the kind of action I feared most. After the roll call my friends and I tried to go back to the stables, but we were not allowed to leave. We were trapped. There was a lot of confusion. We could not understand what was happening. But we knew something was going on. Anxiously, we tried again to go back across the street but the guard refused saying, "Nobody can leave the camp." That is when we realized we were in deep trouble. We had no choice but to stay and no assigned place to stay either. I saw prisoners and the Jewish Police running around. We stayed away from them. Worriedly, we began to see SS guards in full battle gear and trucks and motorcycles surrounding our camp. They remained at a distance of about 1 km. Around 10 PM the darkness was assaulted with floodlights as assembly sirens wailed. Once we were assembled, Commander Grzimek spoke, "You are going to be transported to another camp. You do not need to bring anything because you will be going to a very hot place. Anything you have in your pockets or any belongings, leave them in the baskets."

This would be the liquidation of Szebnie. Moshe Katz and I had some money. It might be hard to believe but we found ways to make some money. Meanwhile, if we were caught with it, this could be the reason for our executions. So we hid the money behind a brick and made sure our pockets were empty.

My friend Moshe Blauner remained in Szebnie, as he wished. There was nothing we could do to convince him to come with us, he just refused. Moshe Katz and I could have stayed too. We spoke about it but could not see the sense. Here was a Commandant who was a heartless murderer and a camp that was being closed. I have gone over what happened thousands of times in my mind, and I still can't come to terms with it. Moshe Blauner was like a brother to me.

What puzzles me is that we did nearly everything together. Moshe was the closest in age of the Blauner brothers, to me. We went to school together. We were in the same class, together. When the kids in our class studied religion and the Jewish boys were excused, it was me and Moshe who left to play stick ball together. Even when things got bad in Grybow, Moshe left his family, just like me and went to do roadwork in the North, and of course, that's why we both ended up in Szebnie. So why he decided to stay I'll never know. My only guess is the speech we all heard about, you don't need anything, "...you will be going to a very hot place." I can only imagine him thinking if I'm going to die, not by fire. It all seemed hopeless for all of us, no matter what choice we each made. But Moshe Katz and I made a pact, "We will figure something out."

190

So, we agreed to leave as my best friend took his chance, staying.

The trouble was, too many of the other prisoners had the same idea as Moshe Blauner - to stay. The same night, the camp was evacuated right on schedule. Those of us leaving formed into lines, five deep by twenty rows. This created neat blocks of 100 prisoners. We marched out of the camp in a group. I was in the first group. Out of the corner of my eye I saw Moshe B. for the last time. He said goodbye with a gesture. I could not return it without fear of reprisal. Resigned to my fate my feet moved me forward.

Three hundred prisoners were authorized to clean up the mess after we left, however over five hundred remained. Soon, the Commandant would have to deal with this. Based on his past, I knew he believed the prisoners were not people to him. They were instead, sub-human, and he needed little reason to thin the herd. Worse he had the authority, given to him by the criminal Nazi regime, as well as all the tools he needed to do it. We already knew what he had done in the past, so we knew he had no compunction, at all, to carry this out.

Within a few days of the evacuation, Commander Grzimek gathered the remaining prisoners for a special roll call. I did not see it, but I can imagine him astride my horse, Maciek, moving about the men as they assembled while his adjutant announced, "If anybody is here illegally, step out of line." The announcement, I know to be true. Where I'm hazy is I'm not sure if anything different would have happened if anyone would have stepped out of line, no one did. While the men remained assembled, trucks arrived, and everyone was loaded on board. Just as before, the trucks drove a short distance to the nearby woods where all the prisoners were ordered to get out, were lined up and executed.

Do you remember the free Polish man who worked with me at the stable? The fellow who checked for me if I escaped would the Underground accept me? After the war I saw him again. This is how

I learned what happened to Moshe Blauner and the rest. This is how I lost one of my best friends. Szebnie is where his story ended but mine still had a long way to go.

Around 11 PM we began our march about three kilometers to the rail station at Moderowka. Along the way I heard sporadic shooting and shouting as I put one foot in front of the other. There were few lights if any at the rail station. It was so dark I could hardly see a thing. During this march a few of the prisoners escaped. That must have been the reason for the shooting. But most of us kept walking. Cattle cars were waiting to transport us at the station. But first before we got on the train, Ukrainian SS guards began to shout at us, "Take your clothing off." The guards must have heard stories of how the clothing of the condemned contained valuables. They must have wanted whatever meager things we, the condemned, had for ourselves.

Naked and intimidated by guards with their pain inflicting bludgeons, vicious dogs and guns, I was among 3000 men and 1,200 women who were crammed into a series of empty cattle cars. They stuffed as many of us into each car as they could. I did not count but there was no room to sit once they had loaded us in - every inch of the car was filled with people. We were treated worse than animals. Suddenly the door was snapped shut, the outside lock was engaged and we were trapped.

Chapter Seven

The Cattle Car

Naked and frantic we felt ourselves being jammed tightly against each other until every inch of space in the cattle car was filled. I could hardly breath and I could feel others gasping for breath as well. The car was dark and the mass of humanity struggled to adjust itself to allow each individual to have a bit of space.

The weak quickly succumbed. As they lost consciousness they slipped to the floor and died. The space they had occupied gave the living a little more room. The lifeless bodies couldn't help but be trampled under foot. But the torture was over for them.

The floor of the car was covered in straw and lime. But it did not take long for the stench of human waste to permeate our sealed and rolling tomb.

There in the darkness we stood, beyond hope, having no idea where we were going other than the sadistic clue from Commander Grzimck that it was "a very hot place." For me the only consolation was that my dear friend, Moshe Katz, was in the car with me. Although we had plenty of time to say goodbye our only conversation was about how to survive.

We remained trapped in this inhuman prison for three days and nights, although the length of the journey was only about a hundred miles. Our train must have had the lowest priority because we watched other trains speed past us. But for us time was measured in moments and each moment was an eternity. We were exhausted, naked, without food or water, and resigned to whatever Fate had planned for us. I thought for sure I would soon see my family. No one could have imagined what would happen next.

Late on the third night of our journey the train slowed and then stopped. We had arrived at Auschwitz. Most of the survivors of the journey would not survive their first day in this fiendish place.

After three harrowing days and nights our train had arrived at the commercial station 3km from Auschwitz.[8] The rail line at Auschwitz was not completed yet so this was the closest station. All of us were still tightly crammed standing in the cattle car. None of us had a sip of water nor a morsel of food the whole time. By the time of our arrival the air was stale and the stench was choking us. I could not help but feel dead bodies under my feet mixed with urine and excrement. I also had no idea what time it was, except that it was late at night.

The cars stopped and we waited until it came time to unload. I first heard a big thump on the roof. I remember my listlessness just before the doors were unlocked. I hoped to fill my lungs with some fresh air and escape from these tight quarters, maybe even get some water. My mouth was terribly dry. Once the doors opened, I felt the rush of fresh air. It was followed by a blinding white light. Floodlights assaulted my vision. I jumped free from the car amidst shouting, "Raus!"

The bright light blinded me, so I turned away and looked back at the car. That is when I realized the thump I had just heard above my head was two soldiers standing high above us with their weapons ready. I can only guess they were there to eliminate any chance of disorder or maybe escape by a stampede, after all, they were treating us like a herd of animals. At least, up there, they could not hit any of us with sticks. Since I was in the dark for the last few days the bright light made it almost impossible for me to see at all. I was disoriented. A guard pushed me into line. Raus! Things were starting to come together fast. It must have been quite a foul and pathetic sight to see all of us, both men and women, naked, in the night, after that harrowing adventure in the cattle car. I breathed deeply and tried to regain a small measure of my strength and composure. We were all weakened and slightly delirious. The unloading

194

proceeded, car by car. As it continued, I started to gather my wits. That is when I realized the floodlights were coming from the hills.

The unloading was going on in an organized and deliberate way. We were being channeled into a clearing. Doctors stood ready to review everyone. As my eyes and mind continued to adjust, it became clear to me, I was in a life or death selection. While standing, I tried to shake my body back to life. The night air was

fig 71

cold and brisk. Instinctively, I wanted to make sure I looked strong and healthy when they would decide my fate.

Guards with German Shepherds were stationed on both sides of us. If the line became unformed, the dogs would snarl. As I got closer, I saw elite SS, dressed in white uniforms marked with medical symbols. Nearby, I saw a group of officers of higher ranks milling around surrounded by more guards. They were all immaculately dressed - we were naked. As I got closer, I noticed one of the doctors wearing a monocle over his eye. They were assembled in teams working to hurry the large influx of people along. Just a few days before, this naked mass was camp Szebnie. Now most of the people I saw before me would be condemned to die.

Beyond the guards, I saw a large group of people forming on the right. Step to the right, said the doctor to the man a few people in front of me. Another man, condemned. This evening these few doctors would decide the fate of all of us. I took another step towards them. Soon, it would be my turn.

If you were to step on a beehive that is the kind of chaos that ensued as the cars were opened. Except that the Jews were naked, men and women, dirty and half alive, and they had no weapons. At

195

least a bee has a stinger. I lost Moshe in the shuffle, Roman too. At least I had the Lipczers, Joshua the eldest stepped up to the doctor in front of his two brothers. He did whatever he was told. I was still clearing my head. "Links," was all I heard. His younger brother stepped up to the doctor, the middle one.

Another car was opened, a dog growled, people were asking each other questions about what was happening, Raus! The guard pushed us along. "Links," I heard again. The two Lipczer brothers were off to the left side, safe for now but at the time I could not tell the difference. They were exceptions. The bulk of this mass of humanity was directed to the right. I was close.

The youngest brother stepped forward, Usher. As I saw him I stepped forward. A few years before I had stepped into his family's clothing store. His father was fitting someone for a new outfit. Mr. Lipczer, his measuring tape draped around his neck like a tallit while a yamaka rested on his head. Their family was Orthodox. His assistant wrote the notes as he called out the sizes.

Like a slap in the face I came back to my senses and realized what was happening, Usher, standing in front of me was turning around for the doctor. I was within earshot as I heard the doctor of life and death ask, What is your profession? This was my only warning as to what to expect when it would be my turn. I could not hear Usher's answer. I think he said, Those are my brothers, pointing left. Abruptly without discussion the decision was, Step to the right. The brothers were separated forever. The only solace I can give Usher is he never felt the sustained abuse of Birkenau.

I had already been through a few selections and what I thought to be the most important thing was to show the bastards no fear. So, I shook the fear out of my body as I took another step forward. It was my turn. The elegant doctor with the monocle welcomed me tersely, "Show me your tongue." Without speaking I did as I was told. "Turn around." Again without hesitation, I turned. Looking me straight in

196

Birkenau Front Gate fig. 72

the eye, he asked, "What is your profession?"

I puffed up my chest and told him, "I am a Horse Adjutant."

At first they did not understand and spoke among themselves. Then they laughed. They must have thought I was lower than a horse, a naked Jew boy who said he was the assistant of a horse, at once pathetic and funny. No Jew, especially not a child, could be the Adjutant of a Commandant or any German soldier for that matter. The doctor's composure returned to austere as he peered through me. This time with intense clarity and without a lick of humor he repeated, "What is your profession?"

So I elaborated, "I groomed and took care of the horse for Commander Grzimek."

They thought that was funny too, but now they understood. In good humor he pointed me to the left, "Links."

There was a small group of prisoners standing on the left side. Without thinking, I started toward the larger group on the right. An SS guard grabbed me by the neck and said, "You cursed dog," as he pushed me to the left." I found myself waiting on the left as the selection continued. That night I saw hundreds go to the right. Moshe soon joined me as well as Simon Unger. I am sorry to say that those selected on the right were immediately loaded onto trucks, and sadly, none of them survived. They were sent directly to the gas chambers followed by, ...a very hot place. *Yitgaddal veyitqaddash shmeh rabba...*

Moshe told me his own story about the selection that night. He said, "I looked young. So, they did not do much, except, quickly look me over and decide I was still useful as a worker. So, I too was told to go to the left." I know by the way he passed over the question so fast that he really did not want to talk about it. He intentionally left the details out, preferring to change the subject as quickly as he could. These were terrible years, and Moshe certainly is not alone in not wanting to recall every detail. For him, it was better to ask about me, "Leon, how are *you* doing?"

As I stood there naked, I realized I was with about 50 or 60 other people. Meanwhile on the other side I saw trucks coming and going taking one load at a time of hapless victims. Oddly, I noticed not all of us were naked. There, with us, were the Ordnungsdienst, the Jewish police, in their telltale uniforms with the stylish hats. They still had their belts and shoes too. I was freezing and wondered why they were allowed to keep their uniforms. I guess I should not have been too jealous since not one of the people wearing uniforms were chosen to be on my side. In what was characteristic Nazi fashion, as a way to cover up what happened, they were all sent to the gas chambers to be destroyed, their usefulness over. Their uniforms just made it that much easier for the selection committee to pick them out of the crowd.

Eventually there was a full group of 100 naked prisoners on my side. As soon as this number was achieved, we were formed into a walking group, 5 across, and marched towards the gate. I could still hear trucks coming and going and train cars being unloaded. It would be a long evening for the selection committee.

We walked three kilometers to the camp in the cold and dead of night. We were still naked and thirsty but the movement felt good. While we marched, guards and their dogs kept us in line. Approach-

198

Auschwitz Prisoner photo
Yad Vashem fig 78

ing the huge compound, I saw smoke from a set of chimneys off into the distance. At this sight, somehow, I knew all the rumors about the crematoriums were true. Before long, we walked through the gates of Birkenau, and moved directly to the quarantine center. We might as well have crossed the gates of hell.

Every new prisoner that did not go directly to the killing factory went to the quarantine center. It was a deadly serious place. Floodlights were scouring the darkness, guards in towers watched from above, and small red lights flashed around the perimeter. These, I would learn later designated the high voltage electric fence. For now they were just a part of the blur. We marched into a center where the block directors and SS officers started to select us again. I was assigned to Block 2. Moshe and I were separated. I was alone. He was assigned to Block 7. There must have been 28 or 30 blocks in the entire compound. Each block held about 500 prisoners. The total was about 10,000 to 15,000 prisoners, and that was only at Birkenau, Auschwitz II. Auschwitz I, nearby, was similar in size. The main features of Birkenau were a large brick gate, an assembly square, and the vast array of barracks and strange buildings that dotted the compound with smoke stacks that never ceased pouring victims into the sky. The crematoria operated around the clock.

Wooden Shoes & Tin Pan fig 74 and 75

While being processed through the quarantine center, I got a tattoo on my arm, *161744*. It was done very quickly. Finally, we were issued clothing, but not before being tormented by the other prisoners who handed it to us. Oddly, we were given civilian clothes. What made them different was that they had a red stripe on the side and a yellow six pointed *Star of David*, about 3 inches wide over the breast. However, I will never forget the shoes, because they were made of wood and since they would not bend they were bound to be a miserable problem.

By this time I was unbelievably tired, but mostly thirsty, and now I was also tattooed and dressed as a prisoner. The blockleiters gathered us up, "Hâftlinge folge mir," (Prisoners follow me), and took us to our respective barracks. Maybe here they will give us some water and let us sleep. Little did I realize, my night had just begun. I walked with a group of 200 men to Block 2.

My blockleiter, Katarzynski, was himself a Polish prisoner. You would think he would have had empathy for our plight because of this, but instead, he earned the nickname, *Bloody Mietek*. It wouldn't be long before I understood why. He also had an assistant who was a famous boxer prior to the war. They both carried

200

long wooden sticks. Once inside the bare-bones barracks I saw the rest of the prisoners who were already there. As we stood in this unfamiliar place Katarzynski[9] proceeded to give a strict lecture on the rules. In his crass and simple tongue he told us, when we will wake up, how much time we will have at the latrine, and where we will assemble in the morning. As you might expect, while he was doing this, many of us grumbled, faintly, with dry throats, Water?

Bloody Mietek fig 73

For the crime of asking for water, he took one of us to the middle of the barracks, laid him on what came to be known as *The Chimney,* a small stack of bricks raised from the floor used for heating. Then he took a stick, placed it on the fellow's neck, and without warning, jumped on it, instantly breaking his neck. He died thirsty. Malevolently emboldened, and certainly deranged, *Bloody Mietek* got close to each of our faces and challenged the rest of us. Who else wants water?

Understandably, we were horrified and silent. Our silence seemed to last forever as he continued to chastise and provoke another incident. The rest of the barracks cowered, hiding their eyes. They must have seen this type of behavior before. Finally, he broke

Armband of a Kapo fig 79

the silence, "If you behave you will live longer. Normally, a Hâftlinge in my block does not live longer than 4 weeks." He paused, panning our faces to make sure the point sank in, then he continued, "If the fire does not get you, pointing outside to the big chimney, I will." I was now almost 17 years old, with 4 weeks left to live. Thirsty, tired, scared, numbered, and sad, I was far too exhausted to focus on any of this, so I stood and listened trying not to bring attention to myself until we were dismissed. I found a place to lie down, and tried my best to sleep on the wooden slats. As cramped as I was in these new tight quarters, I was thankful to have enough space to lay my head down and fall asleep, escaping my living nightmare, at least for a little while.

When I awoke, I realized our blockhouse must have been a horse stable. Over time I saw that it was in 24 sections with three horizontal levels leaving 72 sleeping platforms for 500 prisoners. The only way to fit all these people onto those platforms was to place 3 or 4 together. So we slept shoulder-to-shoulder. The block-houses were designed to fit the maximum amount of people into the smallest amount of space. Every inch was used. I was on the top level. It was very crowded. The only thing extra was a little straw that acted as a carrier for disease more than insulation from the cold. Disease could easily run rampant in this squalid environment.

As I rested, I heard coughing and moaning. I would not get much sleep that night or any night in Birkenau. The only thing good about the barracks was that Katarzynski had his own room. At least when he was in there he could do little harm. Across from his room was one of his assistants. I don't remember his name but I do remember he was a professional fighter before the war. Needless to say he was in great shape. This was a terrible place. The grim reaper would be wide-awake during my entire stay. Each morning those who died the night before were piled by the door.

My block included at least 50 Russian prisoners of war. I ended up with a group of them, but soon, I would learn, even prisoners of war were treated better than Jews. I met one named Sasha, who must have been an officer before he was captured. He went out of his way to give me encouragement. To start, he gave me a familiar nickname, only it was in his native language - Malczyk, or young boy. I'll never forget his prison uniform. It had a large SU painted on his back; Soviet Union.

This was the first time I was assigned to a general concentration camp population. I was confined and quarantined with Jewish prisoners, Polish prisoners of politics and captured Russian combatants. It would not be long before I realized my barracks was close by one of the infamous crematoria. The smell of humans burning, day-after-day, is something I will never forget. But, when I was there, think about the odor. However, I never escaped the smoky beacon on top of the smoke stack. It was an eerie and unmistakable omen of evil that I could see from most any place in the camp. To avoid

Drawing Auschwitz general conditions in the barracks
fig 80

thinking about this I kept my head down and focused on maintaining my wits. I was just trying to survive. I was only 16. I was so young. It was a time I was just trying to figure out the world, but this was not a good place to figure out anything, better to just keep my head down and take one awkward step at a time.

At 5:00 AM a harsh metallic noise punctuated the morning. It was a flat piece of steel hanging on a pair of posts that was hammered to wake everyone up. There was still no food, but they did finally give us some drinking water in the form of roasted chicory, a popular substitute for coffee. All our meals were given to us in a tin pan. We had no spoons. Gold would be less valuable than those pathetic pieces of tin. I took mine with me everywhere. Everything I had, I kept under my cap or on my belt. It wasn't much. If I were to lose the pan I would not get another and be forced to eat everything with my hands.

My first bit of nourishment since the train ride was a dark

Drawing Auschwitz general conditions in the barracks
fig 81

liquid doled out of a barrel. It had been 3 days since I last saw food. Images of Tarnow still flooded my memory. I drank every drop. It wasn't much. By 6:00 AM we had to be ready to walk in our wooden shoes to the assembly area. That did not work out too well. People were walking with an unnatural step because these shoes were in some cases too tight, others too loose and for all they would not bend. We also had no socks or insulation of any kind leaving our feet to freeze in the winter. Mine are still numb and stiff to this day. To ensure we would be ready for assembly on time the blockleiters and their assistants were yelling, Raus! And their sticks were always nearby to ensuring the Hâftlinge were moving.

Sasha made sure I lined up correctly for the assembly. On the way he told me, "Malczyk nie boysa Budziony pridjot toda," (Young one, don't give up, General Budziony is in the field nearby). Every day he would remind me not to give up. In a place like this it was easy to give up and hard to survive. I saw many prisoners pass away exhausted, emaciated and forlorn. For hope, I also thought of my father and the words of the Tsadik of Tyczyn, "He will live longer than the rest of us." The words felt hollow in this place, but it was better to let them reverberate than to think about my predicament. The smoke never ceased to remind me where I was. It would never stop as long as I was there. I kept my head down... The guards found our walking comical. It was, but I wasn't laughing. Every time we went to assembly I followed Sasha, the young man following the old, with the SU on his back.

Assembly would take place regardless of the weather. In the rain we would get soaked, but we could not move from our position standing and looking forward as the rain drenched us. And afterwards, we would never have time to dry off. If it snowed we would stand there, in our wooden shoes, feet close to frozen. After roll call, Sasha would leave to go to the kitchen. It seemed the Russians were in charge of the kitchen at the camp. I don't know how any prisoners had control of anything. Once Sasha smuggled a potato for me. This was brave and very appreciated, because everyone was being searched, randomly. He knew I was suffering badly but he never let me give up. Frequently he repeated, Malczyk, don't give up. Those few words nourished my sense of survival. I needed as much of any type of encouragement as I could get.

Once the assembly was over, I went to my assigned work too. But, for me, each day it was something different. I did not have a permanent job. Peeling potatoes, one day, was the best work duty I could be assigned because I could eat the peels when the guards were not looking. It hardly mattered they were raw. My only concern was the fear of getting caught. If that happened, I would be beaten. Facing starvation the choice was simple - damned if you do and damned if you don't.

Incidentally, I could see glimpses of the outside world through the fence. A few large horses with riders could be seen. At

206

one point I saw the commandant riding with one of his officers. When I saw them I thought of Maciek and wondered how he was. I hoped he was in a better place than me.

Once after peeling potatoes for an entire day, I tried to keep some of the shavings to eat them later. Anything would be better than starving. How wrong I would be. On this day I was singled out and searched by Katarzynski and his assistant. When the few peelings were discovered Bloody Mietek went mad. I am not sure why his punishment was so severe. It doesn't matter. First, he knocked me senseless with his stick and I fell. Then he kicked me repeatedly as he cursed and yelled.

Sasha was nearby watching but he could not intervene. I got up dazed. That is when Katarzynski swung around and hit me full force in the face with that dammed stick he always carried. I fell again. Stars were filling my head, blocking the pain, if just enough to remain conscious. Both my front teeth were broken. I tried to regain my footing as blood gushed from my face. Sasha bravely stepped in and pushed me, "Run, Malczyk, Run!" I ran to the opposite side of the barracks and hid in the open, as best I could. I don't know what happened to Sasha for helping me but the maelstrom was over as the rest of the prisoners filed into the barracks.

There was never any lunch. Dinner was carried into the block by four men using sticks to hold a barrel. It always came through the back door near where I slept, as far away from Katarzynski as possible. Sometimes, deranged prisoners would attack the food. Katarzynski and his assistants would hit them with sticks. Once, he told one of the Häftlinge, "You want soup so bad? You shall have it," and thrust the man's head into the soup nearly drowning the man. Later, it was doled out of the barrel in the form of a thin cabbage soup. Many times there was no bread. Since, the solid food was sporadic, I could never save anything. Even if I did, I had nowhere to keep it. This was a starvation diet. Thousands must have died of malnourishment. In Birkenau, I would consider this second only to the gas chamber as the cause of death. Disease might have been the official cause but the weakness caused by having too little to eat made it almost impossible to fight disease.

Four times a week we received 35 grams of bread, three times a week we got 45 grams. This was combined with a thin soup that we got twice a day. I calculated that without the torture of the intensive work we could each live about 7 months. With the cold and the constant harangue 4-6 weeks was tough. The only hope was to last this long and get transferred to another camp where it would not be so brutal.

Everyone was trying to survive. Food was critical and in short supply, so there was little reason to attempt to take care of everyone. I was on my own except for Sasha and his friends. Many died in the block. Every day a few prisoners would never wake up. They were piled in a corner. I was among only 600 who barely survived the selection from Szebnie. Most of these would never survive Birkenau. With no way to help myself, I knew our blockleiter was right, 4 weeks to live echoed in my mind.

At the time of this realization I was already there for a week. I was now 17 years old, condemned, with only 3 weeks left to live. But this was not living. It was instead a walking nightmare. In desperation, I tried to figure out how to survive or even escape. I felt that the only way to survive was through work. However, by this point, I was being weakened, steadily under fed, and lacking any way to help myself. Plus, it was hard to avoid being beaten. I knew my chances of survival were slim. A small glimmer of hope opened as they selected me help build a railroad. Maybe this could be a permanent job.

I was tasked among hundreds of men to move stones. The purpose was to build up the land to support the heavy rails for a train. The train they were building pointed directly to the gas chambers. This was to be an even faster way to kill people. I could not think about the purpose. Nothing made sense except the next step and the guards yelling. We had to walk 2 km with these heavy rocks, bring them to where they were needed then return for more, no stopping, no standing, endless, mindless, work, a long line of men toiling. I worked hard. Soon, I was tasked with carrying the rail. Being the tallest, it seemed, almost the whole weight rested on me. I was now a slave laborer in an extermination factory.

One day while doing this work I saw a Pullman train with 15 cars full of people slowly approach the dreaded end of the line. This was a real train with regular seating but unlike a normal destination this was Birkenau. What struck in my mind that was different about this train, was that it was filled with nicely dressed Germans. They must have seen me too. I was among the hundreds of men they saw while looking out the windows moving rocks. I must have been less than 100 feet from their train. I was so close, I could see their eyes and they saw me too, toiling with the hundreds of prisoners. They disappeared and were never seen again.

While this was happening I could not help staring, but not for long. I forced myself to avert my eyes for fear the guards would single me out for punishment. My face was still swollen and tender. I could not risk another beating. Because we were busy working, this was one time when the Germans did not stop our efforts and isolate us in the blocks while the train full of condemned people arrived. Later, the Sonder Kommandos, who worked with the people who were gassed, told us these people were Jehovah's Witnesses who refused to fight for the Third Reich on the Eastern front.

I would soon realize there were 2 classes of prisoners. Prisoners of politics and war, like the Soviets and the Poles, or prisoners of race like the Jews and Gypsies. Only prisoners of race were part of the deadly selections within the block.[11]

With little to no hope, I continued to consider ways I could

Kommando Canada
fig. 82

escape. Moshe Katz was gone. He was sent to Buna. At the time, I did not know what that was, but anything had to be better than here. But nothing could get past the electric fence. I saw dead prisoners in a puddle near the high voltage sign, the red flashing light that foretold the danger highlighted their bodies. One of these poor fellows must have stepped into a puddle that was too close to the fence. As soon as he became entangled in the electric field another prisoner tried to help but one touch proved deadly, they both were electrocuted.

By chance I saw my old friends Roman Blauner and Simon Unger. They had been looking for me. They were both wearing blue and white uniforms and they were assigned to the D Section. Their jobs were to take the clothing from the people going on their final walk to the gas chambers. Their kommando had an odd name, Kommando Canada, but its formal name was the Aufrâumungskomman-

210

do or clearing gang.

I showed my friends my beaten face and broken teeth. Roman told me something that gave me a small measure of hope, "There is a Polish political prisoner here from our hometown, Victor (Wiktor) Mordarski. He helped us get our jobs. I will ask him to help you too." He then told me, "Leon, your arrival was called the naked transport. I saw you when you arrived and knew you needed help. This is the first chance I could get to help you. Hang in there." I shook my head in acknowledgement I would do my best. He was right, I was just hanging on.

Wiktor Mordarski
fig. 83

Things got worse after seeing Roman, I became very ill with diarrhea and fever. In my delirium I saw my old home and my family, and the friendly smoke from the small stove. I woke and realized I was still in hell. At the time, I had no idea what to do about my sickness. I could not show Katarzynski any weakness, or ask him for help. He would just as soon finish me off and put me in the corner like the others. Besides, he knew I was sick because I needed to frequently go to the latrine. The trouble was that the bastard would not let me go. He was happy to extend my misery. When I got near the door he would hit me with his stick, prolonging my torture. I let him hit me a few times. I did not feel it nor did I allow it to hurt me. I just needed to create a diversion, so I could run past him to the latrine. While he was abusing me he would also threaten, "When the next selection comes, I will make sure you are einschreiben." (on the list)

My misery knew no bounds, but I was not alone. All of us

were suffering. My sickness also did not let me rest at night, nor did it excuse me from assembly in any weather condition and a full day of work. I had to go frequently. But we were not supposed to go to the latrine during the night. Instead, at night, a portable tub was set up for pee only. If you had diarrhea you had to do your best to wait until the morning. Sometimes this just wasn't possible. The worst would be to soil your clothing. There was nothing to change into. So you just had to find a place to let it go and hope you did not get caught.

Thankfully, Roman did tell Victor about me as soon as he was able. Shortly afterwards, Victor came into my block looking for me. He was dressed in an elegant blue and white uniform and he had a leather vest over top of this, with a white armband. This designated him as a political prisoner. Victor was an impressive man even though he was a prisoner. When I spoke with him the first time I was in bad shape. He saw my battered face, and broken teeth. I also showed him a few welts. I must have been in bad shape because as we spoke he put both of his hands on his head and said, "How did this happen? Who did this to you?" Besides being beaten, I was sick and he was trying to figure out just how bad. Weakly, I told him, I came from Grybov. They murdered everyone. He said, I am also from Grybow, My accent was Yiddish, his was Polish. I knew this since Roman had already told me but it sounded wonderful to hear the familiar sound in a comforting voice.

Then I told him my immediate problem, the bloody diarrhea and fever... My voice trailed off. He said, "Leon, they put you in the worst place. Is the block elder abusing you?" I told him, "He is chasing me whenever he can, always with the painful stick. I have to run like a rat to escape getting beaten." Before I could finish, he had to go, "Leon," he said, "I know what to do."

Later that day, Victor sent Abe Fenigstein and Roman Blauner to help me. Thankfully, they brought medicine. As Abe handed a paper with the medicine inside, he said, "Swallow this paste with the black coffee." I put it under my cap for the morning and tossed and turned through the night. I don't know what the medicine was but it was like raw dough, and it helped. Soon, my fever and diarrhea stopped.

In December 1943, before Christmas there was another selection. It was one of the largest selections to the gas chambers ever in Birkenau. Earlier that week the top Nazi brass had visited the camp and said, We must make room for more prisoners. So, the doctors went to work. It started with an assembly within the barracks, only for the Jews. The announcement came by surprise, in the form of a shout, All Juden must undress and form in a line on the right side of the barracks. In my block alone there were 300 Jews standing in that line. About 200 Russian and Polish prisoners witnessed this. During this selection about half of the Jews in my block, went directly to the gas chamber. This was happening all over the camp in every block, thousands of Jews were chosen to die that day. I too, was in that line. I cleaned my face with my dirty hands as best I could. When it was my turn, the doctor said, Show me your tongue. At least by this time I was familiar with the drill. Once again, I intended to not show any kind of fear. I proudly stuck my tongue out with every ounce of enthusiasm I could find. And at the same time I smiled as brightly as I could with my eyes.

I don't know where the strength came from, but I was not afraid. I guess it wasn't strength, but bravado, in the face of oblivion. What other choice did I have? Turn about, said the doctor. He must have seen the welts on my body from being beaten by the blockleiter, as well as my broken teeth. I was not in good shape, but I was young and even though I was weakened, I could still show him some vim and vigor. I stood at attention waiting, he paused a moment considering life or death. Finally he said, Links (go to the left - Life).

Once again I passed a life or death selection. This was a close call. Many others were not so lucky, for them, the doctor would say to his assistant, Einschreiben, or put him on the list. When Katarzynski saw what was happening with me, while he was standing safely on the side, he brashly interrupted the doctor, just as he said he would, "What are you doing, letting this boy live? He is an insolent Jew, einschreiben." He made a motion of writing with his hand. The doctor admonished him curtly, "Do not mix into my affairs." As they were having this exchange, my poor fellow Jews and I, standing naked, watched and remained expressionless. I was at the total mercy of the outcome. Most of the others would not live another day just as the blockleiter had predicted when we were placed into his vicious care. Four weeks was a very long time in Birkenau, especially for a Jew and once they sign your number, einschreiben, you're finished.

Victor was the blockleiter for barracks 14 in D section. His block was where people with sickness recovered after the infirmary. Somehow, he also had access to the camp records. Soon after the terrible selection Victor gave my blockleiter orders to send me to him with my records. When doing this, he also warned him not to touch me. So I left and went to the D section, I remember the day well because it was also my birthday, I just turned 17. When I arrived, I immediately realized the mood was completely different here; Victor was friendly. He asked, "Leon, do you know anything about my family?" I was sorry to report to him, "All I know is that they arrested your sister." He probed for anything I might be able to share with him about his family.

I did not know much more. "Leon, he said, "Listen carefully, I will try to help you, but you can only stay here 4 weeks. First, I will give you a little extra food. Then, I will send you to the infirmary. I will tell them to keep you a few weeks too. Just stay there as long as you can."

I didn't know anything; I just did as I was told. I was only in the infirmary for about two weeks when there was yet another selection held around the whole camp. Going to the infirmary, in my poor shape, most likely saved my life. It was another big selection, and again, at least half of the Jewish prisoners went to the gas chamber. New deliveries of people arrived all the time. The blocks would never be empty for long.

I was lucky to be in the infirmary. Here, I met the blockleiter; it was none other than Mendel Scher, another old neighbor, and the same young man that was picked in the first hostage taking in Grybow. This was when the Judenrat made its feeble last stand and was mowed down. First, he asked, "How are you doing?" I was weak. It was easy to see this place was killing me, slowly. He understood the diarrhea and general illness, but I also reported to him the beatings. Upon hearing about this, he bristled in anger. Then he asked, "How did you get here? "

There was no good answer, but I told him about Grybow, and picking up the bodies, and the roadwork, and Tarnow, and Goth's boots, and being plucked from the mass grave, and Szebnie, and my horse, Maciek, and Tadeusz, and the naked transport, and Katarzynski - the bastard, and Victor. Together, we ate from a barrel of soup and had a little bread. During my stay we had plenty of time to talk. There was also a little extra food while I was there. The people who died, left theirs.

After 4 weeks I felt a little stronger but I had to leave. So I went back to Victor and pleaded with him to find me a permanent job. He said, I have to send you away until I can do this. I was disappointed but I trusted Victor. Good jobs were scarce. Victor saved Roman and Simon by assigning them to Kommando Canada but I was too young to be even considered and I wasn't allowed to stay with Victor either. He said, Leon, I am sending you to Block 28. You must wait there until I can get you assigned to Buna.

I asked, "What is Buna?"

He said, "A ticket out of here. It is the factories close by. That is where you can survive. Just hang on until I can get you there."

I had already beat the odds by 2 weeks. But I did not want to take any more chances. It was urgent that I get out of Birkenau as soon as possible. Anything would be better than this place. At least, when I went to Block 28, it was run by a good man. I can't remember his name, except that it was French.

While I hoped for anything better than Birkenau, every day I still went to the general assembly. Since I was young and was unassigned to a permanent kommando it was imperative during these assemblies that I be given work. Victor warned me, You must be functional to the Germans. Without a purpose they would have little reason to give you room and board. As he said this, I thought, a wood board and gruel. I had many jobs, none were good, but I liked the carpentry shop because it was inside, out of the cold, and more importantly, I could get an extra piece of bread with a little soup there.

On another day, I went to help build the railroad tracks again. I tried not to think about their hellish purpose. I was laying the rails again. This time, I worked with both prisoners and civilians. The civilians would drive the spikes with a sledgehammer to set the rail while we prisoners would use tamping stones to help level the iron bars for a smooth operation. The kapo set the pace. He would shout to a group of us, Pick up the rail. Again, since I was the tallest, it felt as if I carried most of the weight. We carried it towards where it needed to go, but the wooden shoes made this much harder to do. Then the kapo again shouted, Put it down. The prisoners quickly let go of the rail leaving me with all of the weight. If I hadn't let go right away, I would have been crushed.

To survive a single day took every ounce of my wits. Yet I would be here for months. Insanity would be saner than this reality. And without some kind of help soon I was surely doomed. Victor was my only hope. The rules were so strict there was no way to follow them without getting a beating. Guards would yell, and slug you with clubs, all for what seemed to be no reason other than to appease their sadistic appetites.

When there was a large transport to the gas chamber the blocks were closed. During this time no one could walk outside. I'm sorry to say the blocks were closed frequently. The facilities were terrible or non-existent and the people in charge had little reason to care. They could just as easily feed the gas chamber as take care of the prisoners. There was never any place to just sit down, except the wooden beds at night. Worse, if you were too weak, or if you fell down, you were as good as dead.

If all of this was not brutal enough, for awhile I was assigned to the Straf Kommando, prisoners who were being punished. I'm not sure what I did to deserve this. Our work detail was outside. We would march through the gates as musicians played. They were prisoners too. On the way out we were trained to take our caps off and turn our heads in unison towards the SS officer in charge. He would take a count both before we left and after we returned to make sure all of us were present and accounted for. They would not tolerate any escapees. Once we walked past the checkpoint we would turn our head back to forward and put our caps back on. Each day we walked about 3 kilometers to the Vistula River. Our mission was to drain the swamp.

As slave labor this was some of the most brutal work possible. It was cold, wet and muddy, but worst of all, it was relentless hard work and if anyone slacked or slowed down the guard's vicious dog was right in his face. I once saw the dogs even kill one of the prisoners by crushing his neck. As an added punishment for the rest of us, we were required to carry him back.

My job was pulling the field kitchen. Since this was a grueling kommando the prisoners were given an extra helping of food.

Staf Commando - Field Kitchen
fig 84

Days passed doing this. I had nothing to look forward to. Hope seemed to fade forever. This was my worst kommando. But somehow I never gave up. Coming back from one of these excursions, I saw Victor, and I pleaded with him again, "Please, you must find me a steady job before it is too late. I cannot survive in this kommando." He looked at me and my cracked front teeth. I'm sure he knew I was right. Then he said, "I am sending you to the infirmary for a few days. I am trying to put you on a transport to Buna, but you will have to hang on until I see an opportunity to do it."

Luckily, that day, he sent me to the infirmary and once again, the blockleiter was my old friend, Mendel Scher. However, by this time the situation was desperate in his block. I could tell as soon as I walked in because I saw only dead people. Mendel came to me and said, "I am sorry Leon, I can not keep you here." I was stunned and dejected. He was, however, able to give me some bread and soup. I drank as much as I could and we were able to again speak a little about our old town again. But I could not stay long, so I went back to Victor. There wasn't much he could do either except send me to a block where he knew the blockleiter would not harass me.

I did as he told me and waited for a chance to go to Buna. However, this did not excuse me from lining up and being assigned work every day. And again, I had no choice but to go to whatever job they assigned me. Before long the kapos treated me like a scapegoat. Sometimes, they would make me march all day for no other reason than to see how awkward my shoes were. It was an ordeal to march in wooden shoes, but more dangerous to stop. People around me wasted away to skeletons. Few found their last breath lying in the street, beaten down from extended hunger, worked to death. Many were completely disabled and mentally disoriented. These people earned the nickname Muselmann. It was an association with the act of a Muslim in prayer, but in this deadly place it meant a deranged, starved person who would sit on the ground like a Muslim and die in that position. This association was actually too kind, more likely they would act in a manic way right before an ignoble end in the mud or against the wires. Some intentionally even became targets for the guards' guns.

Conditions were so bad even one of the kapos escaped, but he was caught and all of us were assembled to watch him hanged. My misery was unbounded. The night was never quiet. It was constantly interrupted with sporadic agony while the tower guards kept busy shining their searchlights.

When I spoke to Victor, he told me, "I am so sorry, I can only do so much." But at least he was still trying to get me out of Birkenau. He was powerless unless the Germans ordered more people for

Buna.

Luckily, with his persistence, I did get assigned to Buna. If this did not happen there is no way I could have survived. Somehow I made it. Thank God for Victor. I found a record of my transfer years later when I contacted the Auschwitz archives. By giving them my tattoo number they were able to locate a record of a health report used to certify the health of exactly 100 prisoners prior to being sent to the factory detail.

Well after the war a book was published called *The Vanished City of Tsanz, by Shelomoh Zalman Lehrer.* Its author, another survivor, died in 2010. On page 353 it speaks of a man named Blauner from Gribov who worked in Canada Kommando. He must have been referring to Roman. The story goes, ... a transport arrived from Hungary and a selection took place. Mothers who were carrying children were all sent directly to the gas chambers. Blauner noticed a robust-looking woman standing at the side with two children. He tore the children from her arms and called out to the SS guard, She is strong and suitable for work. The SS guard agreed. The woman, not realizing that this step was to save her life, showered Blauner with curses and wildly scratched at his hands. After the liberation she sought him out and thanked him for saving her life. She apologized for the scratches and curses she had inflicted upon him. At the time she did not know that within an hour no remnant would remain of those mothers who had been carrying children.

Chapter Eight

Buna

Victor appeared at my barracks the night before I was to be transferred. He said, "Tomorrow you will be leaving." I was elated. He continued, "One of the reasons you had to wait so long is that I did not want you to go to one of the small work camps, like the coal mines, nearby. I think your chances of surviving there would be slim. Instead, I was waiting for you to go to Buna. But, I could not do that until they ordered more labor, and in your case teenagers. They don't accept many teenagers."

I listened. I knew that Victor was also a prisoner, like me, so there was only so much he could do. He had already saved me when I was in the direst of needs, and now, hearing I will be leaving tomorrow, it felt like he was again giving me a great gift; my life. Before he left, the last thing he said to me was, "Leon, you must not return here. Once you leave you can never come back. If you are sent back for any reason I will not be able to help you."

Before he walked away he looked at me deeply and as I peered back I saw my father saying, "You are young, you will survive and live longer than any of us. *When* you do, tell our story to the world, they must figure out a way to stop the madness." I shook my head, silently vowing to do what he said.

To me, Victor was a saint. He saved many people, I only know a few, but I bet there were hundreds. I believe this is true because he was the liaison between Birkenau and all of the prisoner labor requests.

The next morning I walked over to his barracks. There was no daily assembly in the rehab area, so I was able to walk on my own. An SS Striben officer was waiting with his assistant, a teen, wearing a blue and white striped outfit, not like my regular clothing

221

now tattered with a painted red line down the leg. My record was in the officer's hands. In 2010 a copy was sent to me by the Auschwitz records bureau. It has the strangest title for a report, Fleckfieber-trockenbluntersuchung. This word is difficult to translate. It means a dried blood test for typhus. I don't remember having my blood drawn, but the test is completed by checking blood samples allowed to dry on a slide with a microscope. This test was important because typhus can spread like an epidemic and was rampant in Auschwitz II. So the blood test was to ensure the health of the factory workers, and more importantly to the Nazis, the factory itself. One prisoner with an infectious disease could hurt or even halt production. This document was a clean bill of health for the listed prisoners. You can see one hundred tattoo numbers on the form. Mine is the 7th on the list, 161744. It is under the hâftlinge column. You can't tell by the list but it includes both adults and a couple of teens. I was one of the teens.

Everyone arrived at Victor's barracks with all of their belongings, a tin pan and the clothing on their backs. We were told we didn't need the pans anymore, and as strange as it may seem to you, since this was an essential part of staying alive in Birkenau, I found it hard to put it down. But I had no time to ponder the loss. I was expected to immediately release it and line up 5 across. Like this, a group of 100 of us walked in formation to a station where a line of trucks stood ready to go. Our wooden shoes creating the unmistakable Birkenau prison shuffle.

As I got on the truck, I thought of Moshe Blauner. Even though I did not know what happened to him, I remembered the line of 16 trucks similar to these back in Szebnie and how Moshe Blauner and I watched everyone getting on them from the safety of the stable. I'm sure they did not know where they were going or were more likely told they were just being deported. It wouldn't be long before we all knew the answer. They hardly left the camp when we heard

222

the shooting, followed by a pyre that burned all night. Thick smoke blanketed the stable that night, mixed with a sickly, unforgettable odor. Even the horses were agitated. I learned from an eyewitness that as the fire burned the bastard Gestapo celebrated. Throughout that night I heard shots from machine guns tearing holes in the night. Each star, the result of another tear, or so it seemed. I thought, whatever would happen to Moshe could not have been good, but I hoped for the best. I sat down in the back of the truck heading to Buna and tried to think about something else. Even though I was told I was going to a better place, I wasn't sure about what to expect. I would find out soon enough though, as my destination was only 6 kilometers away.

This whole prisoner exchange was a business for the SS. They sold our labor to the giant factory. And while the factory was happy to have the cheap labor, we were lucky to have anything to do that would give us a chance for survival. As the trucks drove away, I saw Birkenau fade into the distance, its crematoria chimneys still bellowing vile smoke. Surrounded by my fellow prisoners we all vowed never to return. It was more like hope than a vow. After the war I did go back once more, partly to make sure it was destroyed, and partly to insure I remembered everyone that was now gone forever. I paid them homage with a prayer.

During my four month stay in Birkenau at least 100,000 people were murdered by deadly gas and then turned to dust in six crematoria[12] While another similar but smaller number died nearby in the original camp Auschwitz I. Under this smokescreen of mass murder, atrocities like that of Bloody Mietek pale in comparison, But, I had to stop thinking about this as the I.G. Farben Buna-Monowitz Chemical plant, otherwise known as Auschwitz III, came into view. I stopped daydreaming and cleared my mind in preparation for *who-knows-what*. Surviving Birkenau was the most difficult thing I ever did, yet I had a long way to go before I would taste freedom.

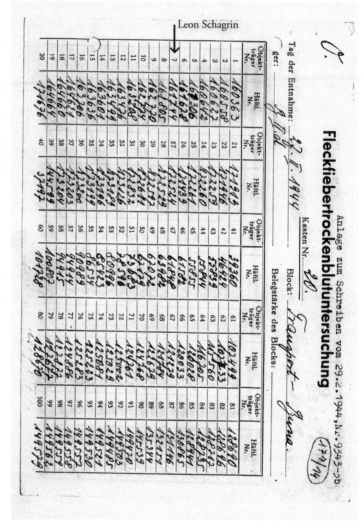

Typhus tests for 100 häftlinge from a slide of dried blood.
Typhus was rampant in Auschwitz this was a way to keep it out of Buna.
Leon Schagrin is # 7 on the list. Tattoo number 161744
Document was courtesy of the Auschwitz Archive. 2010

fig 95

224

When we arrived an SS Striben officer was waiting with our records. We got out of the trucks and fell into formation. First we were counted by his assistant, a young boy wearing a blue & white uniform. The boy reported, 98 men and 2 Jungen. The Striben officer noted a complete shipment of 100 hâftlinge. When he was finished we walked directly to the quarantine center where we removed our old clothing, took a shower, and received a tight haircut, the tighter the better. Since, hair was a main carrier of human lice, and lice brought disease such as typhus, it was best to cut the hair as close as possible. While getting cleaned up I thought about what Victor said, "Don't get sick and don't come back. I won't be able to help you."

I scrubbed extra hard while thinking about this. It had been a long time since I had my last shower. The warm water felt great. Once I was clean, I went to the clothing station and was carefully measured to achieve the closest fit. Then I was issued two sets of clothing, one for the summer, and one for the winter. I guess they were planning to keep us around for awhile. I was also given fresh underwear. This was an important part of proper hygiene. The suits were not fitted to me, but they did get close. The result was much better than the clothing I was wearing in Birkenau After the right size was found, my tattoo number was attached to the breast.

The uniform was blue & white striped with a yellow star to signify my race. Last, I was issued a cap and shoes. Not wooden shoes but real black leather shoes that could bend with a normal step and even a pair of woolen socks to go with them. After months of walking in hell with wooden clogs, socks and shoes did much to lift my spirits.

When we were cleaned and processed, the blockleiters were ready and waiting to take us to the barracks. They had our records in their hands as they stood at a distance to make room for everyone to find their masters. Since I was with only one other teenager it did not take more than a moment to collect us and check our records.

Next I met Zigfreid, my new blockleiter. Over the next year I would realize he was a pleasant fellow with empathy for my plight but when I first met him, I had no idea what to expect. After spending time with Bloody Mietek there was plenty of reason for concern. During my stay, however, he never hit anyone, nor did I ever see him even raise his voice. Incongruously, he had a green triangle on his perfectly fitted blue & white uniform. This marked him as a dangerous criminal. It was just like the SS Officers in charge of this camp to choose a criminal to run a block, especially a youth block. But these were very strange times, and so many people were *wrongly* convicted, just like me. However for extra measure, when I realized he was a convicted criminal, I think this is the first time I remembered to pray in awhile. Silently, I said to myself, I hope this man is nothing like the bloody bastard from across the way.

We walked into the barracks, and instantly I could see a difference. The bunks were only two levels, not three, and the room was much smaller, perhaps 200 people could be housed in this block and another 200 next door. It was not overcrowded, one Jungen hâftlinge to a bed. I was elated to have my own bed but somehow there was a nagging thought about all the others, the ones like me with no place to sleep. Everything was in perfect order as the block master started to speak. His tone was pleasant and I was relieved, but still a little on edge.

While he was showing us around, the place was empty. Everyone was at the factory or working around the barracks, except us. *I'd like* you to be clean at all times, he said. This was going to be much different than the horrors of Birkenau. He was asking for obedience, not demanding it. By the time I arrived in his care, I was brutally trained so nothing he said was a surprise, except, the way he said it.

Listening attentively, I knew things would be different here, better, and because he was asking, instead of telling, it was a refreshing change. He continued, ...and *I would like* the bed to be made, so that I can bounce a coin on the mattress. As he spoke, I saw the luscious mattresses, and could not wait to have a chance to try them out. It had been years since I slept on one of those. I thought this was going to be more like a military school than a concentration camp. In fact, for me, Buna was like a hotel compared to Birkenau.

The block master finished, "This is the Jugenbloch. It consists of block 48 and 49. There are no adults allowed in this block, at any time. If you want to visit someone in the adult blocks, you may do so after the last meal of the day or on Sunday." I thought, "Sunday?" A day off from slave labor? Then, he gave me a little soup to eat, and allowed me to get used to the barracks. I idled the rest of the afternoon walking around the grounds testing out my new shoes. They were not really new, but that didn't matter, they were new to me. I cleaned them with a soft rag. At the same time, I thought, I am never taking them off. As I cleaned them, I could not help but remember Dr. Ameisen lying on the ground, in Grybow, with those nice shoes, or cleaning Goth's bloody boots in Tarnow on that terrible day of the liquidation.

In the early evening the rest of the young men filed into the barracks. Looking around, I saw my peers, other teenagers. The youngest was about 13, and I guess, I was one of the oldest, at 17. They were a well-groomed, friendly bunch, representing nationalities from all over Europe, including Holland, France, and Hungary. Later in the year Greeks and more Poles would arrive. Each nationality stayed together and spoke their own language among themselves. To communicate between the nationalities we spoke German. Everyone needed to at least understand German, or suffer the abuse of the guards. Many of them could speak Yiddish, but none was spoken. No one went out of their way to look for trouble. We all had the same uniform, including the little yellow star. I don't know why, but in July 1944, five or six months after my arrival, the yellow star was changed to a red triangle with a thin yellow horizontal stripe on top. All of the boys' voices were quiet, even subservient. I know the reason for this well. It comes from years of abuse, and the deep sense of loss brought on by being displaced and incarcerated. We were always in fear of reprisals and as young Jews, each of us carried the heavy burden of friends and families displaced or destroyed, like mine. Over the next few months, I heard this story over and over.

I had plenty of time to talk to the kids in my barracks. Our conversations were about the fates of our families and where we came from and we talked about our jobs in the factory. Later in the year, we spoke about when there will be another air raid alarm, and our biggest fear -- rumors that they might liquidate the camp and send us all back to Birkenau. The best thing we could do to survive was to just stay healthy and keep working. The rest would be God's will warped by the Nazi high command and further mangled by war. Everyone knew their personal health was paramount. Once admitted to the infirmary, the chance of survival would plummet. Selections were frequent there, because the sick had no use in the factory and the SS had plenty of fresh labor to replace them. They needed little excuse to make room for fresh labor. I believe they would only get paid if the worker worked. There were no selections in the barracks like Birkenau. The selection occurred only in the infirmary at least as far as I knew since I wasn't in the barracks. I am not aware of a single survivor that was shipped back to Birkenau from Buna, and I only know of one that survived the infirmary for an extended period, my friend Moshe Katz. How he did this, I can only imagine, most likely had to do with his uncanny and infectious personality. Everyone loved Moshe.

I had no particular friend or buddy, like Sasha, in the Jugenbloch. Thankfully I also did not feel threatened every moment of the day. No one was chasing me with a stick or treating me like a rat. For

228

the most part I kept to myself. There was nobody from my region of Poland within the barracks either. By this time, I didn't fully realize it yet, but I was one of the very few left to tell the tale. Today, I am aware of less than 10 people from my hometown that survived. It is painful to think about. At the time I couldn't. I just needed to focus on survival.

Moshe was nearby in the adult barracks, but I did not see him very often even though I was allowed. He was having a much tougher time than I was. All the adults had a much harder time than the teens. I think our youth barracks was set up as a model for the high command to slap each other on the back and say, see what a good job we are doing, and thereby show the world their magnanimity. A few of the young boys in my barracks were the camp's runners. They would deliver messages and orders for the Gestapo. One of these was named Schusterman. Another was the assistant of the Scribben office. He was the boy that helped check us in when we first arrived. So far I was lucky, but soon I would meet my Kommando chief. I hoped he would be humane too, and I could work inside, out of the freezing weather. I went to bed hoping I could survive here. Tomorrow, I would know. In the night I could see the reflection of the red light flashing, warning of the electric fence surrounding my camp. A dog barked. Floodlights scanned the area. I was a prisoner thankful to be no longer in Birkenau, but still very much is a high security prison. Before falling asleep I could hear my father saying, Survive... tell the world... find our bones... As my father's image faded I saw Victor faintly saying the same thing with one added thought, ... "find a cure for the madness. Centering my thinking on this helped me to sleep well for my next unknown challenge. The mattress didn't hurt either.

A tune is still stuck in my head from those times. The Dutch boys would sing it frequently, It was something like, yupee youppe yeah..., I have no clue what it might mean or the rest of the song except that, for me, it has a haunting sound that is better left untranslated and mysterious.

Every day except Sunday, I woke up, had breakfast and ersatz coffee and followed the others to the Appellplatz, the wide open area used for roll call. Right before roll call, I had a few minutes to orient myself. The Buna - Monowitz, I.G. Farben synthetic chemical plant was gigantic. It was more like a city than a factory. After the war I heard about 70,000 people worked there. The staff was a combination of both employees and prison laborers. My camp was a half-mile away, but the factory was so large I could see the outline of it whenever I looked to the north. Looking to the west Birkenau, was out of sight, but not out of mind. I knew it was still a short ride away, and as long as the crematoria were working, I was in danger.

I did, however, see a barracks while looking that way. It was filled with British prisoners of war. The bell rang, so I had to stop trying to figure it all out and line up with the rest of the prisoners in front of our assigned kapos. I was among thousands of prisoners, each with a different triangle or symbol representing their particular curse for being here. We all stood at attention. Rain or snow, weather was no consideration. The wide open square was asphalt, the sky was huge, we must have looked like a sea of blue & white stripes from above. My group, the teens, was spread among many kommandos. The line-ups were always long and seemingly pointless, but none of this was my primary concern. Staying warm was what mattered the most right there and then. Even in my new clothing, this would occupy most, if not all of my energy.

The British prisoners of war were treated differently than the rest of us. I don't know why, maybe the Red Cross, or the fact that the German Air force guarded them instead of the SS. As we lined up for roll call, they would march into Buna. They did so with a military cadence, singing British songs, loud and proud. It was quite a spectacle to see them marching. Sometimes, just by the luck of timing, we would be marching close to them. We all walked the same road to the factory. I will never forget one of the songs they sang. It had a special kind of twang, only the British could sound out properly.

It's a long way to Tip-per-ar-y
It's a long way to go
It's a long way to Tip-per-ar-y
It's a long way to the Sweetest Girl I know.
Goodbye Piccadilly,
Farewell Leicester Square,
It's a long, long way to Tipperary,
But my heart's right there.

I was assigned to Kommando 80, otherwise known as the Schlosser Kommando. My assignment was decided before I arrived. I had to be thankful for this opportunity, as the alternative was almost certain death. So far, the Jugenbloch *was* far better than Birkenau. The difference, for me, was like night and day. But, Buna was still very much a concentration camp, replete with high voltage wires surrounding the barracks, guards with machine guns everywhere, SS officers in high profile and trained dogs along with their associated guards, pacing back and forth. At least, Buna was not an extermination camp, on the contrary, it was a factory and because of this, they needed labor just as much as raw materials.

The primarily mission of this factory was to make synthetic rubber, rubber that could be crafted into tires. Since tires were an integral part of keeping the war machine rolling our jobs and the factory were important. The manufacturing of rubber is also where the name Buna comes from, Butadiene (Acetylene), one of the main ingredients. My division, the Schlosser 80 Kommando, was making ethanol, a highly flammable material used in the production of rubber. Because it was a very dangerous material, warning signs were posted everywhere. I would now have to get used to a new kind of deadly danger, the explosive potential of ethanol. Buna was a very dangerous place during peace time requiring care at all times to maintain safety, but this was a time of war and a plant of this scale was a prime target for the Allies. One spark could set the liquid off. I grew up in a time of horses, sabres and rifles and I saw the tanks rolling in beginning the new epoch of industrialization and warfare. I could imagine the punch of these tanks to be fierce, but looking at those giant vats filled their explosive power was something I could not comprehend. I couldn't even think about it. It was better to just focus on doing my work, one day at a time.

On a normal day, right before roll call, if it was cold, I would huddle near a wall for warmth with the other prisoners. When the bell rang we would quickly line up into formation. Once dismissed we would walk to the factory maintaining our formation. And just as I was taught by the Straf Kommando, we would begin our day, walking past the SS officer in charge and turn our heads in unison as we took off our caps in a sign of subservient obedience. All of this was happening as grand music was playing, courtesy of the Buna prisoner band. And, just like Birkenau, once we were finished walking past the SS, we would turn our heads forward, and put our caps back on. The assistant to the Striben officer would report how many prisoners each kapo had as they were leaving and on the way back, he would do the same, the number was expected to match. If these numbers did not match there would be hell to pay. As we walked by I heard the kapo report 87 hâftlinge and 2 jugendlitche.

The walk to the factory was about a half mile up hill. I did not mind the incline. The factory grounds were well maintained and my shoes felt like heaven. Even if there were a big rain it would not result in flooding or muddy grounds near the barracks at the bottom of the hill. But we would get soaked and stay that way for hours. The

232

entire barracks area was built on asphalt and it had adequate storm drainage and a special kommando was assigned to work on drains. About 10,000 or as many as 15,000 prisoners lived in our camp. All of us appeared for roll call each morning, and then walked along this route. It must have looked like a giant blue & white snake slithering along towards the factory in the morning. Then, around 6 pm, it was the same routine in reverse, and just like as on the way out, the prison musicians welcomed us back, as we took off our caps in obedience to our self-proclaimed masters.

When we arrived at the factory, I would see other workers, not just hâftlinge. Both Germans and Polish civilians worked side-by-side with us. I even saw a few disabled German veterans hobbling around. But, the thing that stood out the most, besides the giant factory, was hundreds of British prisoners of war. This was the first time I would be among them up close. Many Brits were assigned to work at my Kommando.

The first time I entered the workplace everyone went directly to their stations, except me. I was not yet assigned to a specific task, so I waited a moment to let the shuffle subside and approached the man in charge and introduced myself, "Sir, I am here to help you." Looking at me, a teen, for the first time, he said, "Hello, I am Walter, the chief engineer." Obviously German, wearing overalls and a medal of honor around his neck, The Iron Cross. Walter was in charge of this project, and me. It's funny what you remember about people, I'll never forget him wearing that medal every day. As much as he was proud of it, I think, for him, it was a kind of talisman to ward off the Gestapo. He glanced at my record and my broken smile and decided he would call me by a familiar name, Junge. I hadn't heard that since Tarnow, and I wasn't about to connect those horrible thoughts with the man standing right in front of me. Regardless of his medal, he seemed to have kind eyes. Walter turned out to be a decent person. He did not talk much, preferring to remain focused on his work, but he did things to make me realize he was a caring individual. The first thing he did was to take me on a short tour of the part of the factory he oversaw.

The Iron Cross fig 96

It was in a small shop in Buna. Walter was the engineer in charge. The room was square, about 20 x 20 feet with blueprints, a drawing table and cabinets filled with plans. We shared it with two German Soldiers who were welders, Fritz and Wietzorek. They came to work dressed in uniform. Wietzorek wore an airforce uniform and was missing a leg. I pulled their tools to them as well as delivered the pipes. From this point forward I became Walter's apprentice. If I kept this up, in time, I would become a welder or a plumber. But for now, I was just a young man following simple directions.

It did not take long for me to discover that Walter was a fine man. Many times he would leave food in his canteen and without saying much he would ask me to wash it. I would take it to the sink and when no one was looking hungrily wash this down. He expected me to do this. As much as I was being fed better in Buna, I had lost a lot of weight in Birkenau, and I had a voracious appetite. I remember seeing his smiling face when I returned from cleaning his canteen. I smiled back, with my two cracked front teeth. Maybe, the reason Walter did not talk too much was the oppressive atmosphere that permeated the entire complex. The Gestapo was always near. Or maybe, it was just his natural tendency. I suspect it was a little of both. If he was caught talking nicely to a hâftlinge, like me, the Gestapo might wonder where his loyalty lay. For them it was better that the fear be shared by all, Germans and prisoners alike. In that respect Walter was a prisoner too, even though he was a hero of his country. Rather than think of any of this it was better to just

234

keep quiet and even though I felt I could survive an extended period in Buna, lacking any unforeseen accident, the environment was stifling. SS guards policed the facility constantly and their punishment for infractions, both real and contrived, was harsh. I saw plenty of warnings for the ethanol but none for the Gestapo. Not that I needed any reminder of what those shiny black boots were capable of inflicting.

I had a good job and new clothing, extra food and, most importantly, my job was indoors. Also, Walter made me feel appreciated. As he would approve drawings he would call me to deliver them to the appropriate welder. Speaking in very short sentences, always with the familiar name, he would say, Junge, take this ... After awhile, I was assigned to a particular welder. I helped him by moving the pipes as needed, as well as filling them with sand. The reason we used sand was that when the welder would heat and shape the pipes, the heat would be uniform because of the sand, creating a fine curve. Pipes like this were assembled into longer columns and then snaked around the large tanks to make the ethanol. You could smell it throughout the area where I worked, a sickly sweet smell that was always present.

Being young, I was running all over Walter's section of the plant. I remember a few times I even climbed to the top of the vats around the long circular staircase and surveyed the whole area. In retrospect, I was on top of a bomb. But being young you don't think about things like that. I had a lot of leeway as Walter's assistant. Because of this I got to know many of the civilian workers and other prisoners. I felt they all liked me running around with my friendly broken smile. I'm sure while all of this was happening, Walter watched me out of the corner of his eye and like a father didn't mind letting his child wander. As long as I was in his domain he could decide what I was and wasn't allowed to do. He never stopped me.

The base product of the ethanol we were producing was coal,

a special type of coal. The giant vats were helping to extracting the liquid energy out of the black rock. I don't know the chemistry or the engineering, but I do know that it took tremendous amounts of coal to do this. The result was a man made mountain of used coal called koks (coke). We disposed of this koks on the edge of the compound near the fence that surrounded the factory. Many of us realized that in the event of an air raid this would be a good place to hide. It was about 2 km from the factory and would not be a good target. Even if a stray bomb fell that way it could absorb a pounding. With all the concern for safety at the factory there was none for us in the event of an air raid.

Even though Walter did not talk much, I was not restricted from talking. So, I talked to everyone, a little here, a little there. Nothing to draw attention to myself, just small talk and practice with my language skills. Whenever I spoke in the language of the person I was speaking they appreciated my understanding of their native tongue. Doing this made for better friendships. Carefully, embedded into this small talk was useful information. The civilians were the best source of information. Since they went home at night, they had access to the news. I wanted to know all I could about what was going on in the outside world. Their information was sketchy, but I knew for sure, that the war was still raging, giving me hope for rescue.

Meanwhile, the British were also teaching me their language. And their favorite thing to teach me was how to curse. The British or perhaps more specifically, the Scots, were cursing constantly, all day long. "No fucking bloody way." They would say about this or that, the pain and humor at once inseparable. We got along swimmingly. At the time, I had never heard language like that, so at first, I was surprised, but soon I learned how to mimic them. Whenever I did, they smiled, and shook their heads approvingly. I smiled back, my two cracked front teeth revealing the abuse I had been through.

236

A few times, I would visit Moshe Katz in the adult barracks. It was great to see him. The adult barracks was hell compared to mine. It had three levels like Birkenau and was fully loaded with 500 prisoners per barrack, wood slats to sleep on and poor rations in the form of a thin soup. Each morning those that died in the night were piled by the back door. The good news was we were both surviving. We had both been through being torn away from our families, Tarnow, Szebnie, that dammed cattle car and a very hot place. Thankfully, he did not have to fear for his life every minute of the day either. He had a good kapo too. Each visit with him was no longer than a half of an hour.

We spoke about Szebnie and how we both missed Moshe Blauner. At the time, we did not know of his demise, so we still held hope for him. Moshe Katz would tell me about his job at the factory. I told him about Schlosser 80 and Walter. He was doing construction and odd jobs. I was the apprentice of a German hero. At one point, I asked him if he thought the camp would be liquidated. He said, I don't know about that. It is better not to think that way. We will find a way to get through this. Just try to stay strong. In practical terms this meant well fed and healthy.

It was freezing cold. Even though my clothing was wool it was not enough to protect me from the cold. Leaving the barracks after working all day was not a good idea. Normally, I would come to the barracks toward dark, eat and have just a little time before I would need to go to bed so I could do it again. At least the food was a little more nourishing and a little warmer than at Birkenau. It was delivered in a metal barrel instead of wood. I got into a routine and before I realized it I was 18 years old. Overall to me, Buna was tame compared to the chaos of Birkenau.

I don't know if it was true, but someone told me our food was sprinkled with special chemicals to reduce or eliminate sexual desire. What I do know is that during my entire period of being incarcerated, I did not grow hair on my private parts. Maybe, it was the lack of nutrition, or a fear response from being in concentration camp. I don't know. I do know, for the greater part of my childhood, I was in a desperate, life-threatening situation, living day-by-day, sometimes hour-by-hour. My family and community were brutally destroyed so girls were the last thing on my mind. But, they were on someone's mind, because this camp had a barracks they turned into a brothel that was strictly under the SS control. German soldiers and non-Jewish kapos were given permits to visit there. I remember seeing some of the girls, prisoners like me, only a little older. They must have had more food since they did not appear as skeletons - on the contrary, they were good looking and shapely. I saw them rarely. When I did, they were always walking with an SS guard.

Since the factory had both prison staff and non-prison staff there was a day off. For me this meant a chance to clean the barracks and my shoes. Sometimes there would be time to visit Moshe.

I went to see Moshe frequently. But, one time I went to see him he was not there. No one knew where he was. I became upset and started to ask everyone. Finally, someone said that he was in an accident and got hurt badly. You can find him in the infirmary. Just hearing the words infirmary put shivers down my spine.

Moshe was assigned to a very tough Kommando. One of the tasks he was forced to do was dig sand and put it into a rail car. This was back breaking work in freezing weather. He was doing this with a few other hâftlinge. It was a precarious task. A rail line was set up with small cars along a mountain of sandy soil. A small locomotive would push 7 cars into place and each small car would be assigned two hâftlinge. With meager tools they set out on their task. Each had only a shovel. Nearby they also had a metal rod to move the car closer to the mountain as they dug away at it and a railroad tie to stop the cars from moving back down the incline. A guard stood hovering nearby holding his machine gun as the prisoners toiled.

238

Rail car used for moving sand. British War Museum fig 97

The line of cars would slowly get heavier. As soon as they were filled a small locomotive would take the load away and then quickly return with more empty rail cars. Day after day of mindless work but at least the effort helped keep the prisoners warm. It was very cold. At one point the rail cars on the incline started to get away from the prisoners. To stop it or even derail it they tossed a railroad tie under the wheels. This caused the cars to stop but not before smashing the wood into Moshe's left inner thigh creating a hematoma under the skin.

Moshe was hurt badly but he did not know it at the time. He felt the pain, but he did not realize how badly he was hurt until the next day. Preferring to continue working he refused to tell the guard or anyone other than the other hâftlinge what happened. It was an insider rule to avoid the infirmary at all costs or risk a deadly selection. The reason why he did not know how bad it was until the next day was that the damage was beneath of the skin. The next morning his leg was in bad shape, red and purple and dangerously colorful. In the night Moshe temperature spiked with a fever and when he showed his injury to the block elder there was no choice, he had to go to the infirmary. Since he was still able to walk, he held his shirt tightly as he fought through the cold, it was close to zero degrees. Even with this cold when he stepped on his foot, he felt hot pain. He was admitted.

The infirmary had to open the wound to allow it to drain. This was done without any pain medicine. For the next six weeks Moshe remained in the infirmary. On the third week the dreaded SS visited. They were doing a deadly selection. When they came upon Moshe's bed he tried to sit up and make his eyes bright, alive, and able to work soon. After looking at him they asked the male nurse, 'How long does this hâftlinge need to be in the hospital?" Without hesitation the nurse shot back, 'Four days.' He lied. With the wound draining something was very wrong. The officer accepted the answer he received and walked over to the next patient marking his number on the chart.

In this way Moshe passed a deadly selection. When they were gone the nurse put him into the surgical rotation and in a miracle no one can explain another surgery was performed and the wound was repaired. Moshe remained in the hospital for a few more weeks dreading the next selection but knowing there was nothing he could do about it. He had to take his chances; there was no way he could survive in a work crew.

Moshe said, "The male nurse was friendly. He was Polish. The only thing I can remember about him is that he was from Krakow. Unfortunately, I don't know his name. I think the surgeon, doctors and the nurse were all prisoners, just like me, but I am sure they must have had SS oversight. After the surgery, I was weak but getting better. While I was in bed I had time to think about all the

240

patients around me. So many of those patients would never get better. Each day a few died. In a strange twist of fate the nurses marked many to be alive even after they died to obtain extra rations. Those that died helped to save the rest of us because their rations were given to a few others and me. Just a few extra calories could make a huge difference in surviving another day. As I got better the nurse got me on my feet and I started to help by cleaning dishes or whatever else I could with my limited mobility. During those times we spoke about things we both had interest in, like Polish songs and culture."

Moshe's natural tendency is to make friends regardless of the situation so I am sure this friendship also meant much more, as his life ended up depending on it. Moshe told me, the day before the next selection the nurse told me of the black storm coming. He said, "Moshe you must leave today. There will be a selection in the morning. You must not be here or they will take you." There was no choice. Moshe was not healed but faced with certain destruction he had to do what he suggested and left. But just before Moshe left the male nurse said, "If you come back after they are gone I will accept you again." Moshe was counting on that. All he had to do was survive the day. Limping he left the medical barracks and went back to the general population.

Moshe continued, "I was still hurting badly but there was no excuse to miss roll call or work afterwards. That first day after a 6-week hiatus in the hospital I was assigned one of the worst kommandos of my incarceration. Kommando 92, working with a group of Gypsies who were in charge. Our job was to lift heavy bags of cement from a train and move them to where they could be used. Obviously limping, I was a target to prey upon instead of someone to give just a little bit of extra care." With tears beginning to form in his eyes thinking about that time long ago he said, "They would beaten me like schoolhouse bullies to bring them some of my meager portion of food and if I complained or did not comply they would double the workload, forcing me to lift two bags of cement instead of one at a time. I had a huge strain on my already wounded leg and if they were to hurt me badly enough it would not matter for at that time my life was almost worthless they would just as well bring my bones back to camp in a wheel barrel, as long as I could be counted and did not escape. Escape was the furthest thing from my mind at that time all I wanted to do was stop my leg from throbbing. This was a very dangerous group to be among, especially for me."

Moshe continued, "That night I attempted to re-enter the infirmary. Worried, it was almost impossible to find the male nurse that offered to help me. But with persistence I did. But trouble is that when we spoke again that night it was like I was talking to a stranger. I begged him to be readmitted and instead the nurse said, 'what do you want? What do I owe you?' Since I felt like I *knew* the fellow because of all the conversations and time we spent together I had to assume that he was being watched. This wasn't the same good natured, kindhearted man that saved me. I was beside myself. I could not go back to the Gypsy kommando. I think this was one of the lowest points in my life. I'm sorry to say this may have been the one time I gave up hope. Repulsed, I slinked back to my barracks limply in the freezing cold, tired, hurting, hungry, and worn out."

"On the way back I happened upon a prisoner that I knew from Tarnow. It was Chaim! I was miserable but very pleased to see the fellow who had been deported was standing in front of me, alive. I told Chaim what happened, about the runaway train hitting my leg and the infirmary and how somehow my foot was saved and I was still walking, barely. But alas I told him how hopeless I felt, too. At that moment Chaim offered me hope, when I needed it the most. He said, 'Moshe, I am working with Kommando 116. We know about Kommando 92, the Gypsies. We know how mean they are. My kapo is kind. He was a bookkeeper in Holland, a Jew, and our foreman is

242

788.

Nr - 10186

Lfd. Nr.	Häftl. Nr.	Name	Zugang	Abgang	Bemerkungen
17961	157216	Somogyi, Ludwig Jr.	16.12.43	7.7.44	nach Birkenau
17966	164465	Dax, Charles Jr.	"	7.7.44	Entlassen
17971	164472	Kubelski, Elias Jr.	"	30.12.43	Entlassen
17979	160243	Ress, Ludwig Jr.	"	23.12.43	Entlassen
17980	161007	Degen, Noach Jr.	"	23.12.43	Entlassen
17981	148339	Farenfeit, Mordka Jr.	"	22.12.43	Entlassen
17982	144231	Frost, Chaim Jr.	"	24.12.43	Entlassen
17983	102631	Birah, Wojciech	"	23.12.43	Entlassen
17984	161434	Katz, Hesa Jr.	"	25.1.44	Entlassen
17985	115211	Kaar, Maurice Jr.	"	7.1.44	Entlassen

Buna infirmary register
Häftl. Nr = Häftlinge number or prison tattoo number - Zolang = Arrival Date 16.12.43 = Dec. 16th, 1943 -
Shogang = Release Date 25.1.44 = Jan. 25th, 1944
Entlassen = Released fig 98

German but he was a brought here as a prisoner and has so far been a good man. I have never seen him hit anyone. There are only 32 of us in my group, but I will ask if they will take one more.' I knew this was a risky thing to do but I was in dire straits. The next morning at roll call all of the prisoners lined up behind their kapos. But Kommando 92 was missing a man, me. Since it was before the count the SS did not get involved, only the Gypsies knew he was missing. They were looking for him with their eyes but could not break the roll call to search all over. If they found him they would beat him for not showing up. Kommando 92 was hard to keep manned because of how tough they were. Now they were down another man."

Moshe was hiding between other prisoners behind the kapo for Kommando 116. They made sure that no one would see him, at least not easily. When the roll call was over the prisoners started for work. Moshe was now a part of 116 and the Gypsies could no longer count on him, he would be protected from this point forward by his newly adopted kommando. They had no way of making him come back once he was assigned.

Kommando 116 was like earning a new lease on life. They were moving metal pipes and bottles of gas for welding. Since the gas was located at a different train depot as the metal pipes a small group was formed of 6 men. Two Poles, two adult Jews, and two young men like Moshe. Together they went looking for the gas with a permit. These were good people. The Poles even got care packages delivered to them from family many contained food, a few extra calories and thankfully they shared their bounty. This kommando was nothing like moving cement. When a bottle of gas was ordered it could arrive the next day. They had plenty of time so they acted busy but worked slowly.

At one point the kommando was asked to dig a hole for a piece of heavy equipment. Moshe was feeling better so was able to work diligently. The work had to be completed in just a short while.

244

While doing this he caught the eye of a German welder, a good man. He told his kapo that Moshe should report to him in the morning. From this point forward Moshe had a savior. He would walk with his kommando but then report to the welder. His job was to hand him tools and pipes. The fellow was from Hamburg, He was handsome and pleasant, a civilian. Frequently he would leave some of his food and have Moshe clean the plate. He would have done this like a dog if he had to but in a more civilized way brought it to the tool shed where he was out of sight and ate every last morsel. The fellow did the same with his cigarettes. He would take a few puffs and put it out of sight, somewhere he knew that Moshe could also share. After awhile Moshe was feeling better but the fellow wanted to take a vacation.

Just before he left for Hamburg Moshe was worried what would happen to him. But the welder had the same concern and told the kapo, "When I leave for a short vacation I want Moshe to clean my tools and report to my station, as if I am here. I will expect my tools to be perfectly clean when I return." In this way Moshe escaped further hard labor.

When the fellow came back from his trip, Moshe asked him, "How was Hamburg?"

Forlornly he said, "Gone, all gone."

Moshe prodded, "What do you mean?" "Bombed to the ground, nothing left. This is all I could bring back." He took out two small rolls from his pocket and shared one with Moshe.

Once Moshe and this same man were in a hole with a broken pipe trying to fix it. The job was messy but made for good friendship when working in unison. Moshe by this time felt comfortable enough to ask him a tough question, he said, "Freidlinger, are you a Nazi?" The response rang true even if it was not what Moshe wanted to hear, "There is nothing else but to be a Nazi."

The collective hopes of the prisoners, like me, started to rise, as the Nazi defeat loomed more assuredly. We were especially elated when planes flew overhead with the designation of the American Air force. They were bombing in the vicinity. In fact, it seemed all the Allied forces were closing in at the same time. As the Americans bombed, the Russians were gathering at the Vistula River and the long awaited combined Allied Normandy invasion was finally, fully engaged and on the move. It was no secret. The change in the attitude of the guards within our camp was palpable. Air raid sirens sounded frequently interrupting whatever we were doing. The Germans would go to their bomb shelters. Most of the time we would not know what to do with ourselves. There was no bomb shelter for hâftlinge. My biggest fear was my proximity to the ethanol. This was second only to the camp closing and being shipped back to Birkenau. Those large flammable tanks would be a prize target for the bombing. And even though I worked close enough to them to be vaporized I would risk just about anything to avoid going back to Birkenau.

For years, my greatest wish was for rescue but even though it now appeared possible, I could count on nothing. To protect the factory and its valuable materials, the Germans did their best to conceal the buildings with camouflage. They did this by using barrels of liquid that would be set on fire to create smoke. The Nazi regime was collapsing in front of our eyes, and they knew it. Parts of the factory were pulverized although we still went to work. When the air raids occurred it was like a carpet of bombers. Like clockwork, they would always arrive between noon and one in the afternoon. You could almost set your watch to their timeliness.

As soon as the bombers appeared sirens started and the barrels would be lit to create smoke. The smoke burned my eyes terribly. During the air raids all the prisoners ran away from the factory as the guards retreated into the bomb shelters. Many of us ran to the mountain of used up coal. Anti-aircraft fire created small

246

clouds in the sky. Their sound punctuated the drone of the propellers and the whistle of the bombs falling. It was very frightening, the air was concussing everything nearby and the ground was shaking. The planes were also dropping aluminum to stifle the anti-aircraft fire. They bombed the entire region not just my camp. The British barracks was hit. I hoped no one was inside. Prisoners were dying exposed to the shells. It was impossible to avoid. The Allied planes were not getting a free ride either. I saw planes fall from the sky. But the superiority of the Allies was overwhelming the Germans, the planes kept coming and the bombs kept falling.

The first time Walter spoke to me as a person I listened intently. It was July 1944, shortly after D-Day. He took out a map and said, Junge, I want to show you something. He showed me where he was from, Leipzig. Then he asked me, Where do you come from? I pointed to Nowy-Sacz, below Warsaw and then over a little to the east, to Grybow. Upon learning where I came from he asked, Is your family alive? Forlornly, I said, No. I believe they were all killed by gas in Belzec. I pointed a little further to the east to where Belzec is located and thought, the bones of my family. Then, I repeated the story of Belzec told to me by the locomotive engineer. As I did this, anger filled his face.

When I was through there was a long silence, then he said, Junge, the Russians will be coming soon. Excited and concerned at the same time, I asked him, What will happen to us?

His response reaffirmed my concern, "The Gestapo cannot kill everyone."

Of course I wanted to be liberated, but I was concerned the Nazis would try to erase their crimes, and Auschwitz was one of the biggest. After a short pause he continued, "Junge, I think we will pay for this for a thousand years."

We spoke a little longer. He asked if I had brothers or sisters. I told him, "Yes, I do. I had a brother and four sisters. I had two more sisters but they died as toddlers before the war. None of them are alive."

"Do you have any other family?"

I shook my head, "Sir, from what I know, I think all my relatives were killed at Belzec. They were all held in a field with thousands of others and waited until it was their turn to be killed by gas."

When he heard this he shook his head in knowing understanding and seemed to ponder the depth of the disaster I had been through.

As a way of commiserating he shared his own grief with me; he told me he had lost one son on the Eastern front, and another on the Western. With this he was very sad and you could tell he was deeply reflective. That was the whole conversation, and the most I ever spoke with him the entire time I was in his care. Maybe, it was his sons he was thinking about, when he gave me those extra morsels of food? Or maybe it was his sons he was thinking about when he contracted the SS for labor and asked for a Jewish teenager? Caught up in the war, one of the few ways the Germans could save the Jews was to give them a job. Maybe this was his way of repenting because the little I knew of him he was a good man.

Even though the bombing was relentless we kept on working and trying to meet deadlines. The whole complex was crumbling as the SS stepped up their patrols and aggressive behavior. They were very concerned about escape or worse, a slave revolt. There were many more of us than them. I saw them checking hâftlinge looking for anything that did not belong, especially civilian clothing or weapons. Bursting into Walter's area, one started to check me. He pushed me aside and started to pull things apart. When Walter saw this he became forceful in his speech. With authority in his voice he said, I am responsible for this junge. He has no civilian clothing or weapons. By his word alone, they stopped searching and left.

248

Painting of Auschwitz Bombing
Unknown Artist
fig 99

The sustained bombing in our area, started in August 1944 and it did not stop until Christmas Day, December 24th, 1944. The entire region was saturated. The factory took a pounding but the bombing seemed to bypass our barracks. The Americans consistently bombed during the day, and less frequently, the British bombed at night. Once, I tried to count the planes, I lost track quickly. The planes were flying in formation. They looked beautiful from my viewpoint. Every time they got close anti-aircraft guns pounded the sky. The Americans lost a lot of planes because of this. But they owned the sky. I did not see any of the German's planes attempt to challenge their supremacy.

By the time the bombing stopped, the entire Buna factory complex was in ruins. It was a miracle I was not killed. Many of the

Bomb Shelter / Auschwitz - Birkenau fig 100

prisoners in Buna died from this friendly fire than from the guards or even malnutrition. Safe inside my barracks or at least as safe as anyone could be with bombs dropping, I saw a bomb drop nearby in the field outside my window. With all the destruction going on around me this one bomb, the one that would have surely destroyed me was a dud. It did not detonate. If it exploded as intended I would not be here today.

During one particularly heavy pounding, all of the prisoners including me ran once again to the mountain of coal. We ran as fast as we could. It was a good distance to the mountain from the factory. The bombing was directly on top of us. We were running for our lives. I reached the coal, and hid as best I could. Bombs were falling all around. Prisoners were being killed, the factory pulverized. I was still in the open, but this was the best I could do. The mounds of coal offered some protection and the brim of the hill kept the huge explosions mostly on the factory side of the spent coal. Watching this scene was at once beautiful, and frightening. The bombs were dropping all over the factory. While I was at a safe distance, or so I thought, the ethanol tanks were hit and a fireball erupted. Just as I predicted it was followed by secondary explosions.

The smoke rose high in the sky. All around the perimeter I heard anti-aircraft guns continuing their volleys. Flak was all over the sky. Aluminum chaff floated down like confetti. The bombers were trying to confuse the anti-aircraft fire. A few of the American planes were caught in their nasty web. They careened out of control and crashed. I hoped to see parachutes but saw none. Even though we were being pounded by them, I wished for their safety. As the grand panorama played out, the Germans cowered safely in their bunkers. Many of my fellow prisoners would not know what hit them. For those it was over fast. A few were maimed, of these, the lucky ones were forever scarred, while others died more slowly. That day we took the biggest pounding.

Air Bomb like the one the landed near me and did not explode

fig 101

This bombing turned out to be the final straw. After it the whole camp was closed down. My fear rose quickly, thinking the rumors were going to be true. We would be shipped to Birkenau and destroyed. There was no factory left by the time the bombing was over. During the raid, explosions were everywhere. The sound was deafening but the concussion of the nearby air was the worst. Everyone on the ground was disoriented, some bleed from their ears.

Near the end of the bombing one plane found itself directly over the coal mountain. Before I could comprehend what was happening, another bomb dropped. The whistle was right above my location. It exploded. I felt something wet on my neck. Instinctively, I put my hand there and realized I was bleeding profusely. A piece of shrapnel or coal must have caught me in the neck. I was hurt and bleeding badly, but the artery was not severed. I never lost consciousness. I knew my wound needed attention but I was frightened. Under no circumstances did I want to be sent back to Birkenau. I covered the gash as best I could, but there was no way of adequately doing this. At least the artery was not cut or I would have bled out. Looking around me others died, red marking their blue and white uniforms, as they lay motionless against the black rocks.

During the chaos of the bombing raids, three prisoners attempted to escape. They were caught and quickly hanged with all of us in attendance. Regardless, of the crumbling status of the factory the SS were still intent on maintaining strict control of the prisoners.

The three men stood by the gallows. Each wore a noose around his neck, their heads were uncovered. You could see their eyes. They were already in bad shape from beatings. It was Sunday. We were called to the Appellplatz for a formal roll call. I knew it would not be good. We lined up block-by-block behind our blockleiter. I was with all the teens. Everyone was present and accounted for as SS Rokacz addressed the prisoners. He was wearing his best uniform and a helmet with a spike on the top. I was not too far away. Everyone had to face forward. I had no choice but to watch.

Rokacz was standing on a specially made platform that had a few stairs. He spoke with a big megaphone. An entire company of SS was there to create the maximum effect. He wanted to make sure everyone saw him. They were facing us with their machine

252

Monument in Israel to the three hanged in Buna:
Yehuda Leo Diament
Nathan Weissman
Janek Grossfeld
The text says, "The three were arrested, tortured
and hanged for leading a resistance movement
among the inmates of the extermination camp."
fig 102

guns ready. There must have been over one hundred Gestapo perfectly dressed as he spoke. I could only hear parts of it. "By order of the Reich Fuhrer ... Diamond, ... Weissman, ...are to be hanged for the crime of attempting to escape and foster an insurrection." Years later, I found a book with a monument for the hanging. It lists the names I accurately remembered with the correct spelling and the third I didn't, Grossfeld.

The gallows was very close to my barracks. They were built for this event. It was made by tilting a few pairs of poles, securing them with support on the sides. It was all set upon a platform and there was a small stairs to step up onto the flat surface. Three ropes were set up for the three victims. They were evenly separated from each other. The ropes were looped through a pulley. It was designed so the ropes would extend on both sides of the platform. Fellow prisoners were lined up on both sides holding the ropes. The condemned stood on stools. Right before the order was given one of them shouted, "We are the last." Anyone could see the camp was falling apart and our liberation or destruction was imminent. It was a very ugly scene. As soon as the man shouted in defiance SS Rokacz gave the word to the prisoners holding the rope and they pulled. The stools fell into the platform and the men fell quickly, snapping their necks. Their bodies quivered a little and then remained still. As soon as this was over they hung there for a few hours until they were removed. The message was received loud and clear. No escape, and no associated insurrection would be tolerated.

The combined bombing and onslaught of the Allied troops was steadily taking a toll upon the Germans, Buna and all of the prisoners. The factory was the prime target so it was bombed regularly. Eventually, its back was broken and we could no longer work there. In one of the ironies of war, I learned years later that my own cousin Sam Keen, was a navigator bombardier in the US 8th Air Force and it was his group that bombed my camp in Buna while I hid behind a pile of coal. Showing me his actual briefing orders for the bombing of the I.G. Farben, Buna works I read, Saturate and Destroy at any price. As I read this, I imagined him above me as I cowered near the black rocks. Many prisoners died in those air raids. The bombing was successful and Buna was destroyed. The entire factory in chaos, and me, I had no work assignment, and a wounded neck. Because of this, I stayed in my block for one entire month, lingering with nothing to do. Luckily, we were not sent to Birkenau, I'm sure this must have crossed their minds too. But we were worth 3 marks a day and collectively since there were so many of us that could be of some value to the SS. It wasn't going to stay this way, something would have to change soon. A few work groups were assembled and given

254

jobs. One dug out the bomb that did not detonate.

Finally, on January 15,1945 the whole camp assembled at the Appellplatz. All the remaining prisoners were in attendance. Hundreds were missing, and presumably killed. I stood at attention for the last time while Captain Rokacz of the SS announced the plans for the camp. Holding up the megaphone he first spoke in German, then again in Polish, The camp will be closed tomorrow. I gulped hard. In the morning you will all assemble here then we will walk out to the railroad station. Anyone who cannot walk will remain here and go to the krankenstube (infirmary). If you are not hurt and not assembled to walk, you will be executed. Anyone who cannot walk should stay in the camp, by order of the Reich Fuhrer.

I asked my block elder Zigfreid, What should I do? He said, "You have a fever, and an infection from the wound in your neck; you must stay. Take your portion of bread and wait in the barracks. I will have you taken to the krankenstube." The following day, I saw thousands of prisoners march out of camp, my friend, Moshe among them with his bad leg. I had mixed emotions watching them leave. I knew the German structure was falling apart but these were my friends and community of prisoners. What would happen to me when they all left? Those that left went on a terrible adventure. It came to be known as *The Death March from Auschwitz*. After everything I had been through in Buna I was now being sent to the dreaded infirmary and all of them into the freezing cold.

Years later at a Holocaust conference in Israel 1981 a man walked up to me and spoke in French. I could not understand him. I asked him to speak in another language. He switched to German and said, I know you. I did not recognize him. He continued, "Let me see your neck." I showed him the scar I received in those last days of bombing. He said, "Leon, I was the fellow that brought you from the Jugenbloch to the krankenstube before we all left Buna." It was good to see him, especially to know he was still alive. The man introduced himself as Shusterman, my fellow Jugenbloch prisoner. He survived.

Moshe Katz told me what happened on the death march. He said, "We were marched out of Auschwitz to nearby Gliwitz. With my bad leg, I did the best I could. In Gliwitz, we were put into a camp overnight. Then we were herded onto a train that took us to Buchenwald. Upon arrival, we unloaded from the train and marched in formation to the local concentration camp. The next day we lined up for roll call and afterwards work assignments. I was selected to build a barracks in a small camp called, Holcen. To get there I boarded a truck. I stayed there for 5 weeks until the barracks was built. Then on April 5th, I was sent to Bergen–Belsen, another concentration camp. However, on the way, the train stopped at the Cele station. As we stood in the darkness and confines of the cattle car I heard a drone of propellers diving towards us. At the time I could not see anything but I learned this was a British Aircraft raid after we were strafed. Within seconds of hearing the plane diving, it started its strafing run followed by bombs dropping on top of us. Wood splintered and some of my fellow prisoners were shot. They must have been thinking our train was a military target. They were right to believe this, because the train carried ammunition on one side, and heavy equipment on the other. We, the prisoners were in the middle acting as a human shield. The doors to the cars flew open and the prisoners started to run. We ran as fast as we could. I hobbled. The bombing ignited the ammunition and a large explosion followed. The moment I heard this sound I dropped the ground and waited. Then, I continued into the woods. When it was clear to resume, the Gestapo gathered everyone who was still alive, and we marched to Bergen-Belsen. You would think the prisoners would escape during this chaos but there was nowhere to go and the surrounding area was hostile to Jews. It was best to stay together.

The Cele station was a disaster but I think the Germans were more concerned we would escape and cause havoc in the country-side. We thought the best chance for survival was to stay together. So, instead of helping to clean up Cele we were brought to the concentration camp. First there was another selection, but this time no gas chamber. There was also no food, except a single piece of bread per prisoner and this small piece of bread ended up having to last 8 days at the time when we had no idea when we would ever get food again. The conditions in the camp were atrocious. At one point I was grouped with eight hundred prisoners and crammed into a single barracks. At night the doors were locked. This resulted in hundreds dying of asphyxiation. I survived, and was liberated on April 15th, by the Americans."

Quar.Kartei: _____ 125 _____
Zug-Buch: _____
A.m. Weimar-Buchenwald, 26. Januar 194_
Kartei: _____

Eingang der Zugänge vom 26. Januar 1945

Vom Kl. Auschwitz

Polit. Polen:

Nr.	Nr.	Name	Vorname	Geb.	Ort	Beruf	Nr.
1.	121845	Adamczyk	Franz	16. 9.23	Kosi	Maurer	
2.	124255	Birnbaum	Jozef	4. 8.20	Krakau	Schloss.	16898
3.	120500	Blach	Stanislaw	8. 5.58	Preszow	Berga.	8990
4.	122168	Bozykowski	Adolf	12.12.24	Ulchowihe	Arb.	9103
5.	122773	Buczaszek	Stefan	25. 1.13	Andrichow	Arzt	20526
6.	122257	Budynowski	Jan	20.10.21	Moszczowa	Schloss.	9150
7.	122143	Chrobak	Ferdynand	9. 6.25	Stracenka	"	9171
8.	122305	Dylewski	Stefan	21. 2.25	Sucho-dol	Arb.	
9.	123619	Gacuk	Wladyslaw	1927	Kozy	Arb.	
10.	122304	Grocholski	Bronislaw	14.10.27	Podhajce	Schwass.	9085
11.	123530	Gutann	Moses	18. 2.04	Bendzin	Schloss.	9192
12.	122575	Kasyniuk	Jan	10. 5.28	Bidek	Landarb.	169160
13.	122713	Kalecinski	Franciszek	20. 5.08	Belchatow	Arbeir.	9172
14.	122193	Kocur	Johann	13. 6.87	Bestwin	Maurer	126246
15.	122310	Kopyto	Georg	31. 1.16	Hohenlinde	Arb.	99062
16.	122750	Kowalski	Jerzy	27. 4.23	Czerwinek	Pfleg.	119683
17.	122279	Kwasny	Gustaw	5.10.09	Grzepinik	Schloss.	135568
18.	121697	Luben	Becalel	8. 9.20	Gras	Schloss.	114804
			(18 - Mischl. 1.Graden)				128141
19.	122276	Lena	Jan	5. 9.93	Lma	Mauer	
20.	122129	Lukasik	Stanislaw	17. 8.04	Chrzanow	Fräser	9132
21.	122342	Majcherosyk	Franciszek	28. 9.26	Wegulica	Arb.	9189
22.	122774	Makowski	Antoni	25. 7.10	Bochnczew	Arzt	131791
23.	122775	Nowakowski	Edward	1.18.11	Warschau	Schloss.	131752
24.	122721	Konaranca	Adam	16. 5.03	Wyslawlew	Autoschl.	132478
25.	122778	Pospieszynski	Mieczyslaw	27. 1.10	Blotiny	Schloss.	169710
26.	122664	Rutkowski	Bronislaw	30.10.05	Warschau	Arzt	79881
27.	122135	Salacinski	Antoni	10. 3.00	Bialogora	Dinadru.	12019
28.	122130	Sobel	Jan	10.10.20	Bilowa	Glaser	8407 H
29.	122624	Solski	Artur	23. 3.14	Warschau	Metallar.	122618
30.	124149	Styrsower	Zygmunt	19.12.97	Mechanik	Werkzeug.	18757
			(30 - Mischling)				
31.	124432	Tydor	Aleksander	10. 1.01	Krakau	Schloss.	62061
			(31 - Mischl. 1.Grades)				
32.	121902	Zajac	Jan	24. 6.92	Franciszow	Landarb.	9187
33.	122152	Zajac	Michal	15. 7.98	Daviampol	Lisarre.	159203
34.	122776	Zianowicz	Ryszard	28. 8.26	Zabkowice	Schles.	
35.	122184	Zealik	Kazimierz	8. 2.26	Pektop	Landarb.	9126

Polit. Polen- Juden:

36.	124071	Abelowicz	Chaim	28.10.10	Blonin	Schneid.	95043
37.	123534	Abend	Baruch	15. 7.23	Tyszya	Schloss.	166890
38.	123651	Abramow	Dawid	25. 2.06	Minsk	"	17170
39.	123509	Abramowicz	Hilel	16. 2.19	Bielzn	Schneid.	97245
40.	122039	Abramowicz	Salona	3.11.22	Lodz	Maurer	9599
41.	122098	Abramowicz	Samuil	20.11.20	Czerwinak	Schuhm.	83713
42.	123429	Abramowski	Meizer	8. 9.14	Druskieniki	"	9114
43.	122245	Abramson	Kirz	-. -.12	Lodz	Maler	14230
44.	121662	Adalberg	Josxek	19.11.23	Xraxy-Stow	Schloss.	127914
45.	122560	Adler	Laib	18. 3.11	Lodz	Dreher	143863
46.	122165	Adler	Wolf	2. 1.06	Warschau	Mech.	117463
47.	121385	Ajnfeld	Boroka	14. 6.08	"	Schloss.	171917
48.	120925	Ajznmeser	Dawid	28.10.22	Kasienice	Schloss.	18865
49.	120491	Ajzenberg	Nachyn	4. 5.25	Brady	"	1885
50.	121006	Ajzenberg	Uywa	15. 3.09	Lwow	Schneid.	1571

0027972

- 12 -   26. Januar 1945

651. 121... Kapelmajster   Icek   6. 4.25 Kielce   Tisch.   B658
652. 123311 Kapolusz   Mendel   30. 4.25 Litzmannstadt, Schl.   148079
653. 131576 Kapelusznik   Pinkus   0. 5.23   "   132544
654. 123406 Kaplan   Boleslaw 25. 1.26 Warschau   167706
655. 120584 Kaplan   Chaim   24. 5.96 Bialystok   "   171586
656. 124059 Kaplan   Dawid   29. 9.22 Pruzana   "   99362
657. 121686 Kaplanski   Gerszon   24.12.24 Opatow   Mechan. A19399
658. 120658 Kapler   Mieczyslaw 20.5.11 Kozienice   Tapez. A65006
659. 123455 Kaprak   Szmul   34. 9.24 Plonsk   Schl.   79759
660. 121747 Kapuscinski   Berel   26.12.12 Warschau   Setzer 33176
661. 121590 Karp   Chaskiel 12.12.26 Starachowice Schl.   A19940
662. 123563 Karp   Mersz   1. 9.20 Litzmannstadt.   "   144052
663. 123146 Karp   Szymon   25. 9.14 Litzmannstadt Fris. 144044
664. 123868 Karpusinski   Izrael   26. 1.25 Kielce   Schl.   33143
665. 123100 Karsch   Chaim   26. 6.21 Bialystok   Techn. 171820
666. 123666 Kaszczburski   Berek   23. 1.25 Bialystok   Druck. 171527
667. 120607 Kaszub   Fiszel   29. 3.17 Krosniewice   Fleisch.142418
668. 120579 Kaszub   Rubin   7.10.20 Krosniewice   Schn.   148435
669. 120600 Kaszub   S...aje   --.--.00 Krosniewice   Fleisch.142611
670. 120606 Katz   Mendel   15. 3.09 Blaszki   Schn. 123101
671. 121847 Katz   Moses   1. 4.25 Nowy Sacz   Schwbie.161274
672. 120655 Kaufman   Berek   1. 5.15 Gora Kalwaria ASchl. B514
673. 123021 Kaufman   Wolf   10. 6.15 Bobowa   Schl.   161260
674. 120654 Kaufmann   Make   11. 7.08 Litzmannstadt Arb.   34255
675. 121024 Kawer   Benjamin 25. 5.25 Szczekociny   Maler   9021c
676. 121423 Kawer   Lajzer   16. 4.14 Ostroleka   "   96962
677. 122256 Kawka   Michal   11.12.22 Krosniewice   Bahn.   144367
678. 120546 Kazanowski   Chaim   10. 1.27 Piotrkow   Schl.   24356
679. 123416 Kazimierski   Moses   22. 7.14 Demsburg   "   167260
680. 120759 Kazmir   Abram   12.11.19 Petryna   Tisch. 79444
681. 123526 Kanoglewicz   Bernat   2. 4.14 Plensk   Elekt. 64158
682. 123061 Kellner   Mechel   3.12.15 Zmigrod   Tisch. 161296
683. 123367 Kempinski   Jakob   26.10.12 Pielun   Schl.   33164
684. 123570 Kepinski   Jeremiasz 25. 9.25 Litzmannstadt   33152
685. 123516 Kerner   Gedalja   23. 1.22 Warschau   123169
686. 120691 Korechbaum   Jakob   14. 1.09 Samahil   Bäcker 144557
687. 121904 Kesten   Jakub   25.11.25 Rochnin   Elekt. A19355
688. 122710 Kestin   Josef   25. 6.24 Karczin   Zimmerm.90645
689. 121143 Kiersz   Abram   25. 6.09 Piotrkow   Schl.   BBell
690. 122363 Kierszenblat   Szmul   20.11.20 Ostrowiec   B1817
691. 123531 Kirkner   Benjamin 12. 7.10 Krinki   Schn.   B1999
692. 121164 Klagebald   Barush   25.10.23 Stary Oncz   "   B492
693. 123533 Klainer   Icek   16. 8.21 Krzesko Nowe   B b044
694. 122260 Klajman   Abram   20.10.20 Ostrowiec   Metalla.161244
695. 120606 Klajman   Jankiel   4. 4.24 Kalwaria   Tisch. 12390
696. 121749 Klajner   Moszek   16. 7.27 Ostrowiec   Schl.   B5009
697. 121227 Klajman   Moszek   3. 6.05 Starachowice   Huta. A19192
698. 120646 Klaparda   Chaskiel 13. 4.24 Starachowice Schweis.A19215
699. 121895 Klapwald   Samiel   1. 1.00 Krakau   Bucht. 16563
700. 121699 Kleyster   Meyer   17. 2.07 Kowanoz   Schn.   BZ305
701. 120612 Klein   Beno   15. 1.05 Sierads   Schl.   160131
702. 124207 Kleinberger   Simon   4.10.20 Brzasko   Tapez. 161546
703. 120775 Kleiner   Jakob   3. 5.25 Krakau   Tisch. B4595
704. 120785 Kleiner   Salek   15. 1.25 Krakau   "   B6894
705. 120476 Kleiman   German   5. 5.24 Nowy Sacz   Schmied 161555
706. 123636 Kleiman   Moraka   22. 5.00 Litzmannstadt   144832
707. 120847 Kleinzahler   Faiwel   15. 0.23 Nowy Sacz   Maurer 161513
708. 124169 Klepfisch   Abram   1.11.92 Radom   Zimmerm.160177
709. 124168 Klepfisz   Rudolf   10. 3.27 Wien   Maler   103170
710. 120579 Klieger   Mozes   0. 9.11 Aubensierz   Schl.   103474

0027983

Tarnow

Nowa Synagoga Jubileuszowa w Tarnowie.
Neue Jubiläums-Synagoge in Tarnów.

Tarnow Synagogue
fig. 68

Tarnow

Interior of the Tarnow synagogue
please notice the central columns
fig. 142

Tarnow ghetto

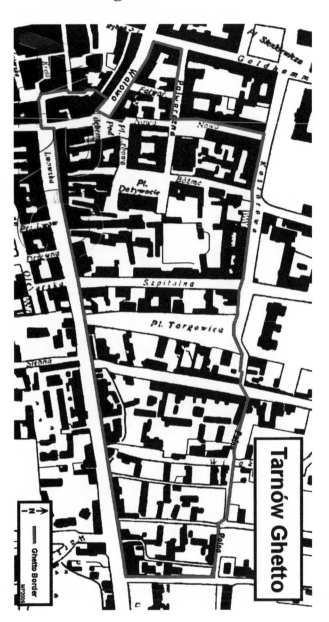

Tarnow ghetto
fig. 61

Tarnow ghetto

Tarnow ghetto 1939/40 German Officers with the Judenrat

fig. 141

264

Tarnow ghetto

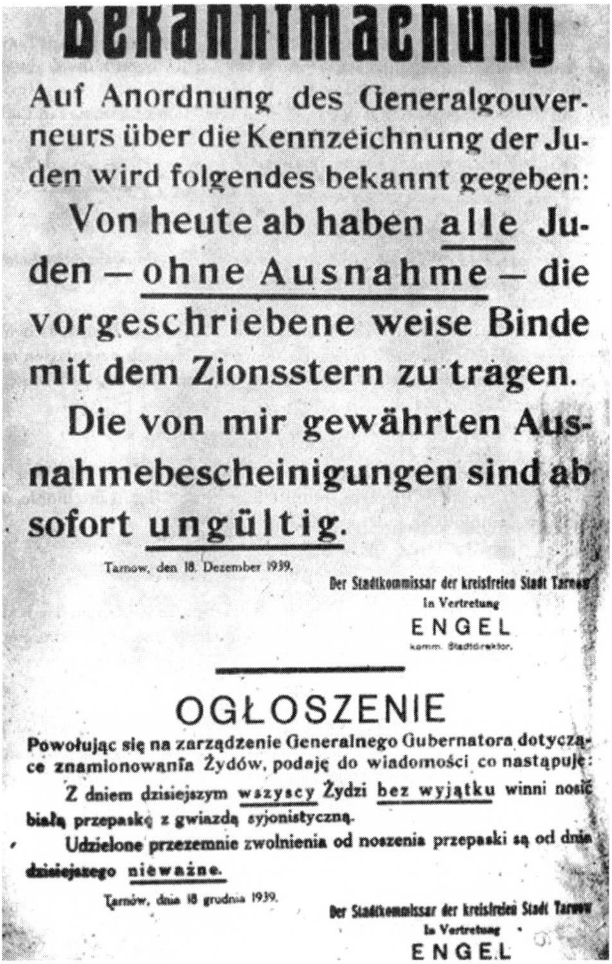

Bekanntmachung

Auf Anordnung des Generalgouverneurs über die Kennzeichnung der Juden wird folgendes bekannt gegeben:

Von heute ab haben alle Juden – ohne Ausnahme – die vorgeschriebene weise Binde mit dem Zionsstern zu tragen.

Die von mir gewährten Ausnahmebescheinigungen sind ab sofort ungültig.

Tarnow, den 18. Dezember 1939.

Der Stadtkommissar der kreisfreien Stadt Tarnow
In Vertretung
ENGEL
komm. Stadtdirektor.

OGŁOSZENIE

Powołując się na zarządzenie Generalnego Gubernatora dotyczące znamionowania Żydów, podaję do wiadomości co następuje:

Z dniem dzisiejszym wszyscy Żydzi bez wyjątku winni nosić białą przepaskę z gwiazdą syjonistyczną.

Udzielone przezemnie zwolnienia od noszenia przepaski są od dnia dzisiejszego nieważne.

Tarnów, dnia 18 grudnia 1939.

Der Stadtkommissar der kreisfreien Stadt Tarnow
In Vertretung
ENGEL

All Jews must wear a Star of David Armband without exceptions.
A poster from the Tarnow ghetto
fig 62

Tarnow ghetto

Tarnow ghetto - June 1942
fig. 65

Street scene from Tarnow ghetto
fig 66

Tarnow ghetto

Tarnow ghetto - Jews crouching prior to deportation
fig. 63

Tarnow ghetto - the collection of Jews to be taken to Belzec.
fig 64

Tarnow Post-War

Tarnow Synagogue
the central columns are all that remain
fig. 67

Auschwitz Region

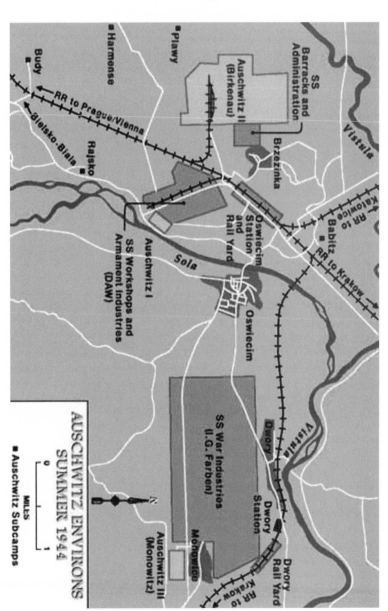

fig 85

Auschwitz II - Birkenau

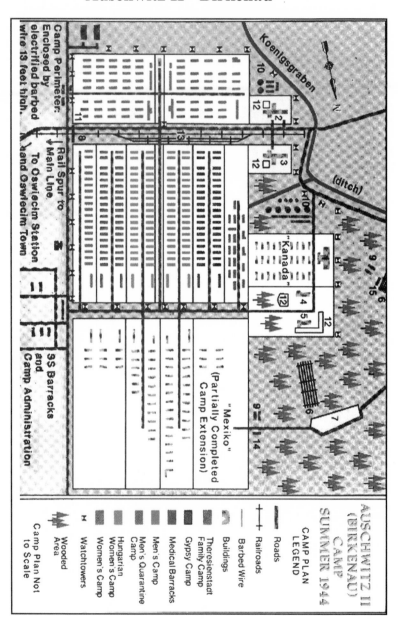

fig 86

Auschwitz II - Birkenau

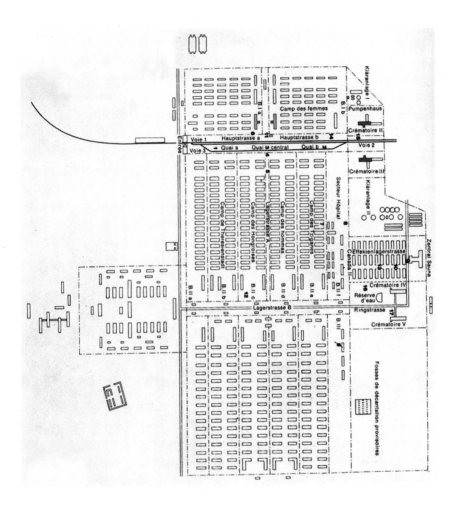

Auschwitz - Birkenau Plan - fig 87

Auschwitz II - Birkenau

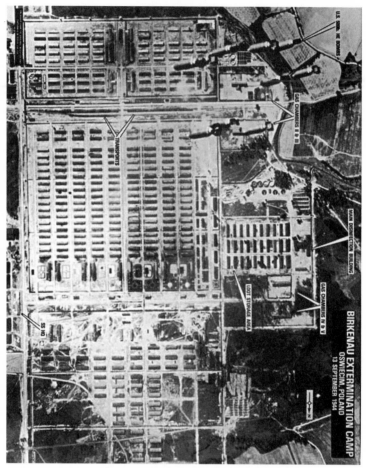

Aerial Map - Birkenau - Sept 13th 1944

Top right - Bombs being dropped over the gas chambers of Birkenau.
The bombs in the photograph continued on their ballistic route and hit
the Buna factory. A number of stray bombs hit Birkenau too and caused
light damage. The formation of the camp is clearly visible, as is the train
standing by the platform.

fig 88

Auschwitz II - Birkenau

High Voltage Danger
fig. 92

Artist's perspective of Birkenau
fig. 90

Auschwitz II - Birkenau

Auschwitz Barracks notice chimney in the center.
fig. 91

Auschwitz Latrine
fig. 89

274

Auschwitz II - Birkenau

Auschwitz Crematorium
fig. 93

Auschwitz III - I.G. Farben - BUNA

I.G. Farben 'Buna' complex
fig 94

276

Chapter Nine

Liberation

By this time all the walking prisoners had left the camp leaving the entire Buna complex a ghost town with the only sign of life the Krankenstube. Composed of two barracks the dreaded infirmary was now guarded by only a few elderly soldiers. Together, we were the last of camp Buna. Within its confines there were about 400 total beds. All of them were in use, but not for long. Only about 25-30 of us could still walk, the rest were deathly sick. Many had injuries from the sustained bombing. Some were missing appendages if they were lucky, others were far worse if they were hit anywhere else. We were all in a race against time. When one of the unfortunate passed away the icy cold inside the building preserved the body. So, by the time we moved them, they were like blocks of wood. Since we had nowhere to move the bodies we stacked them outside. Here, the snow covered their grey skin and tattered blue & whites.

For the rest of us, the living, it wasn't enough that we were wounded, malnutrition was as deadly as any other injury. At least there was still a doctor and a male nurse but they had to support the entire infirmary. Needless to say, they couldn't do much. Even if they could, there were no materials, no medication, no running water, no electricity and worst of all no food. Nothing but the roof over our heads and the useless old guards who would not even let us scrape the ground outside the fence to look for a potato. This would be our last stand and the outcome was far from clear. We knew, a short distance beyond the fence, there was a small cache of frozen potatoes not far from the gates, and we wanted to find them badly.

To treat my neck wound and attempt to clean any infection, the doctor used the only thing he had, melted snow. With this he did the best that he could. Yet, even in my condition, I was one of the lucky ones, especially since I was well fed before the camp cleared out. So, even though my wound was severe it did not stop me from moving around, and as soon as I was tended to the doctor put me to work. My job was to clear the beds of those that passed. While doing this I discovered a room with a pile of frozen limbs. I took one look at them and closed the door. I have no idea why they were collected instead of destroyed. Even though many of the bombing victims were at the infirmary, only some had lost appendages, and this was too big a cache of body parts to account for by those injured. I am positive I never saw anyone in the factory or during the roll call with crutches or a missing limb except a few Germans who returned from the war.

After moving a few bodies each morning I did not have much to do. None of us did. Mostly, I languished with the rest, waiting, fearful of a truck to arrive that might take us to Birkenau, or excited that a liberator might show up at the door to give us our coveted freedom. It was a toss up. My life remained in limbo. Anything could happen. Still, the most pressing problem was the lack of food. Without it I had to conserve the little energy I still had. We all did. No one knew when we could expect any support or if they would reach us in time. The little energy I had I used to scavenge for food. Cold, weak and tired, everything slowed down to a crawl except my thoughts that were punctuated by the sounds of battle. Possibly hallucinating, I heard my father's voice, "You will survive. You will live longer than everyone else..." I had already outlived my whole family.

Survival would be a different story. My life hung by a thread. With no food, we were all wasting away. So, a few of us got together and became fixated on the field just outside the gate. We knew there was a stash of frozen potatoes left by the trucks when they dumped them for our commissary. Near delirious, all of us walking skele-

Krankenschwester (Nurse) Armband fig 134

tons, we started to head towards the gate, but when we got close, the old Nazi guards fired upon us. Confused by where the shooting was coming from and dismayed by not being allowed to rummage for the frozen morsels, we scattered and turned back to avoid any more shooting. At one point however, I did manage to scrounge some dry onions, but all they did was make me very thirsty. At least there was plenty of snow with more falling from the sky to quench my thirst. I don't think this was what the ancient Israelites meant by manna from heaven.

I struck up a conversation with the male nurse. He was a pleasant fellow from Warsaw, and a prisoner just like me. I told him about my hometown. He told me about his. I asked him about how he came to Buna. There were so many sick and dying around us, but there was little we could do to help them. We spoke for a long time, and I asked him, "Do you know my friend Moshe Katz? He got hurt by a railcar on his inner thigh." While talking to him, I remember looking at his eyes. They seemed to remember but he acted the part of a fool. It didn't matter whether he knew of him or not. I was just trying to occupy the time. I'm sure he saw hundreds of terrible tragedies, so I did not press it. It is hard to explain when you're in such a dire position but sitting there, talking to him, I missed the organized life of the camp, my friends, and especially the meager but consistent food. Not knowing what would happen next weighed heavily upon me.

By the time of our rescue my body weight was only eighty pounds. Being six feet tall I was dangerously thin. Yet, in spite of everything I had been through, including the infection in my neck, I was in relatively good shape compared with the others. Most of them were in bed, and needed attention. I could not do much to help them either. Feebly, I did try to help a few, but the little I could do was offer kindness, and a bowl of melted snow. Our only collective hope was the sounds of the battle all around us, both day and night. During those cold beautiful nights right before the liberation, I saw the skies light up, not with twinkling stars or lightning, but with the sparks and sounds of battle. Anticipating freedom I closed my eyes and dreamed of better days. By doing this, I also removed doubt and negative feelings from my future.

Finally, after ten days of fasting, on January 27th, 1945, the liberation of Buna came to our front door. It was in the form of a full Russian attack. I remember it clearly. It was a very cold but beautifully sunny day. White snow was everywhere. The temperature was well below freezing. Some light snow was still falling. The attack was being held back by whatever meager resistance the old SS guards could muster. It wasn't much. You could hear the attacks get louder as the Russians approached us.

From my view, because the camp was in a low part of the valley, I looked up into the hills for a glimpse of the liberators. It was easy to see smoke but much harder to see the soldiers in their white camouflage against the white snow. As they got closer, however, I heard bullets whizzing by me, hitting my barracks and splintering the wood. Eventually I heard Russian voices. They were very close. Carelessly, possibly deranged, I stood outside, unprotected, hardly reacting. I must have been dazed by the lack of food, or fever, or shock. It was probably a combination of all of these.

After a final barrage of gunfire I heard a joyful battle cry, Hoorah! The infirmary was the closest barracks to the action. It was located near the rear of the compound, which happened to be directly towards the fighting. At the very end, the battle became fiercest, and the artillery got so heavy that one of the barracks caught fire.

Soon the first Russian soldiers arrived in white camouflage battle gear. It was still morning. I could hear their voices. When one approached me he used his rifle to direct while speaking, "Go back inside the barracks." I understood his motions better then his voice, and did as I was told. Upon entering the Krankenstube I reported meekly, "The Russians are here."

Upon hearing the news of our liberation my fellow prisoners could only moan with happiness and relief. Not one of them shed a tear, including me, as we had all lost that ability long before our release. I think that is one of the side effects of malnutrition. Half of those liberated were comatose. Many lay still. The liberation came too late for them. They had lost the race. At 11:00 AM the Russians formally entered the Buna compound and their foot soldiers fanned out in front of two riders on horseback. What they saw must have been appalling, a mountain of bodies, starving prisoners, and a ghost town filled with blue & white striped zombies.

Focused on the immediate threat, with voices full of urgency mixed with the anxiousness of battle, one of the riders asked, "Who is a Nazi? Show me!" Of course, this was said in Russian, but I did not need any translation. By this time most if not all of the guards in the foxholes and bomb shelters were already dead and the camp was empty except for us. We were close to death too. So, the answer came in the form of silence. None of us knew. Interrupting the silence, a second rider approached. He was saying the same thing, but he said it in a familiar voice, one that gave me inspiration. It was in my native tongue, Yiddish.

"Ver ist a Nazi? Is imizer da ver ut gi helfed di Nazis?" It was followed by something I longed to hear, "Du Bist Frie, Eri canst gayn haym" (You are FREE. You can go home). Surveying our sad situation, he looked at me directly and said, "Zun kenst gayn?" (Son, can you walk?) "If so, you can follow us, otherwise, wait here and others will take you."

I wasn't about to stay there when I could get food anywhere but where I was. So, I followed them, traveling east on foot about 2 kilometers to a Red Cross aid station. But, before I left, I took 2 pairs of pants, and 2 jackets from the dead. It was very cold that day, and I badly needed the extra clothing to stay warm. On the way to the aid station everyone I saw was asking where I came from, my blue & whites telling the story. I would respond, "Auschwitz" followed by, "Hell on Earth." This would always be followed by the same question, "Did you know my brother _____?"

When we arrived at the aid station I was greeted by the Russian military police. The first thing one of them told me was, walk low, bullets are still flying. Looking at my neck, another asked, "What is wrong with you?"

He could see my neck wound but wanted to hear my voice and know my own opinion of my condition. In response, I said weakly, "Can I have some food?"

Even though he did not get the answer he was looking for,

my response was sufficient for him to figure out I could walk and talk and needed food desperately. No matter what was wrong with me the most urgent problem was the lack of nourishment.

He asked, "Where do you come from?"

I told him, "Near Nowy-Sacz, *Grybov.*" Rescued, I no longer felt the pretense of having to hide my Yiddish tongue.

He nodded his head knowingly as he continued to speak in Polish, "We will send you to Krakow and from there you can get a ride to Grybow."

I said with my parched voice, "Can I have water?" He handed me his canteen but I did not realize it was filled with vodka before I took a big gulp and passed out.

I remember waking up a little later on a truck heading to Krakow. Resisting the throbbing in my head, I raised it enough to see dead bodies still lying on the side of the road. The fighting must have been recent. I was FREE, but so very tired. With the little energy I had left, I wondered what would be left of war torn Poland. Soon, I would learn the scale of the damage. For now I could only rest.

When we arrived in Krakow, I learned the Russians had occupied the city only about 10-12 days before my rescue. It was around the same time Buna was evacuated. But, at least the city was essentially intact; it survived the bombing. Buildings still functioned and it was bustling with people. I was in bad shape and very weak and still wearing my blue and white striped uniform." The truck brought me to a field hospital. As soon as I arrived, I was given some fresh bread to eat. It was a wondrous thing. While I ate, the nurses properly washed and disinfected my wound. Before long, I was eating with two hands. A nurse saw me doing this and admonished, "Slow down, eat with only one hand."

The next thing they did was strip me down and scrape my back. I had a lice infestation on my lower back. This was a common problem affecting millions of Poles almost to the level of an epidemic. The lice cause typhoid fever and worse. To cure me once my back was scraped I was sprinkled with a strong pesticide. Then my clothing was cleaned as well as possible and I was given the same clothing back, my old blue & whites. It would be weeks before I changed clothing again and by that time I had another infestation.

At the hospital, I was safe but confused, instinctively I still felt like a prisoner and I couldn't shake the feeling of expecting to go back to the work camp. The feeling of freedom was new to me and it would take some time to get used to it. Those years I lost were critical growth periods for me. I entered the war as a child, and came out a full-grown man. It would take a long time before I got used to thinking for myself, but the Russians treated me kindly, and soon, when I was well enough, the Commander approached, and asked, "Son, where do you want to go?"

Chapter Ten

Chaos

The thought never crossed my mind. I had nowhere to go. However, there was only one place I wanted to be; Home, I told him. I knew this was not the answer he expected, so I followed with, *Grybov*. He understood, "Go to the Vistula Bridge, he said and the military police will take you toward your home."

On the 2nd or 3rd of February 1945, I arrived in Grybow courtesy of a Russian transport, and as soon as I arrived I made my way directly to my neighbor's home, Tadeusz Skrabski's. The compass in my head was set to my father's last wish, which was directed to him, Tadeusz, if Leon survives, promise me, you must take care of him, When his family saw me, they started to jump for joy. I hugged his daughters, Janka and Jadwiga. Then, I held Tadeusz like I would my father, holding back the tears that I could not produce. He was elated to see me too, "Leon, I knew if anybody could survive, it would be you!"

Once past the formalities of knowing I was alive, I began to take a more detailed assessment of the surroundings, picking up on things that changed. First, I noticed that his hand seemed to have healed; then I glanced over at my old home and saw horses in the yard and my brother and sisters playing, while a rooster was looking on as he perched on a fence surrounded by hens, all pecking the ground. Oddly, the small garden near the well was over grown. My mother would never have allowed that. I saw smoke coming from my chimney and noticed the fireplace was in use. Was my mother waiting for me?

Tadeusz saw what was happening. Realizing, I was both here and there, in a kind of dream state. For my safety, he held me back.

All I had been through flooded back into my mind allowing

me to comprehend that my family was gone forever. Yet, there *was* a horse and even a carriage in my yard, and I had never seen either of them before. Peering more carefully, I realized those kids were not my brother and sisters. What were they doing at my house? I became incensed. Tadeusz could not hold me back any longer. I tore away from him and stormed open the door of my old home. I was not happy with what I found. It was occupied, but not by my family. "Who are you?" I shouted, "Who gave you permission to move into my house?" The answers were not forthcoming. It took no more than a few moments to realize this must have been a collaborator.

I did not wait for any answers. Instead, I told him forcefully, Get out of here. Get out of my home! Over the next few days I learned all the Jewish homes were in use. Nobody expected the Jews to return. They were all gone, forever. Right then I promised myself that there would be at least one home returned to its rightful owner, mine.

By this time, I knew a few of the Russian authorities, so I contacted them to remove the collaborators from my home. At least at my old home they fled, but once it was empty, I also knew I could not live there anymore. It was no longer safe in my own hometown! The war was just about over with the Allies fast approaching Berlin, but even though they pushed westward they left large pockets of resistance in the hills nearby. For me, the front to the South was only 90 miles away. Grybow, and the whole region was virtually Juden-frei. So the Jews lost everything, their businesses, homes, property and lives, and the people who now held their possessions did not want to give them back or suffer from claims on their newly found treasure. And me, I was some kind of miracle, a survivor, and even though I had a good neighbor to take care of me I felt alone.

I could not sustain thinking about this for too long. I had to accept that war was chaos; besides I was still very weak and I needed to rest. At the time, the only thing that would be right, in

286

my mind, for my old home, would be that Tadeusz would take over the property. I did not want any compensation. He had already done more then enough to earn my eternal gratefulness. I just wanted to thank him for everything he did and tried to do for my family and me. When I told him how I felt, he said, Leon, I won't take your property, unless I can give you a fair payment for it. He took out cash, but I pushed it away. Eventually, he did end up giving me some money, which I accepted.

After about two weeks of living at the Skrabski's, the snow and freezing weather let up enough for Tadeusz to find me some new clothing. When he did he said, Leon we are going to burn your old clothing. I finally took off my blue & white prison uniform for good. Living in these clothes for so long and being in the poor conditions I was subjected to my lower back was infested with mites and lice. To finally rid myself of this pestilence my back was dusted with pesticide and skin scraped to ensure it was all gone. The raw skin was then washed carefully. It was important to keep the house clean for the health of all its occupants, my saviors.

More importantly, I slowly recovered in their care. It was another cold winter, but this time we had coal and furs, combined with food and friendship. And just like old times, at one point that winter, the snow reached two meters in drifts. Once in awhile, you could still hear the long guns abrasively interrupting the serenity of nature. At least I felt safe, and free to roam as I pleased. I wasn't thinking about the Polish Underground, nor did I go out of way to provoke anyone, and no one went out of their way to harass me either. It was a good feeling to be home and free, but I also felt the emptiness of the streets, my culture had disappeared, only remnants remained.

While wandering around Grybow, I saw the Russians rebuilding the bridge nearby the old Roman Arch Bridge that was destroyed, and struck up a conversation with the Commander. His name was Captain Goodman. He was a Jew, from Moscow. It was

Grybow post-war
St. Catherine's Church without a Steeple.
fig. 135

Old Roman Arched Bridge near Leon's Home.

Prior to demolishing the bridge, the Germans first loaded trains with heavy rocks. The weight of the cars amplified the damage. Leon's home was located so close the roof was damaged

fig 136

289

good for me to see him in a position of authority. Most of the workers on this project, however, did not speak Russian. They were instead, Muslim laborers, from Uzbekistan. The Commander quickly befriended me, Son, you are the only Jew I know of that has returned so far. I knew this was true.

Sadly, I knew none of the new storekeepers. The town seemed quiet and normal enough, but there were no longer any people in black outfits with curly hair in front of their ears holding books or praying, and the Jewish temple was desecrated. Today, 2010, 55 years later, it is still without windows, essentially, lost in time even though it is a beautiful brick building. I can't help but wonder in the good years, how the temple and the church stood side-by-side for so many years. Maybe, with a little luck, and proceeds from this book I can help restore it?

One day, I took a long walk with Tadeusz. He took me to his mother's. It was about 2 km. To get there we walked through the town. On the way he pointed up to the church and I noticed the steeple was missing. He said, A German machine gunner took up position in the steeple and to dislodge him the Russians blew it right off the building. We kept walking up a hill. On the way he pointed to a bunker. I peered inside briefly, and saw dead German soldiers. Snow surrounded the edge of the hole. The dead soldiers were in murky water. It was March and the spring was soon to unfold. It was better in my mind to let the worms and rodents clean the bodies than to go anywhere near that stench.

I think I was the first Jew to return to Grybow. A few others trickled in after me. A way of life was over. The Jewish community was no longer sustainable in this part of the world. Among the first to return, was a group of Polish men now Russian soldiers. They too came back looking for their families. One was none other than the older brother of my best friends, Roman and Moshe Blauner, Max Blauner. He returned in full combat uniform holding an auto-

290

Max Blauner in uniform
fig 137

matic weapon. The tide completely changed. When he discovered
I was in town he immediately
sought me out. We were elated to
see each other.

After a strong embrace he
looked at me with a serious expression, "Leon, you cannot stay here;
the fascist Underground is killing
Jews. They will not think twice to
kill you too." Even though I felt
safe at the Skrabski's home, I had
to listen to Max's advice. He continued, "I just came from Lvov.
We had a few skirmishes on the
way here." After taking a moment
to accept some bread from Tadeusz, he said, "Leon, I am going
to take you with me as soon as I
can get a permit from the Russian
command. Stay out of sight until I return. When I come back, we
are gonna get them. You can help us hunt every one of the bastards
down. None of us will rest until they are wiped from the earth." I
could easily see he was incensed. He just returned home finding his
family gone, forever, just like me, and I still had to tell him about his
brother, Moshe. Regretfully, I did. I told him I thought he was gone,
but I tried to balance this with some hope by saying, I saw Roman
leave with the whole camp, I think he is going to be OK.

Max left to get me a permit. He found it in the Poznan area
of Poland. This is near the border with Germany. It was the same
place the bastard Zimny Mroz came from. Max had a friend there.
A fellow named Getz, the son of a wealthy family that owned the

local wood mill. Getz, also happened to be the head of the *Narod-nyy komissariat vnutrennikh del*, better known as the *NKVD*. This would later become the Russian Secret Police, the KGB, but then it was just the beginning of the new Russian influenced Polish regime. A permit was readily issued, and Max came back for me just as he promised. As soon as he came back he picked me up and we left. I thanked Tadeusz and his family. As I was saying goodbye, impatiently, Max tapped my shoulder, "Let's get 'em!"

Max was right. The war was just about over, but the Underground was dangerous. For many reasons they did not want the Jews to return. It was still a deadly serious situation. I learned of an incident very close to town, while I was there. A Jewish family, including a husband and his pregnant wife with their kids, were returning from Russia when the train they were on had a short stopover about 6 km from Grybow between Grybow and Nowy-Sacz at the Ptaszkowa rail station. During that short stop, the local Underground stormed the train, found the Jews, took them off the train, and executed all of them at the station. It was no secret, I found a news article about it in the local paper.

In light of this I realized my host Tadeusz again took a great risk by taking care of me. His entire family could have been severely beaten or killed had I been sought after. I wonder if my close relationships before the war with non-Jews played a role in keeping me safe, but no one overtly said they were helping me. It's not like the whole community came by and said, Welcome home. No one did. Nor did the Skrabski's need to draw attention to themselves, either. And me, I could have been shot at any time, with no questions asked. Because of this, I also realized just how lucky I was that I had such good friends.

With a permit in hand, I left Grybow with Max to start a new life. This time, I expected never to come back. We traveled west, towards Germany and stopped near the border on the Polish side. Max's plan was to help me enlist into the Polish army. That is exactly what happened. Meanwhile, I kept eating every chance I could, regaining my endurance and normal body weight. So, by the time I left Grybow, I was close to full strength and mental acuity, and before I knew it, I was no longer a prisoner, but a soldier. Fully armed, and part of a fighting unit.

There was a strong sense of vengeance in the air. The new Polish armies, combined with the Russians, were still blistering mad for the years of abuse and punishment at the hands of the Germans. They wanted to hurt them badly. What could be justice in comparison to the atrocities? Everyone was disrupted by the war, not just the Jews; everyone on all sides had friends and family who were missing or killed. The Russians alone, lost over 26.6 million people, the Americans 418 thousand, the Germans 6.6 - 8.5 million, France 567 thousand, Poland 5.6 - 5.8 million with 2.3 million of them Jewish.[13] and the poor Jews lost 6 million, men woman and children from all parts of Europe.

I don't know how to comprehend such a great number of lost souls. Besides the loss in numbers, the Polish also lost almost all of their upper class. However, no group suffered greater then the Jews. They were subjected to the systematic destruction of an entire race from all parts of Europe. As soon as Max dropped me off, and made sure I was safe, with people he could trust, he went to work. It wasn't simple vengeance but justice he sought. But with the scope of the war as broad and disruptive as it was, what was justice? Hitler did most of the damage and now he was gone and his henchmen were running scared with every armed survivor looking for them.

The Americans set up inspection stations where they would systematically cycle the potential perpetrators through with their shirts off and one arm raised, not unlike the Nazi salute, but a little higher. They sought out small tattoos with blood types printed on them under the arm of the Germans. If they found a tattoo it would

Leon Schagrin one month after liberation (Jan-27-1945)
Auschwitz prisoner number 161744.
Photo made in Nowy-Sanz for an ID card.
fig. 140

mean the person was a member of the SS. Luckily for the Germans nothing like the Nazi extermination factories happened after the war. From the perspective of the men on the ground, Max's perspective, chaos was the common man's plight. Which way to turn? Who still held arms and was willing to use them? What of the Underground movements and their vigilante-style actions?

Max may not have understood the wider conflict, the large chess pieces moving around the board, but he found his own ways of squeezing small reparations out of those who were perpetrators, like the Nazi collaborators, or those who where silent yet still gained at the loss of the Jews and other minorities. And even though what he did was not authorized, or pretty, it should go down in the annals as poetic justice if nothing else.

Max gathered a small group of three trusted friends. They each wore the uniforms of the Soviet Polish Army - the new army, deemed authorized by the new government. It is with these uniforms, of low ranking soldiers that they could do the most damage. Anything above the pay grade of a rank and file soldier would work against the plan. First, they fanned out and gathered information, who was a sympathizer and who was a collaborator. Then they found out where those people lived, and whose home it was it before the war. Soon they also got an official looking car.

Now, as they rolled around in style on the streets in their new car with loaded weapons, chaos in the air, and a mission, they felt like they were at least on top of the local situation. The generals and officers were distracted by logistics, so the whole place was a mess. Next, they illegally crafted papers and an official stamp to evict those who gained from the demise of the Jews. Using these *official-unofficial* papers they began to take vengeance one at a time.

The homesteaders were already on edge, knowing full well that they were now alone in their political bent and no longer had the Third Reich as their savior. As soon as they were issued papers by this gang of Max and his friends, they packed and left, leaving the apartments and townhouses furnished, but empty and ready for new occupants. None went to the authorities to protest, none felt like they had a leg to stand on. Max and his friends had a field day, only descending upon the unworthy.

If Max's small group were caught they would surely have faced a firing squad. But now, armed with property rights, and property, they took the empty apartments and sold them. Since they could make official looking stamps, they could complete the transaction with some other foil, like a document showing the home was vacant before the purchase. Most likely they didn't care. Everyone in the new government who abetted them was happy since there was plenty of money to go around. Max and his merry gang did this over and over.

Needless to say, this could not go on forever. As the chaos around them reigned more vigilante groups arrived with the same methods and procedures. Eventually the low hanging fruit dried up, and they had to move along and find something else to do with their time. There was still plenty of opportunity and Max had learned to thrive in chaos.

Meanwhile, as soon as I enlisted, my training began. This would be a Polish army acting under the Russians. I first trained to be a scout. Once I passed the exercises I became a guard at an open prison camp. There were no electric wires at this camp. But the tide had completely changed. Now I was holding the weapon and the Nazis were being detained and interrogated. This was a busy job. There were thousands of Nazis, both civilians and soldiers. Some were Gestapo members hiding in civilian clothing, while others were collaborators. Each one of these needed to be routed out and punished.

When the war ended in May everybody got drunk, including me. In fact, if you did not drink, you were ostracized. Everyone was singing happy songs. It is hard to describe the happiness. I was happy too. This would be another crossroad for me. It was an opportunity for Max as well. He was offered a job as an officer, but declined, telling them, "If you try to make me an officer, I am *gonna* run away." For anybody else this would be treason, but for Max it was just a matter of fact. He did not want to become an officer nor did he want to be responsible for other soldiers. This would have made it more difficult for him to move around with impunity, which was exactly what he wanted. He needed the freedom. Egging me on, he said, Leon, come with me. We are going to start a business.

Where? I asked.

We will go to the territory liberated by the Russians, he said.

I had to decline; I was eight years younger than Max and I had never finished elementary school. Uncharacteristically, I wanted to learn something and go to school.

Max left without me and ended up in Breslau, Germany. I, on the other hand remained and signed papers confirming my stay with the army. For this I was sent to a regular school and told, "If you enlist, once you are finished, you will be given a job."

At first, Max's business was a little dangerous, but very lucrative. Eventually he was able to go mainstream and earn enough to open his own sewing factory in Stuttgart. To get the money to start this business, he sold things on the black market just like he did when the war started with the small flint stones. But now he would operate on a different scale. To get the ball rolling he sold American cigarettes, smuggling them from Hungary. To get them, he enlisted the aid of none other then the United States army. He did this by befriending an American soldier and paying him handsomely. All he had to do was take his truck to Hungary and just get the cigarettes. Under the auspices of a United States flagged truck he could do this with relative safety and by doing this, they all made a small fortune.

By repeating the process, everyone around him was making money, lots of it. This business might have been a little dodgy, being done on the black market, but everyone wanted the product and Max found a way to provide it. But, eventually his trade route dried up, and he had to stop selling cigarettes. That is when he moved to Stuttgart.

It did not take long for him to find another product in his new city, nylon stockings. He ordered them directly from America, Again, this worked out well. Max was a natural businessman, combining his great sense of humor with a determination hardened from years of backbreaking work in the gulag. The only danger was the authorities. The threat of getting arrested always weighed on him. But the authorities liked stockings too. By the age of 26, Max was well on his way to becoming an established businessman. He had an American car in Germany, a status symbol on its own, his own personal chauffeur, and it seemed nothing could stop him.

Before long, Max found his future wife, a woman who had been hiding right under the noses of the Nazis. She was a quiet Polish girl working at a restaurant in Stuttgart. She worked there, serving the Germans throughout the entire war and because of the fear that still lingered heavily in the community, even though the war was over, she continued to hide her identity. Max met her at that same restaurant. After a good meal and some kibitzing, he asked her for her name. Rose, she said. Then, with his characteristic boldness, he asked her to a dance. She reluctantly agreed, partially not to blow her cover, and partially because she was intrigued.

Rose didn't know what to make of Max. While they were spending time together, she realized he was Jewish, and eventually she felt comfortable enough to open up, telling him her secret. It took great courage for her, because the world was still only beginning to become sane again. Shortly thereafter, Rose married Max, and soon she was pregnant with their first child. (Just last week I went to their 65th wedding anniversary. Surrounded by their kids, and grand kids and all of their friends, the speeches given that day

298

were moving and profound.).

By a strange coincidence, around the same time, Dr. Kohn, the same Dr. Kohn who left Grybow before the war, was living at Max's house. He had recently returned from Russia, and needed a place to stay. Max was pleased to have his old neighbor, especially a doctor, at his home, to help his pregnant wife. However, all was not harmonious in the young lovers home. Early in her pregnancy, Rose became upset with the good doctor, and she told her husband, Dr. Kohn doesn't respect me. He is leaving newspapers all over the floor of the house, and expecting me to clean up after him.

Max was perturbed by what he heard from his wife, so he took the doctor aside and they had a conversation, "Why don't you respect my wife?"

Enjoying the challenge, Dr. Kohn, smiled and said, "You know why? Your wife, she sleeps all the time. She sleeps like a cat. I am throwing the newspaper around so she should do something physical. It is not good for the baby if the mother is sleeping all day."

Max was a practical fellow so, needless to say, the newspapers continued to end up all over the home, and a few months later their first baby, Sam Blauner, was born healthy.

I personally met with Dr. Kohn at Max and Rose's home. I wanted to see the baby and my old neighbor. By this time I was fully-grown and had changed much but he still remembered me and my family well, reminding me of how sick I was as a child.

Even though we were all starting to personally blossom, it was not without danger. Anti-semitism was still strong in certain areas. One field that was now promising for Jews however, was government; around this time, the Prime Minister of Poland, Cyrankiewicz, was a survivor of Auschwitz like me. He clearly understood the depth of the depravity we had been through. Overall, 1945 to 1949 was thankfully a time for a liberal trend in the new Polish government.

When the war ended the lines on the map stopped moving. The Allies took the West and Russia the east with poor Berlin caught in the cross hairs of both. To solve the stalemate the superpowers split Berlin in half. The trouble was the Allies half was totally surrounded by Russian territory. There was no access by road or rail. It was cut off. It was an island in an ocean of red with a hammer and sickle as companions. To keep West Berlin in western hands, the Allies launched an unprecedented airlift. It was the only way to bring in goods to the beleaguered city.

Poland was now firmly behind the Russian Iron Curtain. Many Poles felt hurt and betrayed, feeling the West abandoned them, first, by not following through on the treaties before the war and now by leaving Poland behind the Iron Curtain.

The Jews came back, but so many were now gone it was nothing like it was in the past. Throughout the transition I did notice a respite in religious discrimination, but I'm sorry to say it was just that. It wasn't long until repression started again. At least for a couple of years the Jews could recuperate. They were eager to accept the new jobs, especially in government, and needed them badly. Meanwhile, I liked knowing at least some Jews were representing us in the government. However, none of this was my direct concern. I remained in the army and focused on doing well at school.

One thing changed dramatically after what I had been through, my attitude toward school was completely turned around. I liked school, deciding to major in communications. But, just as I was finishing my formal education, I started seeing anti-semitic feelings emerge again. Much of this was driven by the Allies' relationship with Russia. It did not help that the USA became a sponsor of the new state of Israel. As the West blossomed, the East paid dearly in the form of Communist repression. Me, I was caught in the middle with my love for Israel, respect for the idea of America, a state based on acknowledging religious differences, and my Polish, now Russian dominated homeland.

By 1946, the tides were fully changed. I was now a Sergeant in the Polish army and our charter which turned into my mission was defined by The Polish Supreme Court as the De-Nazification of Poland. The Polish courts ruled that anybody who collaborated with the Nazis, including kapos, Blue police, Jewish police, blockleiters, or anyone in a position of enslaving people, would be brought to the magistrate to face a rehabilitation committee. I was happy they were facing justice by the courts.

One troubling result that spun out of this, was that the Ukrainians, who were in the SS, were immediately court marshaled and sent back to where they came from. This was a slap on the hand, and it would prove to be a problem later on, as these fellows were hardened warriors who were allowed to go home with their status virtually intact. For others executions and imprisonment were commonplace. There was no way to rehabilitate all of them and someone had to pay for all the deaths and mayhem. I remember seeing a group of fellows shackled together with a wooden sign that read *Traitors to the Nation*. I can't say I did not smile. It felt good to be on the side of justice, where right and wrong had meaning. One of the tricks I learned to find former SS members was to look under their left arm for a tattoo showing their blood type. To expedite this, bare-chested men would be lined up and forced to walk by examiners.

Information about where collaborators were came to me from many sources, including anonymous letters sent to the local police station. At one point, I reported to the town of Greenberg to help them root out Nazis. When I arrived, the people were happy to see me. They understood that the tattoo I wore on my forearm was earned in a terrible way, and I would stand for nothing less than justice. I was big and strong with an official army uniform, and most importantly, I now held the gun. As they pointed out collaborators, I caught up with them, and did my own assessment, arresting the ones who fit the profile or were blatantly against the new regime. I was pleased with my work, and happy to help set up a new governing administration.

A survivor introducing himself as Mr. Holzer, pleaded for my help by saying, I am from Nowy-Sacz. He continued, "I survived with my three brothers. We hid with a fine and courageous couple who cared for us as best they could." I thought of my old friend, Tadeusz, knowing exactly the kind of person he was referring to. "Recently, I tried to go back to my old home, and the fellow who was living there threatened to kill me if I returned. All I wanted was my horses and a wagon, so I could start over. I wasn't even trying to take my house back, because I knew it was too dangerous to live there anymore. Can you help me?" I accepted the mission, but I did not follow through with proper written authorization from my Commander. I figured I could go there and be back before I would be missed. So I decided I was going to do this on my own. Not completely, however, as I enlisted the aid of two of my fellow soldiers. They volunteered readily. Together, the four of us went back to this man's hometown.

As we got closer, I passed through my own memories. This was familiar ground, close to my own home. Those were my mountains off in the distance. I thought of my own family whenever my mind wandered, but it did not take much to jog me back to reality. Eventually, we arrived at the fellow's old farm. It was the height of winter. I remember the snow and the cold. Upon arrival, I went directly to the front door, flanked by my fellow soldiers. We were an imposing lot. Mr. Holzer stood behind us. I knocked on the door and it was answered. Confronting the occupant, I introduced myself, and said politely, "Do you intend to give back this farm to its original and proper owner?"

Just as the farmer told me, he said, "No, I will kill him if he

General Karl Swierczewski, March 1947
fig

returns." With this I took a breath and held my gun tightly. The two soldiers bristled as well. He clearly saw our impatience. Speaking with unmistakable conviction, I said, "If you harm this man in any way, I will come back and shoot you myself."

Since I had no written authority for my being there in the first place, my recourse was thin, but I could not stand there and do nothing. I was deadly serious, and he knew it. What we did was crazy and dangerous for all of us, as anything could have happened, but it felt right.

While we stood there, Mr. Holzer quickly collected his horses, and a sled that happened to be filled with potatoes. When he was ready, we all withdrew safely, with the heavy load in tow. Since, I needed to return to base I could not be slowed by the animals. Once we were safely away, I left him with his horse and sled while I hurried back to my destination. He was happy and we were pleased to help. He thanked me over and over. After all of the injustice I had been through, I was glad to do a good deed.

In March 1947, a well-known Polish General and Communist, Karl Swierczewski, was ambushed and killed by the Ukrainian Underground, better known as the UPA (Ukrayins'ka Povstans'ka Armiya). The area he was killed in was a powder keg, and the Polish army was already planning an exercise to clean it up. Using this event as a trip wire, on the same day he was killed, a huge action was triggered. It would be a campaign that would completely decimate the whole area. The plan was to deport everyone in the region and kill anyone who resisted.

That would turn out to be 150,000 people. It sounds crazy but the Communists were in charge and that was their plan. It was also decided that those caught with weapons were to be prosecuted, while those still shooting were to be killed. Although this operation had many of the echoes of the Jewish deportations and ensuing Holocaust, it was not an exercise replete with crematoria and mass killings. However, the toll on the people was severe, and many needlessly died. No one in that area escaped the disruption. It would turn out to be another heartbreaking operation on a massive scale.

The exercise was called Operation Vistula and included Polish, Russian and Slovakian soldiers. It wasn't going to be easy, as the Ukrainians were well armed and dug in on their home turf. The operation was centered in Lesko, deep in the southern Carpathian Mountains, on the border with Russia. This is where the SS recruited its Ukrainian guards and these people still hated the Jews after the war. From my perspective, these were the same Ukrainians who were complicit in the extermination of Polish Jews, including my family. I will never forget how the SS Ukrainian guards acted during the war.

When the operation was winding down at the end of 1947, I returned to school. At the end of the operation, the Polish government announced amnesty for anyone who still had weapons. All they had to do was bring the weapons to a designated place. Many people you would have never expected to have weapons showed up to dispose of them.

Back, at school, I was starting to focus on radiotelephony, and doing well. However, as graduation neared, I started to feel uneasy. I had not felt that kind of uneasiness in a long time, not since my liberation from Buna. What brought this on were interviews with the authorities related to my future job. They were deciding what to do with me upon graduation. To figure it out, they asked me a series of probing questions about my life.

They were especially interested in my family within the United States, as well as my cousin in Israel. It did not take long during these interviews before they became abrasive. The crux of their questioning centered on why I entered Polish under *nationality*. When I was probed, I kept my answers simple. At the time of these inquiries, I was a marked man with an unmistakable prison tattoo.

It was common knowledge that a low number on a tattoo meant the wearer was a political prisoner, but a high number was a different story; it could mean only one thing, the wearer must be Jewish. No matter how I behaved I could not escape being constantly defined by my race.

Once again anti-Semitism raised its ugly head through state sponsored policies, this time from the Soviets. What precipitated it were relations with the United States. Much of it was centered on the US backing of the new State of Israel. All kinds of rumors started. Some of them charged Jews with extraordinary crimes that were hard to disprove and easy to foment, like espionage. According to the rumors I heard, Stalin wanted to remove every Jew from every government position. It was a complete reversal of the current situation. I was appalled to think after what I went through, including the sacrifice of my entire family, it could happen again so quickly. There was no way I would risk going back to a concentration camp or a Russian gulag.

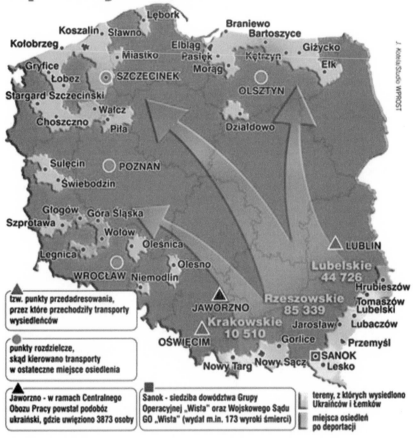

Operation Vistula
fig. 105

Chapter Eleven

Leaving Soviet Poland

By 1948 the former Polish Underground also started getting more prominent with their Anti-Semitic feelings. Now I was sensing the danger coming from both sides, and I knew I had to get out of the army and even more urgently, out of the country. This would not be an easy task for a Sergeant, even though I had already lost everything and they couldn't take much more. But I would have to risk it. Graduation came upon me. I saw my fellow graduates with their families, celebrating. But not me. I was alone. All I can remember was yet another long questionnaire.

There were many questions designed to trap the unsuspecting. For example, "Do you have family in Israel?" or "What is your religion?" and especially for me, "Do you have any markings on your body, if so please explain." I am not sure how I answered these, but one thing for certain that was nagging me, was my tattoo. They knew I was hiding the fact that I was Jewish. Finally, a Russian intelligence officer, and a fellow Jew confronted me. And they took me into a private room and said, "This is not true, referring to Polish *nationality*."

They tried very hard to break me. I am not sure what would have happened if I agreed. But I felt I could not take a chance. So, I held my position. This, of course, made them more upset. Finally, exasperated based on my silence, they said, "You will not get a degree. Instead, you will be discharged."

I was crestfallen, but stoic. I would not be dismayed, after all, I was a survivor and these fellows could not even begin to imagine the kind of challenges I had already been through. They may have been yelling at me, but in the back of my mind all I heard was my father, "You will survive and tell the story of everything that happened." Drifting off, my interrogators shook me, "You will be doing a different kind of work, like a laborer."

Finally, the grilling was over and I left there in a state of limbo. I was to remain in the army, and even get paid, but I had nothing to do. The writing was on the wall for me. If I just let it happen there was no way the result would have been good. I had to act. In fact, I was not alone, Jews everywhere in Poland were under duress. I heard about Jews in the government being replaced with non-Jews, and then sent east to the gulag for forced labor. Time was getting short.

I was living in a minefield. The repression around me was palpable. It was dangerous to talk about leaving. The talking alone was actionable. You could easily go to jail or worse. Treading carefully, I first approached my friend, another Jewish fellow, who was in a responsible position within the government. We met in Krakow. While there, I also met with the local administrator in charge of the jail, Mr. Hammerschmidt. I felt I could trust him too, because he was in both Szebnie and later in Birkenau with me. His tattoo number was almost a match with mine. First, he told me, Leon, you are crazy. Then under his breath he agreed, Do not repeat this but I think it can happen again too. Here was an important government official but he could not even talk openly about the situation. I sensed this was a dead end, so I looked for alternatives.

Luckily, I found Dr. Norbert Kant, a lawyer from Grybow who was married to my cousin. It was his brother who helped give me the idea to get the coal from the railroad station when my family was freezing and desperate for some warmth. I met him at his office next to the Israeli consulate in Warsaw.

Dr. Kant himself escaped the wartime mayhem by going to Russia. Afterwards, he returned as a Major in the new Polish Army. When I met him he was about the same age as my father and more importantly was mostly handling cases like mine. It seemed like

310

his business was booming as he lived in a beautiful home. We had a long conversation. I told him everything I knew. I knew plenty because of my rank, Aryan looks, and the fact that I was still hiding my identity as a Jew. He concurred, making me privy to many anti-Semitic remarks that he heard. Wisely he spoke, "Young man, the thing you are telling me, I know to be true and familiar. I agree with you. It is a matter of time before the situation here gets much worse." I shook my head in agreement, as he continued. "Son, I am preparing to leave. Just like you." It was a relief to share these feelings with him, and since we were in agreement I could focus on the next steps with his expert advice.

He said, "You need to get a passport." To do this you need to find Captain Morganstern in Tsanz. He is working for the Interior Department over there. I had no idea what they even did at the Interior Department. But what I did soon learn was that it was not easy to reach him. Yet, with persistence and patience we finally met and I introduced myself. As I reached my hand to shake his, I said, Hello, I am Leon Schagrin from Gribov. It is the telltale *V*, in *Gribov*, that gave away my being Jewish. He picked up on this in an instant, Are you the brother of Leizer in Israel? I prickled with concern over this initial question. Seeing my concern he put me at ease by saying, "Your brother was in Russia with me."

Relaxed, I knew I was talking with a kindred soul so I answered, "No I am his cousin." Because of my impatience at having waited so long to meet with him I blurted out, I want a passport. Quickly, he made a motion not to talk about this and we left the building as he spoke softly to avoid any prying eyes or ears. Then he said, I can give you a passport to the East, not the West and it may take up to a year for the permission. It was 1952. He continued, "Just fill out the papers. Once completed they are directed to my office and I will see yours." I did as he said using my address in Breslau for the response.

While I waited Stalin died. Things were changing. Months later the mail arrived and I got the coveted passport but I did not have the money for a ticket so I went back to Dr. Kant. We spoke and reminisced and then with little prompting he gave me what I needed, $150 dollars. Upon receiving this gift I told him, "I will pay you back." He gave me a hug, wishing me a long life not wanting anything in return.

With the money I went to the local travel agency. When I met with the agent I wasn't too picky about where I was going as long as it went through Zurich. But I could not tell the agent, instead I had to figure this part out on my own in a way that would not arouse her suspicions. So, I reviewed a few tickets until I found one that would work. Finally, ticket in hand combined with my passport I could almost taste the freedom. Yet, I was far from safe, in fact, with a ticket in my possession I could not chance being discovered by my commanding officer. I was still officially in the army even though not reporting regularly. If they were alerted to my travel, (even to the East), I could be detained or arrested, and anything could still happen to me. The days mattered. I counted the minutes and avoided attention waiting for the big day. My plan was simple. Get to Zurich where my cousin could ensure a safe destination and help me repay Dr. Kant.

The day arrived, December 1954. I got on Moscow Airlines, in Warsaw without incident. The plane was full of Chinese passengers. The plane took off. It was my first plane ride. As it started towards Zurich for some reason we made an unexpected stop in Prague. This worried me, as we were required to deplane and go through a checkpoint.

Again, I was in line with my life in the cross hairs of an inspector. As I waited I could not help my mind from wandering back to that harrowing night when I first arrived at Auschwitz, cold, naked, and thirsty beyond belief, "What is your profession?" Eventu-

312

ally, I handed my passport to the inspector half expecting him to tell me to stick out my tongue. Instead he quickly looked over the papers and then looked at me for a moment. I did not flinch as I heard in my mind, *clean my boots*. Confused for a second I did not hear clearly and he repeated, "Where are you going?" Taking effort to remain relaxed, I answered, "I am going to visit my family". I offered nothing more except a small smile. He didn't know I was Jewish nor did he ask.

That was it. I got back on the plane and arrived in Zurich. The moment I arrived it was as if the clouds opened and sunshine paved the way of my future. Once off the plane I left the terminal. For the first time in my life I tasted the air of Switzerland, a neutral country, and the nagging fear began to melt away from me.

That was the first day I started to feel free. There is no way I can explain what freedom meant to me at that moment. Here, I was my own person. As my composure returned, I went back into the terminal to walk around. It was a beautiful place with many little stores selling watches. There I met my cousin. We shared a few stories as he gave me a gift. It was a watch to commemorate my trip, gold with a solid silver case and an antique carved design. When I opened the box there was a ticket, it read destination Lod, Israel and had the logo of El-AL. Shivers came across me when I touched that ticket. I was speechless.

Gleefully, I boarded the plane to Israel. The atmosphere was completely different then my flight to Zurich. I had not seen Orthodox Jews since I was a child. And here this flight was full of them. I was elated as I arrived the same evening at Lod airport, Israel.

Upon my arrival, I will never forget hearing the Hatikva, the Jewish national anthem. It was new to me but its emotions were ancient. I left the terminal and hopped into a taxi with a bounce in my step. When I got inside the taxi I gave the driver the address and asked him to take me to my cousins' home. The driver was Polish, so it was easy to converse. He took me to the address I had, but he could not find the house. It was a poor neighborhood in the Cholon district of Tel-Aviv. Tel-Aviv was still very much a desert when I arrived.

Dismayed but not discouraged the driver took me for a little tour to the nearby Arab City of Jaffa. There I saw Arabs sitting on the road for the first time cooking shish-kebabs to sell to motorists. We pulled over and they smelled fantastic. The taxi driver spoke with the Arabs, but I could understand nothing. Then he turned to me and said, I told them I have a new guest to our country and he would like that you make him a kabob. He followed by asking for money. I only had $10 and was concerned that I could pay for the food and the car ride. The driver took the whole $10. We both ate kabobs, smacking our lips with each joyful bite. After we ate he drove near a kiosk selling ice cream in Tel-Aviv and then he pointed to house in a very poor neighborhood and said, "This must be the address." I got out of the car and the driver sped away.

Luckily, he was right and I met my cousin there. I embraced him, one of the few family members I had left in the world and told him what had happened with the driver. He said, "It should have cost $2 tops." But, it was too late to do anything about it. I was tired and disoriented and in no position to chase after a taxi. My cousin took me to his apartment. It was very small and he shared it with his wife Pola and their son Joshua. After introductions he said, "It is not much, but you will live here with us for now until you find your own way." I was happy to be with family. I took my shoes off and relaxed.

I was in a whole new world, but I was not alone. The neighborhood was full of newcomers from different countries, many with stories like mine. Among the many, I remember meeting Jews from as far away as Morocco, to the west, and Bulgaria, to the east. I stayed there for about four months. During this time I learned about the place and its language. The first thing I learned was that you had to know somebody to get a job. I explored the surrounding area as well and I stumbled upon a place I liked.

Ein Ha Shfet was a socialist kibbutz populated with American and Polish Jews, near Haifa. Its main business was agriculture and since it was in the north of Israel it felt a little like my old home, Grybow. No longer did I have to hide my identity. On the contrary I was proud of it and so was everyone else. Soon, I was asked to stay and made this my home. I liked this place, but after living here for awhile I realized the kibbutz was even more socialist than Russia. You needed a pass to go out or to buy something. Oversight of my whereabouts was something I was and still am very leery about after what I went through because this can quickly turn into something insidious. Life was good, but I knew I wouldn't stay there for too long.

Meanwhile, life was not so good for my friends back in Poland. The situation for Jews continued to degrade until 1967 when all of the remaining Jews were forced out of the country. Before the Soviet "Iron Curtain" descended I learned from my contacts in Poland that by the time I left I was listed as a 1st Lieutenant with three medals, a Medal of Victory, a medal of freedom and a Shield from Grunwald with a Silver Cross for valor. I have never seen them and wonder how I could verify my achievement. Maybe, someone who reads this memoir can figure that out.

Even though, I left without a degree, I was a fully trained Radio Telephone Engineer so I applied for a job at the Haifa telephone company and I was readily hired. Soon after, I rented a room in Haifa and although it was small I was comfortable. I started as a home telephone installer and then got involved in switching the aerial wires to ground cabling. I knew enough Hebrew to get along and when I got more involved in my job, I started to learn English because phone systems are based on that language. I liked what I

WWII
Medal of Honor

Grunwald
Cross

Medal of
Valor

Leon Schagrin's Missing Medals fig 106+107+108

was doing and began to slip into a nice routine. My confidence blossomed with my abilities, along with a love for my new country. But, I was living the life of a bachelor and starting to think about finding a wife. It was time, I longed for a companion.

I met Betty in 1958 while she was on a trip to Israel from America. She was living in the USA for nine years prior to the time I met her. Here is how Betty characterized our first meeting and our budding love affair soon after.

"All of a sudden I thought like I had known him my whole life. I was living in the United States for about ten years after the war. Both of my sisters were there as well. Life was moving along, I survived the war with my sisters, I was one of the lucky ones even though my mother and father were swept up in the terrible storm of Nazism. My father, a metal contractor who also built balconies was sent to Belzec where no one survived and my mother succumbed to exhaustion and a purported heart attack in the ghetto hospital. I believe she was injected with poison, a common practice which was uncovered after the war. The main doctor was convicted of war crimes after the war. Meanwhile, I was in need of a change. "I wanted to refresh my identity after what I had been through. Plus, on top of this, I was married in the USA and it ended in divorce."

So, I went to Haifa and I was standing on a terrace overlooking Ben Yahuda Street. On another outside patio I saw my friend Cilia and said, "What are you doing?" She said I have family here would you like to meet them?"

I decided to visit with no idea it would lead to meeting someone I would want to spend the rest of my life with. Standing on the side was a young man fixing a radio.

My eyes glistened as I met him and learned he was from a small town near where I grew up. Plus he understood implicitly what I had been through. At the time I did not have much of an idea of the extent of his incarceration. We both liked each other and decided we would meet at an outside restaurant soon after.

The next day or two we were sitting at Hadaris in Haifa. We gradually started talking about the time Leon was in Krakow after the war. I knew the areas he was talking about so this made for an easy conversation. Then I told him about Oscar Schindler and my sister Helen. At the time Schindler was not as famous as he has become. Leon was very interested in my story and happy to hear about this man who took upon himself at great risk the task of saving over 1,000 Jews. Since my sister worked for the camp commandant she was able to sneak me and my other oldest sister food so that we did not starve.

I found myself in Plashow ghetto working at Madriz making uniforms for the German soldiers. There were about 25,000 prisoners mostly from Krakow when I was there. Since I was studying sewing prior to the war this was a natural job for me and I was good at it. I was with women who were much older than me and a few my age as well. When I say much older I am referring to about 50 and below. No one was allowed to work with us that was old. Leon hung on my every word, listening intently. He asked, "Did anything bad happen directly to you?" Losing my parents was terrible. But, it was done in a way that was deceptive so I did not feel the pain except within the context of everyone I was with who was displaced and suffering. It would take years for me to properly grieve their being gone. I don't think this can even be done so I will miss them forever. But, there was one incident that was dangerously close to a terrible outcome.

We were working at the factory. We worked seven days a week. We knew of no other way. One day a Gestapo officer did an inspection on a Sunday and said, "What are you doing here? Don't you filthy Jews know that you are not allowed to work on Sunday, the day of our Lord?" What he did next still puts shivers down my spine. He gathered all of us old and young (5-6) and made us strip. Then one at a time he had one of his henchmen deliver 25 lashes to each of us on the rump. My oldest sister, courageous to the end, volunteered to take the first set hoping that the sting would somehow soften by the time it reached the rest of us. It didn't.

That was the worst direct infliction of pain upon me I can remember. My sister was lashed in this way a second time for a different infraction. None of us could sit for weeks but we were young and healed. At least we could sit, but I will never forget the torture they put us through.

All of the Schindler protected people were transferred to another camp in Brinlistz, Czechoslovakia but it was required that all of us had to go through a quarantine and indoctrination camp – Birkenau. The same place Leon was located, but I was there a little later than him. By the time I was there, he was already in Buna. Unlike Leon I did not go through a life and death selection at Birkenau. Instead a doctor gave each of us a quick look and let us through. I was not skinny since my sister was giving me food to eat prior to

318

coming here. I believe Schindler gave the commandant's wife a diamond ring prior to our arrival to ensure our safety. When I was done telling my story Leon began his. He was 100 times worse off than mine.

Leon being about 31 at the time characterized our love as a *"healing love."* We had both been through a similar experience of depravity, anti-Semitism and torture and we were both alive in Israel. Even Israel was alive because of this experience. The new country was so new that I was told to not use the hot water, not to use the hot iron, and to be careful how I use electricity. The nation was struggling and the 50's were a very tough period on the Israelis.

After meeting Leon I spoke with my sisters in the USA and they warned me that many men were preying upon women, especially ones with American citizenship to come to America. I told them I flipped for this boy and they were just overly cautious. My planned six week trip became 3 months. We dated the whole time I remained. It was a wonderful period in both of our lives. We went to the beach and the movies. We spoke our native tongue of Polish. I had to pay for everything. He hardly had a penny. The little he made in a month lasted two weeks.

As much as we were compatible, we were also very different. I was a few years older than him and my parents were loving and nourishing with me and my three sisters. I could not understand why Leon's father was so rough on him. When I heard this I did not know if I could be close to him.

Despite these small fears we were soon married. We both planned the wedding. Leon did not have family to invite, except for his uncle, the same one that took him in when he arrived in Israel. The wedding was handled by the Orthodox Rabbinate in Haifa. We had about 40 people in attendance. My friends from the USA were there but my sisters could not come. Dr. Kant, the attorney who gave money to Leon in Krakow came to Israel and was there with his family. My brother-in-law in the USA had a brother in Israel who acted not as the best man but represented my mother and father. He took me the chupah. He was also professor in Jerusalem. I wore a light pink chiffon outfit with a short veil.

Leon wore a suit. I bet this was his first suit ever. Leon's cousin Elizer was the best man and also took Leon to the hoopah.

It took Leon only two weeks to ask for my hand in marriage. But at the time, I thought I don't even know who he was. The truth was that I liked him, but to be sure I said, "Let's wait." I had a good job as an interior decorator back in the States, so I was able to stay for awhile longer and see where this would go.

One curious thing prior to our marriage was a public notice in the local newspaper asking everyone as a sort of background check, "Is anyone married to Leon Schagrin?" There were no civil ceremonies like this in the United States. Our marriage was controlled by the rabbinate. Because of this is was handled in a traditional Orthodox manner. And this was not just any Orthodoxy, it was none other than a sect of the Halberstamms. The same Halberstamms that surrounded my community in the old country. I was positive about this because when the rabbi was speaking with Leon it was clear that he knew Leon's family and his hometown. The rabbi first told us he was from Sacz and then said, "I know your family especially your grandfather, 'Enyuten Yosel.' The Red Joseph." This made us both feel connected to our past. He was the perfect person to marry us.

As an engagement gift Leon gave me a necklace with a gold pocket for a photo and a matching ring. This cost him $100, a great sum for him back then. Once married we went to a hotel for a week as a honeymoon and then I had to leave. But, Leon wasn't able to come with me. It would be months and piles of letters before I would see him again. During some of those conversations Leon expressed how he wanted to live in Israel. But I could not do that. I already had an apartment in the USA as well as a good job and I also felt our op-

320

portunities were much greater in America. He had to come to me!

Within about seven months he gained clearance one day soon after he showed up that my local airport.

When you understand our story that you also know we were both mentally damaged, Leon far more than I. The war put us under the constant stress of wondering what would happen next. Wit catastrophe always nearby. Leon and I, both still wake up with night terrors once in awhile, especially now that we are older. Sometimes, he jumps up in a sweat and I ask him what is the matter. He says he was being chased and running with his horse.

We have other friends who went through similar things and many had kids and families. My sister was one of them. But we decided that we would have no kids. Life has its own way on subjects like this. Soon after our marriage I was diagnosed with a tumor in the uterus. After the diagnosis the doctor asked Leon if he wanted kids or his wife. Leon chose me.

For us the war may have ended but we think about it every day, even when we try not to. Leon works as an educator trying to teach young people about the Holocaust. This becomes a constant reminder of our life and times. It seems like it was yesterday.

Leon continued the story: "We got along right away. Betty grew up nearby my hometown, in Krakow. As we spoke I told her about my life and she about hers. It did not take me too long to mention Szebnie and my love of horses before she countered with her own story about a man with a mustache that would frequent a canteen in Krakow. He was an old German fellow that also smoked a pipe. We compared notes and sure enough it had to be Strybuc. When I left for Auschwitz he and Grzimek with 'my' horse Maciek went to Krakow. That is how I knew my horse was there. She even saw it as Grzimek paraded around the area.

It was March. Very soon I knew I had met my soul mate. And on the 26th of June, we were married at a small Orthodox temple in

APR • 59 •

Candid photo Leon and Betty in the USA, 1958
fig. 153

Haifa. Soon after the wedding, she returned to the United States. It was October. I followed in March, the following year. We are very compatible with each other. Our lives have never been easy, but we believe, that because we have freedom, the hard earned freedom of choice, we believe, we can overcome all difficulties. We continue our humble lives today, 2010 the time of the writing of this memoir. We have been married for 52 years and I believe firmly that from the moment I married Betty my life became richer."

Chapter Twelve

The Land of the Free

In March of 1959, I arrived in New York, and into the arms of my bride. Besides my wife, I had some family there as well, three aunts, two uncles and nine first cousins including Raymond Woldman, a United States Federal Judge. Once I was acclimated to life in the USA, I started to look for a job.

I found what I liked at AT&T and was excited to work there. After my initial interview I received a promising call back. They wanted to hire me! All I needed to do was complete a security check. This is when I learned they did not hire anyone who is Jewish. I was outraged, shocked and disappointed all at the same time. Even in America, the anti-Semitism would not end.

Leon Schagrin
United States Citizenship
fig. 113

I left the interview, but before I was gone the security man tried to help me by suggesting, In the future don't write that you are Jewish when applying for jobs. As I left I said, thank you, but I was thinking how much I detested the reason they did not let me work. I did not sleep well that night. As I tossed and turned, I pondered what I had been through and how I would have to again, hide my Jewish identity. When I got a chance, I reported the incident to the Jewish Congress. They acknowledged my experience by saying, "Leon, you are not alone." But they offered no solution. Once again I was on my own.

I was used to very severe environments being a survivor and now that I was 'free' I was not about to walk away beaten, so I tried again to find another job. This time I saw an article in the NY Times looking for a troubleshooter in electronics at the Sloan Kettering Memorial Hospital. To prepare for this interview I put my plan into action and went to the local tattoo parlor. That is where I had this black panther tattooed over my Auschwitz tattoo. Then, when I filed out the forms, and they asked for my nationality, I wrote, 'Polish' and turned in the papers. As I sat and waited for my turn my thoughts couldn't help but return to my past. Eventually, my name was called and I stood up as an engineer introduced himself. He was a retired captain from the US Navy, Mr. O'Donnell. I followed him into the shop where he tested me and I did the tasks he asked, as well. Before I was done he said, "You have the job." I worked there from 1959 to 1966. The staff was mostly Italian. We all got along well. I liked my job and felt good about what I was doing.

In 1966, I went into my own business. First, I started a luncheonette in the Bronx. I knew nothing about this business and my wife quickly became unhappy with the hours. So, in 1970, I opened a Hallmark gifts and school supply store on Long Island. It was a small store. Only 50 by 100 feet but it did OK.

I got the money to open the store from an old friend from Grybow and survivor, Isaac Goldman. At the time he was living in Baltimore. I signed a simple loan note with him and he gave me $7,000 in cash. With the store, in time, I was able to pay back the loan and buy a house. A few years later in 1976, even though I was doing OK, I sold both the business and my house.

The impetus for this was my old friend Max Blauner, the same dear old Max that rescued me from Grybow after the war. By this time he was doing very well in business and he wanted me to represent a Brazilian company called, Dover, that he partially owned. I opened the Miami office for Dover and started selling custom made plastic from Brazil, wholesale. This seemed to go well for a couple of years when I was surprised one morning to receive a telex that informed the company was closing down. It was bankrupt. And I was instantly unemployed.

Working always had its ups and downs for me. Overall, life in America was good. My wife and I, being both survivors, we found many of our friends to also be survivors. We all had so much in common that the bonds were extraordinarily strong. It did not take long to renew my friendship with Moshe Katz at a Bar Mitzvah. We have been in close touch ever since that meeting.

When we met for the first time after many years, he told me a story.

Moshe: "I found myself at a bar getting a drink when I saw a man about my age who looked familiar. I walked over to him and started a conversation. We began to share stories of the war and within about 30 seconds I realized this was Fritz. The same Fritz that escaped from Szebnie so many years ago! He was alive and well, living in the USA. After a few good cheers Fritz told me what happened to him."

Fritz: "Since I grew up around Szebnie I knew the mill operator from before the war. I made up a story to get Strybuc to bring me there so that once I arrived I would elude him. The mill operator saved me and thirteen other people. We were all hiding in a place nearby. That night instead of returning me to camp, as he told Strybuc he would, he took me to the hiding place where I stayed with the others until the liberation. He kept us all safe and well fed. This is how I survived the rest of the war."

Moshe was pleased to see his old cohort, but then proceeded to tell him how his escape almost resulted in the rest of them being executed on the spot. Fritz apologized and then they both toasted, L'chiam, to Life!

Meanwhile, at the age of 55 I had no job again. I started to look for something but knew it was going to be tough. My life switched from years of race discrimination to something new for me, age discrimination. It seemed I would never get a break. I tried a few times but I just could not get a decent sales job. They didn't want to hire anyone over 50. So, I reluctantly took a job as a security officer for about two years until I got a recommendation from the Holocaust Survivors of South Florida. Moshe was one of the founders. Moshe recommended that I run the local office. Shortly, after his recommendation, I was elected as the office coordinator. At the time we had 1,500 members and this became my home for the next twenty years.

Reflecting on my life, I have come to the realization that money is not everything. There is a far more important goal for me, to educate the children and the institutions about what I had been through. When I started, they knew practically nothing about the Holocaust.

To begin this process I got involved with the local Boards of Education and some Jewish organizations. Our mission was to have the public education programs the most important part of the history of World War II, the brutality of the Nazi regime.

By this time the word 'Holocaust' had become the term used to describe what happened to us.[14] It took awhile but we accomplished our goal. We did this in association with the Central Agency of Jewish Education and the Broward County Florida Board of Education with assistance from the Holocaust Documentation and Education Center. Together, we finally agreed upon a curriculum of Holocaust Studies that was approved by State Department of Education. One of the key directives that it approved was that, 'all Florida schools would have a *Holocaust* curriculum during History class.'

At first there was a lot of resistance from different politicians who did not want to include this in the curriculum of the late

326

1980s. So because of this delay, I personally started to give lectures in the high schools and other institutions of Broward County. Once a year we held a 'Student Awareness Day' in which approximately 500 students would take part in exercises. We would break them into groups of 10-12 students and pair each one with a survivor where they would share their story and discuss it with the group. I am proud to report this event continues to this day.

In addition to assisting with the education programs, I began to write petitions and letters in behalf of the survivors' well-being, as related to compensation by the German government. In 1988 I was part of the group that succeeded in changing German laws for restitution to make it easier to get compensation. We did this by participation in the Jewish Material Claims Conference against Germany. During this conference we petitioned our grievances for the survivors. And even though they had a fund, few were paid because they seemed to look for any technicalities to reject the claims. Copies of all the petition papers are in the archives of the Holocaust Museum, Documentation and Education Center on Harrison Street in Hollywood, Florida. It was tough and frustrating work but we did mange to get quite a few claims processed properly. Sometimes, however, it took a few years for approval and the survivors were both aging and needed the money. We learned that over 50,000 survivors' claims rejected on technical grounds. Then in 1995, Germany established a hardship fund for survivors. With this fund 50,000 people from all over the world got a minimum of three hundred dollars a month. This may not seem like much but, it helped and continues to help many poor survivors to make ends meet.

Another issue I became interested in involved the German law recognizing ghetto dweller pensions. Because of this law survivors were entitled to a ghetto pension, however, again, hardly any claims were approved because the law was full of technicalities. To settle a claim required proof of "working voluntarily" and getting paid while living in the ghetto. It had nothing to do with being forced into the ghetto and not being paid at all. This law was not suitable to the survivors as this was almost impossible to prove. So, nobody got compensation.

To combat this we participated in a class action suit and a delegation went to Germany. I was with them.

During our time with the judge we shared with him the bottom line of why we felt the law needed to be changed with this simple phrase, "Show me one ghetto where the people went in voluntarily and got paid." The response was silent because as we knew they couldn't do this because there was none.

We won! This allowed us to take away one restrictive paragraph from the old law as well as add a critical new one. The first was that a claimant only had to produce two witnesses to confirm that he or she was in a ghetto. And the second was that all of those previously rejected have the right to try to apply again.

I, myself, had been rejected prior to this new law. In fact, they brought me and others to the grievance meeting just because I was an example of someone who had their claim rejected. It took 5 more years for a favorable result to weave through the legal process. This is still going on. For instance, they did not want to give anything to children who were hiding. It took three more years to have them approved. This was a big success as these are now old people who need the money.

One of my largest undertakings was to restore the grounds of Belzec. Our petitions were started in 1988, but they seemed to have stalled. So in 1996 I went to Poland to see if I could get something started on this project. I was encouraged to go by Simon Unger and Rabbi Aaron Halberstam, a descendant of the Halberstam dynasty, the same dynasty that blessed me when I was young. He lives in Brooklyn, as a practicing Hasidic Jew following the old ways. They both warned me that I would not like what I saw. It was completely neglected.

I arrived in Poland, and started towards my hometown. Driving past Tarnow, I felt disgust rising up in my memories and I vowed to never enter this town again for the rest of my life. As soon as I arrived in Grybow I went to the place where the mass execution happened. After paying my respects I went to the local monument shop and bought a fitting stone to honor those fallen.

While I was there I also visited the Mol family. This was convenient since the mass grave was located so close to their home. And as luck would have it, the same woman came to the door. She must have been over 90 years old. And she still recognized me, "Oh God, we hid this boy."

I told her, I have returned to say thank you. I tried to give her money, but she refused to take anything. She said the whole village knew what happened and felt terrible for me and my family. She was very happy that I had survived.

I, also, went to the local museum and saw some Jewish artifacts. Since I felt they did not deserve these things I asked to people in charge to allow me to take them back to America with me. Curtly, I was told, I am sorry but these few remnants are now part of the Polish history and culture and they must remain.

I left Grybow and made my way to Belzec. This was not a joy ride. I was going to a massive killing site. My whole family was buried there as well as almost all the Galician Jews. And even though I was deeply saddened going there, I was also solemnly aware of the command my father gave me, If you should survive you must find the bones of our family - to know where they rest. Not too many people even know about Belzec, because once the mass exterminations were completed, it was covered up in an attempt to erase what happened here.

Belzec was different than most other camps because it was

not a concentration camp, but an extermination camp. There were no barracks - only gas chambers and large pits to toss the bodies into.

There was no need for selection. Everyone waited their turn to die. The cover-up was so good that of the thousands killed at Belzec, I am only aware of one survivor. A man who attended the bodies and somehow escaped annihilation once the work was done. The count of people killed here in a short period of time (one single year) was a staggering 600,000.

I wish there was nowhere on earth like Belzec, but I am sorry to say, in Poland, there are many. Walking around these grounds is profoundly sad. Today the site is fully restored into one of the finest of its type. All of the mass gave sites at this location have gone through archeological studies and large walls of concrete have been built around each killing pit. The pits are filled with dirt and bones and topped with a volcanic rock that looks uninviting.

There are, also, fragments of barbed wire in the design to add to the intentional 'stand-off' between the viewer and this terrible event. As a monument, I have never seen anything like it. The whole complex is, also, rather small measuring only about six acres square.

You cannot walk on the volcanic rocks. However, walkways surround the perimeter and go through the center. Walking around here, I cried, "This is where my family is buried! This is where my dreams were turned into dust!" But the first time I saw it, all I saw was trash and disrepair, everything was broken and this added to my mixed anger and sadness.

When I was finished, I walked around the nearby town and talked to the local people. They told me that Belzec belongs to the Jews and that if they want to take care of it, they should.

When I returned home, I started to put a plan into place to rescue Belzec from obscurity by leveraging my connections at the South Florida Holocaust Association. Through them, I learned of a man in Washington, D.C., Jacek Novakowsky, who handles memorials in different countries. On our official letterhead, I wrote a memorandum to him describing the negligence at Belzec and the urgent need to do something about it, before it would be completely forgotten. He read my letter and contacted the Polish ambassador. They said they would be willing to do something but most of the money would have to come from Jewish sources.

The project floundered for many years until, eventually, the rabbinate such as: Halberstam, at the American Jewish Committee got involved. It wasn't too long afterward that the grounds and the museum opened in June 2004.

In the process of preparing the museum, an archaeological team worked on the site for two years. With the help of this expert team 32 mass graves were preserved and artifacts were recovered for display at the museum.

My one disappointment is that the 'March of the Living,' does not bring tours there. I want that to change as they should see this place.

In 2004, there was an international event for the opening of the Belzec museum. This was a huge accomplishment for me, one that I dedicate to my family. During the opening ceremony, all of the European Governments sent dedications. For my efforts in making this a reality I was honored by the Broward County Commission February 5th. They officially declared, February 22nd would be Leon Schagrin Appreciation Day.

That is my story. It is a story that had to be told and which you had to hear. Having read this book, you can no longer avoid your responsibility for doing your part to seeing that such horrors do not go uncontested or unopposed. I have come out of a mass grave to warn you of the ever present danger of racism, bigotry, xenophobia and all the other manifestations of evil that still afflict the human condition.

The rest is up to you...

Belzec Memorial

My wish is that the March of the Living add this site to their agenda so visitors from all over the world will never forget what happened at Belzec.

-Leon Schagrin

Leon Schagrin visiting, *The Bones of my Family*
...and 600,000 others.   fig. 128

Belzec Memorial

Belzec Memorial Plaque fig. 129

Belzec Underground Memorial   fig. 130

Belzec Grybow Memorial   fig. 127

Footnotes

1. Statement on the investigation of the Katyn crime in Russia http://www. Memo.Ru/daytoday/5katyn_eng.Htm

2. The Hasidic Jews in Grybow were descendants of the famous *Tsadik*, the Rabbi Divrei Chaim Halberstam (1793-1876). His teachings were so profound that Jews still make a pilgrimage to his grave each year. Rabbi Halberstam established the first yeshiva in the region of Galicia in nearby Tsanz, better known today as Nowy-Sanz. During his life he was known as one of the foremost experts on the study of Kabbalah (Jewish mysticism). There were two Hasidic movements in Poland. In the north they believed in tradition and opposed anything to do with the mystical. While in the south they embraced mysticism, and tried to bring joy, dance, energy and life into the traditions. Since I lived in the south, I was surrounded by the latter type of Hassidim. It is here, within 12 km of my hometown, where Kabbala or Jewish mysticism took root.
Per Leon - The Halberstam dynasty is still alive and well today. During the writing of this book I spoke with Rebbe Aron Halberstam in Brooklyn, NY. We had a lively discussion wherein I told him, as a survivor of one of the greatest tragedies of mankind, I have a complaint with God. And in a rare moment of levity, he responded, Leon, I think you might win this one. The conversation ended before we had a definitive answer, but it was very good to talk with my old esteemed friend.

3. http://en.wikipedia.org/wiki/Katyn_massacre

4. Vol 1-3, —Gryb€w. Studia z dziej€w miasta i regionu red. Danuta Quirini-Popławska, Krakow 1995 (47)

5. 26,600,000 total Soviets casualties - http://en.wikipedia.org/wiki/ World_War_II_casualties

6.The Ordnungsdienst or order police were Jewish police. As a ghetto institution, the uniformed Jewish police exemplified the dynamics of degeneration that the Germans set in motion. Their job was to regulate the flow of traffic inside the ghettos, maintain law and order, man the ghetto gates,

335

check people entering and leaving, examine identity papers and permits, and search people for contraband. They were supervised by Polish guards and armed German police to ensure appropriate strictness.

7. Simchas / Simchat Torah - Rejoicing with the Torah, a celebration marking the beginning of a new cycle In Torah reading occurring mid-September to early October. The Torah is read portion by portion each week and then repeated each year.

8. Auschwitz,Poland is the common Germanized name of Oświęcim. It was comprised of 3 compounds, the Stammlager or base camp known as Auschwitz I, the Vernichtungslager or extermination camp know as Auschwitz II or Birkenau, and the Labor camp known as Auschwitz III, or Monowitz, also known as Buna-Monowitz (Buna was apx. 10 miles square), Besides the main camps, Auschwitz also had 45 other satellite camps nearby. One of the primary missions of Buna was to produce synthetic oil, like Ethanol which can be used as fuel. http://en.wikipedia.org/wiki/Auschwitz_concentration_camp

The name Birkenau comes from Brzezinka meaning birch tree. This entire region became one of the largest concentration / extermination camps in the world. Oswiecim was owned by a duke who dismayed with its upkeep sold it to a Jew. Property ownership by a Jew of a vast region was uncommon in the past.

9. Mieczyslaw Katarzynski, Born in Warsaw, Nov. 11th, 1920 was a political prisoner at Auschwitz in 1941 working in the locksmith kommando. He was appointed blockleiter in the quarantine center of Birkenau where he earned his nickname, Bloody Mietek. September 17th, 1944 he was transferred to Leitmeritz sub camp of KL Flossenburg. Feb. 1945 he escaped and joined the Czech partisans until May 1945. He was arrested by Polish authorities September, 1945 in Stupca where he used the fake name Jan Witkowski. During his trial many former Birkenau inmates testified and he was found guilty. Execution by hanging July 6th, 1948 - www.axishistoryforum.com

10. not used

11. I was aware that as long as I was still breathing, I was in a far better position than the Jewish prisoners. They were systemically killed just because they were Jews. Surviving Auschwitz - John Wiernicki Polish political prisoner (block 2 Birkenau Polish prisoner-the same as Leon's)

12. http://www.scrapbookpages.com/auschwitzscrapbook/history/articles/DeathStatistics.html

13. http://en.wikipedia.org/wiki/World_War_II_casualties

14. The term, *The Holocaust* stemmed from the Greek word Holokausten, meaning, a completely burnt *kaustos* or sacrificial offering. It was a strange word with a good meaning that became twisted into a modern world. In 1823, it was used to describe the killing of 1,300 people burnt alive in a church, during the invasion of Vitrey-le-Francois in 1142. To connect a burnt offering for God, with mass murder, adds a deadly acid, to the term. In Hebrew, this event is referred to as *'The Shoah'* or *'The Calamity.'* It wasn't until modern times, well after what happened, that the term Holocaust was coined to mean the extermination of the Jews, and others, in WWII.

15. Heinrich Hamann is described by Jan Karski in his book One against the Holocaust.

16. Authors-School Students in Tarnowiec Garbacik Michael, Daniel and Slawomir Rozpara Music under the direction of Jack Bracik
Jasielski Region No 3 (39) 2003
and Joseph Curd Jasło-County-The Family 1945-2000
17. Time Magazine, The Man Behind the Monster By Richard Corliss; Georgia Harbison/New York Monday, Feb. 21, 1994

18. Robin O'Neil. www.jewishgen.org/yizkor/Galicia2/gal001.html
19. JUSTIZ UND NS-VERBRECHEN Nazi crimes on trial. West German trials

20. During the wedding - He told me a mystical story as well. He said I was born under the LW which equates to 36. The story goes that the world is run by 36 people with the sign of 36. And we never know who those 36 are.

22. I was not happy in this photo, taken on Friday, right before high holidays. The photographer waited at our home for four hours because I was nowhere to be found. I was busy playing in the nearby woods and fields with not a care in the world. When I finally arrived my father clobbered me with a stick for being late and we took this photo

23. In 1996 I, Leon Schagrin, went to Grybow and using $2,000 dollars that was raised ahead of time had this monument created to honor the Jews of Grybow, my uncle included.

24. Victor Mordarski was a political prisoner at Auschwitz from Grybow Poland. Being one of the first to be deported he ended up as a blockleiter for the infirmary. In this position he was able to save lives. He saved Leon by giving him typhoid medication, medical leaves and finally getting him transferred to Buna when he was near exhaustion. Victor is a hero for all of time.

After the liberation I went to visit Victor's parents in Grybow. Roman also spoke with Victor and even sent him money. When I met his parents they told me they thought he was dead because in 1942 the Nazis' sent his ashes to them. But, thankfully, these were not his ashes.

Victor survived with Mendel Scher. They were forced to go on the 'death march' when Auschwitz / Birkenau was closed. Eventually they found themselves herded onto a train in Cele. This train was attacked and bombed by the Americans. They escaped into the woods and they both remained free until the war was over. Once the war was over Victor immigrated to England. I credit Victor with at least saving the following people; Roman Blauner, Mendel Scher, Simon Unger, and myself, Leon Schagrin.

25. The Battle of Kircholm (27 September 1605, or 17 September in the Old Style calendar then in use in Protestant countries) was one of the major battles in the Polish-Swedish War of 1600-1611. The battle was decided in 20 minutes by the devastating charge of Polish-Lithuanian cavalry,

338

the Winged Hussars. The battle ended in the decisive victory of Polish-Lithuanian forces, and is remembered as one of the *greatest triumphs of* Commonwealth cavalry.

26. Eli Sommer grew up in Tarnow at Swieta Anna 5

27. After the war Moshe ran a hat factory in New York with a partner for many years. He retired in South Florida and was one of the founding members of the South Florida Holocaust Survivors Group. Morris has a great personality perfect for his favorite hobby, sales.

Morris and Leon survived together in all the worst camps. Understandable Leon could not be closer with him then most anyone in this world.

28. 1933 - Death of Tauba UNSDORFER age 88 (place of origin - Wojnarowa) Mother: Necha UNSDORFER (Father blank) Spouse: Jozef SCHAGRÜN

29. Hersch Schagrin is also Hersch UNSDORFER (the last name of the mother was used in some legal docs)

30. Malke died in Belzec. After marriage she had a child named Salomea in 1938. Malke was born 1915 to Yisrael and Perel Schagin.

Photo List:

1. The White River - (with bridges) - from Slawomir Dziadzio's collection
2. Old Grybow from the Church Tower authored by A. Nitsch, 1945 from Jozef Skrabski's collection
3. Classroom photo from the book. "Sentymentaln spacery po międzywojennym Grybowie" by Stanisław Osika.
4. Krynica ski lift - unknown
5. Lux torpeda - Mariusz Sendowski collection
6. Jarmark Postcards from Mr. Slawomir Dziadzio collection.
7. Artist's rendition St. Catherine's - Shoosty 2011
8. Orthodox Synagogue, Grybow 2011 - Kamil Kmak
9. Artist's Rendition Groszy - Shoosty 2011
10. Artist's Rendition Old Well in Grybow - Shoosty 2011
11. Artist's Rendition of a Spitz dog - Shoosty 2011
12. Photo "Old Grybow from the Church Tower" is authored by A. Nitsch, 1945 From Josef Skrabski's collection
13. Photo http://www.sztetl.org.pl/en/city/grybow/
14. From Jozef Skrabski's collection
15. From Grybow Parish Museum collection
16. From Jozef Skrabski's collection
17. Jarmark Postcards, Slawomir Dziadzio's collection.
18. From Slawomir Dziadzio's collection
19. From Slawomir Dziadzio's collection
20. From Jozef Skrabski's collection
21. From Slawomir Dziadzio's collection
22. From Grybow Parish Museum collection
23. Mendel Klafer - Kamil Kmak's collection
24. Krieger's Shop - From Jozef Skrabski's collection
25. Grybow Church meeting - from Grybow Parish Museum collection
26. Grybow Church meeting - from Grybow Parish Museum collection
27. Rabbi Halberstamm on horse back - from Virtual Shtetl portal
28. Halberstamm wedding - from Virtual Shtetl portal
29. water carrier unknown
30. rural kitchen unknown
31. gypsies Bagnowka website - life in war time
32. Joesel Schagrin - Artists Rendition based on photos from Leon Schagrin - Shoosty 2010
33. Rabbi Halberstamm - unknown

340

34. Rabbi Halberstamm - United States Holocaust Memorial Museum courtesy Norman Salsitz
35. Not used
36. Polish cavalry - Unknown
37. Germans Advance - artist's rendition - Shoosty
38. Soviets entering Poland - unknown
39. God Mit Us - unknown
40. Jackboots - artist's rendition Shoosty 2010
41. Three man motorcycle - artist's rendition Shoosty
42. Star of David armband - unknown
43. Grybow ghetto map - by Stanislaw Oleksy from the book 'Grybow. Studia z dziejow miasta i regionu' edited by Danuta Quirini-Poplawska
44. Grybow map - by Zdzislaw Maczenski, from the book 'Kościoły Grybowa. Monografia historyczno-artystyczna' by Jozef Skrabski
45. Nun from Kamil Kmak family album
46. Franciszek Paszek photo courtesy of Alicja and Grazyna Blicharz.
47. Dr. Kohn home - Jolanta Kruszniewska artist enhanced by Shoosty
48. Siberian Gulag - Artist's Rendition - Shoosty
49. Roadwork in Poland unknown
50. Schagrin Family - Leon and Betty Schagrin Foundation
51. Schagrin Grandparents given to Aunt Rose in America - Leon and Betty Schagrin Foundation
52. Rose Schagrin-Rosen - Bruce Rosen and Family
53. Current image of deportation place - Kamil Kmak 2010
54. Max Blauner's Father - Courtesy of the Blauner Family.
55. Stable in Tarnow ghetto - unknown
56. Example of carriage - unknown
57. Ordnungdienst Cap - unknown
58. Ordnungdienst - unknown
59. Ordnungdienst Stamp of Official Business - unknown
60. Betty and her Sisters - Leon and Betty Schagrin foundation
61. Tarnow ghetto - unknown
62. German Poster - unknown
63. Tarnow ghetto - United States Archives
64. Tarnow ghetto - Photo http://www.ushmm.org/
65. Tarnow ghetto - unknown
66. Tarnow ghetto - unknown
67. Tarnow Synagogue - unknown
68. Tarnow Synagogue - unknown
69. Szebnie Map - Szebnie map is from the book "Szebnie. Dzieje obozów

hitlerowskich" by Stanislaw Zabierowski
70. Leon and Maciek - Artists Conceptions - Shoosty
71. German Shepherd and Soldier - Artist Conception - Shoosty
72. Birkenau Front Gate - unknown
73. Bloody Mietek - Artists Conceptions
74. Wooden Shoe & Tin Pan auschwitz.org.pl
75. Tin Pan auschwitz.org.pl
76. not used
77. not used
78. Auschwitz Prisoner photo - Vad Vashem
79. Armband of a Kapo unknown
80. Drawing Auschwitz general conditions in the barracks - unknown artist
81. Drawing Auschwitz general conditions in the barracks - unknown artist
82. Commando Canada Auschwitz archive
83. Vicktor Mordarski - courtesy Anna Kurdzielewicz
84. Staf Commando - Field Kitchen - Auschwitz Archive
85. Auschwitz Overview
86. Birkenau map - United States Holocaust Memorial Museum, Historical Atlas of the Holocaust. New York: Macmillan, 1996.
87. Auschwitz - Birkenau Plan
88. Auschwitz - Birkenau Aerial Plan
89. Auschwitz latrine - Auschwitz Museum
90. Auschwitz guard
91. Auschwitz Blockhouse - Auschwitz archive
92. High Voltage Danger - Auschwitz Museum
93. Auschwitz Crematorium - Auschwitz Museum
94. I.G. Farben Buna Complex - Auschwitz Museum
95. * Highlight - Fleckliebertrockenbluluntersuchung copy of original document Typhus negative blood test for transfer from Birkenau to Buna- Auschwitz Archive
96. Iron Cross - unknown
97. Rail car used for moving sand. British War Museum
98. Morris Katz - Buna Infirmary Register - courtesy Auschwitz archive
99. Painting of Auschwitz Bombing - unknown artist
100. Bomb Shelter / Auschwitz - Birkenau
101. Air Bomb - unknown
102. Monument to the last fallen in Buna - Holocaust gathering commemorative Book
103. Death March List - Morris Katz - courtesy Auschwitz Archive
104. Death March List - Morris Katz - courtesy Auschwitz Archive

105. Operation Vistula http://www.dpcamps.org/operationVistula.html
106. Medal - Unknown
107. Medal - Unknown
108. Medal - Unknown
109. Leon Schagrin Portrait 2011 - Courtney Ortiz-Cauliflower
110. Leon Schagrin with Jim Boring
111. Leon Schagrin Tattoo photo by Courtney Ortiz-Cauliflower
112. Betty and Leon Schagrin Wedding - Leon & Betty Schagrin Foundation
113. Leon Schagrin USA Citizenship - Leon & Betty Schagrin Foundation
114. not used
115. Morris Moshe Katz 2010 - Photo by Shoosty
116. Max Blauner 2010 - Photo by Shoosty
117. Rose and Max Blauner 2011- Candid Photo by Shoosty
118. Eli Sommer 2011 - Photo by Shoosty
119. Roman Blauner and Leon Schagrin - Leon & Betty Schagrin Foundation
120. Tadeuz and Mary Skrabski - Courtesy of the Skrabski Family
121. Victor Mordarski - courtesy of Anna Kurdzielewicz
122. Leon Schagrin 1950 - Courtesy of Auschwitz Museum Archives see item
121. not used
123. Broward County Proclamation part1
124. Broward County Proclamation part2
125. Artist's Rendition - Leon Schagrin over the Years - Shoosty
126. Artist's Rendition - Leon Schagrin over the Years - Shoosty
127. Belzec - Leon & Betty Schagrin Foundation
128. Belzec - Leon & Betty Schagrin Foundation
129. Belzec - Leon & Betty Schagrin Foundation
130. Belzec - Leon & Betty Schagrin Foundation
131. email 08/11/10 Archiwum PMAB - Auschwitz Museum Archives
132. email 12/02/10 Archiwum PMAB - Auschwitz Museum Archives
133. Hersch and Chaja Schagrin - Leon and Betty Schagrin Foundation
134. Krankenschwester armband (nurse) - unknown
135. St. Catherine's Churh without a steeple, Grybow, fot. A. Nitsch, 1945, from Jozef Skrabski's collection
136. Destroyed Bridge Grybow - from Slawomir Dziadzio's collection
137. Max Blauner in uniform - Blauner Family
138. not used
140. Leon Schagrin Liberation - Photo made in Nowy-Sanz for an ID card - The Leon and Betty Schagrin Foundation
141. Nazi Officers with Judenrat - dokumentationsarchiv Des Ostereichischen Wiederstand - submitted by Judith Levin to Vad Vashem

142. Origin Josef Komilo submitted by Mark Shneberman - Vad Vashem
143. Mass Grave in Biala Nizna, Grybow - Photo Kamil Kmak 2010
144. The White River Swollen with Spring Floods Kamil Kmak 2010
145. Honoring _Broward Country - Leon and Betty Schagrin Foundation
146. Grybow Monument Israel mount Zion - unknown
147. Grybow Monument - Clifton NJ Artist enhanced - Museo of Family History
148. The Panther - Leon and Betty Schagrin Foundation
149. Photographed by an American B-24 bomber from the 464th Bombardment Group during the bombing of the I.G. Farben factory on September 13th,1944 (Sortie no. 464BG/4M97).
150. Sheins_Hardware Dr. Jozef_Skrabski_fot. A. Nitsch 1945.tiff
151. Leon's Nieghborhood - unknown
152. Leon in a School room - candid photo - Stephen Shooster
153. Candid photo - Leon and Betty in the USA
154. Lux torpeda - Interior - Artist Rendition - Shoosty
155. Leon training - Leon and Betty Schagrin Foundation
156. Leon Portrait - Courtney Ortiz-Cauliflower
157. http://www.grybow.pl/pl/14108/0/Zestaw_07.html #124.
158. http-/jr.co.il/pictures/israel/history/f15-jets-over-auschwitz_htm
159. Jewish Federation of Broward County Shoah Honoring 2011 Temple Sha'aray Tzedek - Sunrise Jewish Center
160. Yad Vashem record Malke Goldberg
161. New York Times 1939 map of invasion of Poland
162. Karl Swierczewski - http://www.kuzmicz.pl/historic-background/general-karol-walter-swierczewskis-death

Glossary:

1. Adjutant 1. (n) A helper; an assistant. 2. A regimental staff officer, who assists the colonel, or commanding officer of a garrison or regiment, in the details of regimental and garrison duty.

2. Xenophobic - is the "hatred or fear of foreigners or strangers or of their politics or culture". It comes from the Greek words (xenos), meaning "stranger," "foreigner" and (phobos), meaning "fear."

Links:

Szebnie: http://www.jewishgen.org/yizkor/Nowy_sacz/now850.html

Doomed Soldiers: http://www.doomedsoldiers.com/

grybow: http://data.jewishgen.org/wconnect/wc.dll?
                    jg~jgsys~communiy~-503592

Sokol: http://en.wikipedia.org/wiki/Sok%C3%B3%C5%82

Tarnow: http://www.holocaustresearchproject.org/nazioccupation/
                    tarnowdeport.html

Tarnow: http://www.deathcamps.org/occupation/tarnow%20ghetto.
                    html

Tarow: http://www.holocaustresearchproject.org/ghettos/tarnow.html

Nowy-Sacz/Sebnie: http://www.jewishgen.org/Yizkor/Nowy_sacz/now850.html

Tarnow: http://collections.yadvashem.org/photosarchive/en-us/30351.
                    html

I.G. Farben: http://www.holocaustresearchproject.org/economics/igfarben.
                    html

Buna: http://holocaustmusic.ort.org/places/camps/death-camps/
                    buna-monowitz/

Holocaust insignia: http://www.jewishvirtuallibrary.org/jsource/Holocaust/mark
                    ings.html

Music in death camps: http://holocaustmusic.ort.org/places/camps/death-camps/
                    buna-monowitz/

Copy of e-mail received August 11th, 2010 (E-MAIL 1)
From: Archiwum PMAB - Auschwitz Museum Archives <archiwum@auschwitz.org.pl>
Oświęcim, 11th August 2010
Ref. I-Arch-i/3619/10
In reply to your enquiry the Auschwitz-Birkenau State Museum in Oświęcim would
like to inform that we have searched partially saved documentation, which are kept in our Archives.
Unfortunately, there is no information about SCHAGRIN.
We only know that prisoners' number 161744 received man who was sent to KL Auschwitz from AL Szebnie on November 5/6, 1943. We know that prisoner 161744 was imprisoned in KL Auschwitz II–Birkenau in BIId sector and on February 27, 1944 was transferred to KL Auschwitz III – Monowitz (Buna).
Moreover we want inform you that we have civilian photo of prisoner named Szogriński, Leon.
Source of information: SS-Hygiene Institut files.
The State Museum would like to explain that during the evacuation and liquidation of KL Auschwitz by order of the camp authorities almost all-important documents of KL Auschwitz including prisoners' personal files were destroyed. On the basis of the partially saved documents it is impossible to impart complete information on the all
persons, who were imprisoned at the camp. That why we want ask you to fill and send back attached questionnaire. It will help to collect information about Schagrin.
We suggest you contact in your further search the International Tracing Service: Internationaler
Suchdienst, Grosse Allee 5-9, 34454 Bad Arolsen, Germany
e-mail:
email@its-arolsen.org <mailto:itstrace@its-arolsen.org>

Yours sincerely,
Krystyna Leśniak /Piotr Supiński
Offi ce for Information on Former Prisoners
att. questionnaire (enclosed 2 images - health report and photo 1950)
------ End of Forwarded Message

e-mail from the Auschwitz Archive Aug. 11, 2010
fig 131

346

(E-MAIL 2)

On 12/2/10 6:00 AM, "Archiwum PMAB - Auschwitz Museum Archives" <archiwum@auschwitz.org.pl> wrote:
I-Arch-i/7634-35/2010
Mr. Stephen Shooster
shoosty1@mac.com
In response to your request for information on Moshe Katz, we would like to inform you that in partially saved documentation of Auschwitz concentration camp we found following information about him
 Katz Mozes born April 1, 1925 in Nowy Sacz, was deported to Auschwitz on 5/6 of June 1943 from labour camp in Szebnie. He was registered and received his prisoners' number 161274. From December 16, 1943-January 25, 1944 he is noted in the registry book of prisoners' infirmary in Auschwitz III-Monowitz (also called Buna) On January 26, 1945 during the Auschwitz evacuation he was transferred from to Buchenwald.
 Source of information:
-the list of transports admitted to Auschwitz
-the register book prisoners' infirmary in Buna
-the list of prisoners transferred from Auschwitz to Buchenwald
 We would like to explain, that during the evacuation and liquidation of KL Auschwitz by order of the camp authorities, almost all important documents of KL Auschwitz, including prisoners' personal files, were destroyed. On the basis of our partially saved documents, it is impossible to assent full and accurate information on all the persons who were imprisoned at the camp.
For further research, I suggest contact with the following organization: International Tracing Service in Bad Arolsen: email@its-arolsen.org
Regards
Ewa Bazan
 Biuro informacji o byłych więźniach
Muzeum Auschwitz-Birkenau

Office for Information on Former Prisoners
The State Museum Auschwitz-Birkenau

e-mail from the Auschwitz Archive Dec. 2nd, 2010
fig. 132

Szebnie (sheb-neia) Poland

Frontstalag and Zwangsarbeitslager in Szebniach – Was a German camp for Soviet prisoners of war from October 8th, 1941 to spring 1942 followed by a forced labor camp in Szebnie from March 11th, 1943 to September 8th, 1944.

The foundations of the camp gave a staging point for the Nazi troops, Wehrmacht or Horse Branch. It was built at the turn of 1939 to 1940. It consisted of eight barracks in an area of 10 hectares. In mid-September 1941 the army left the camp and on October 8, 1941 the first transport arrived with about two thousand Soviet prisoners. They arrived at the Moder€wka (now Szebnie station) at the Frontstalag. In November, three more transports arrived and the population increased to between 5 and 7 thousand. In one barracks there were about 300 people. By this time there were 20 barracks. They were all about 40 m x 7 m. These prisoners lived in very difficult circumstances. Not all of them could live in the barracks. The mortality rate was high. In November 1941, 8-10 people a day died. But after an outbreak of epidemic typhus December 12, 1941, the number of deaths rose to 200 people per day. The dead were taken to the nearby depressions, called the 'Bierowskie Docy'. The camp was liquidated in autumn, in November 1942. Between 4 and 6 thousand Soviet prisoners were killed with only about 200 survivors taken to a camp in Rymanow.

The forced labor camp (Zwangsarbeitslager) was launched March 11th 1943, when the first shipment of Jewish artisans from the ghetto in Tarnow arrived. In a short period of time transports arrived from liquidated ghettos in Bochnia, Jaslo, Tarnow, Rzeszow and Przemysl, small camps like Frysztak and Dukla, as well as camps in Plaszow and other desolate areas. At the same time the camp served as a replacement police prison (Polizeiersatzgefängnis) for the Gestapo Jaslo facility. Camp commanders were successively: Scheidt, Kellermann and Blank, and SS-Fuhrer Oberschar Joseph Grzimek.

In early August 1943 the camp inmates numbered 1040 including 570 Jews. Prisoners wore civilian clothes marked with paint and a number sewn on a piece of white fabric. During this time they completed the construction of the camp. The camp measured 557 x 178 meters and was fenced with barbed wire, 4 guard towers and 32 barracks. There were also four fields that were

348

used as places of execution. Besides executions they also performed flogging the goat as well as having a punishment pillar. Dead were buried at the local cemetery. There were also mass organized executions in the nearby forest of Dobrucowa (approximately 1.7 miles from camp) on September 21 and November 6, 1943, shooting about 1,600 people. The corpses were burned on a grate of the rails, and the crime scene was thoroughly masked by placing fresh sod and planting shrubs and trees in the area. On November 4th Oberschar SS-Fuhrer Joseph Grzimek sent 4,237 Jews to Auschwitz. They reached the camp a day later (Leon Schagrin reports that his train did not arrive for three long days and nights , naked, over packed, no food, no water, people trampled under foot). Upon arrival, a selection chose 2,889 people who were killed in the gas chambers. The remainders including 952 males were tattooed with the numbers 160870-161830 and 396 women were tattooed with numbers 66702-67097 and then sent to housing blocks. The remaining 1,200 prisoners in Szebniach were sent February 2, 1944 to a camp in Plaszow.

Prisoners worked mainly in a workshop at the camp and the gravel pit at Jasiocko. The camp owned subsidiaries in Krosno from August 25th, 1943 to January 27th, 1944. They also owned also the former Soviet prisoner of war camp in Rymanow September-November 1943, and a quarry called Cieszyn near Frysztak October, 1943 - January 1944.

Again, the camp was used by Soviet prisoners at the end of March 1944. The camp was evacuated to Grybow in mid-July 14th and August 25, 1944. About 300 wounded and disabled prisoners were left in the camp when the liberation took place September 8th, 1944.

The local population demolished the camp buildings in January and February 1945. A school was built in 1964. A memorial stone was built in front of the main road out of the camp. Also monuments were built on the spot where executions took place in Dobrucowa and at the cemetery in Szebnie as well as Bierowskie Docy. Victims of the POW camp dedicated a poem about the camp as well. It is called, Hunger Camp at Jaslo, by Wislawa Szymborska.

From the book Szebnie by Stanislaw Zabierowski, 1985 Justice

U.S. Strategic Bombing

My own cousin's orders could have been the cause of my neck injuries. The orders even speak of synthetic oil which is what I was making.
Extracts from the U.S. Strategic Bombing Survey, summarizing 15th Air Force bombing attacks in August and September 1944 on Oswiecim (Auschwitz)
....

SYNTHETIC OIL PLANT OF I.G. FARBEN AT OSWIECZIM
NEAR KRAKOW, POLAND

The target is located app. 32 miles west of Krakow and app. 20 miles southeast of Katowice and forms with the rubber plant to the east, one area—grid coordinates 37[ring] 50[ring]. The oil refinery covers an area of approximately 1100 x 1200 yds. and the synthetic rubber plant an area of approximately 1800 x 1200 yds. The plants were owned and operated by the I.G. Farben Trust of Frankfurt, Main. To the south and west of the target, a concentration and labor camp exists which indicates forced and foreign labor at these plants.

The attached diagram shows the target area, the principal buildings and their use as estimated from aerial cover, key to plan. There are over 100 buildings in the synthetic oil plant and aerial cover is available. The target has several railroad lines running through the entire plant.
The target was attacked four times by the 15th Air Force with B-17 and B-24 bombers, the bombs used were 500 GP with 1/10 nose and 1/40 and 1/100 tail fusing.

On Aug. 20th, 127 B-17 bombers attacked dropping 1336 500 lb. GP bombs 1/10 nose, 1/40 tail, alt. of release 26,100 ft to 29,500 ft., time 10:32 to 11:00, 2/10 to 3/10 clouds over target. The main weight of the attack fell on the central and eastern parts; with considerable damage to installations and buildings. It appears that near misses caused a considerable amount of blast damage. Annotated print no. 3071, Aug. 23 shows and DB Report no. 189 list damage by buildings.

Cover was flown Aug. 25, 1944, picture 4173, 4176 and 4178 were taken. Clearance and repair work were in progress. Interpretation Report, Aug. 30th, DP 95 lists as damaged buildings in the primary objectives class no. 80, secondary objective 75 and 98, other objective class no's 61, 64, 70. It is definite that the synthetic rubber plant sustained the greatest amount of damage.

The last cover flown before the second attack was Sept. 2nd 1944 and report DB 199 speaks of repair going on and normal truck and M.T. movement being seen.

The second attack took place Sept. 13, 1944 from 11:17 to 11:20 at a height of 22,300 ft. to 24,000 ft. Ninety-six B-24's attacked with 943 500 lb. RDX filled bombs minus 69 bombs, which had regular filler. Visibility poor, pff technic used. The heaviest concentration was again on the synthetic rubber plant, but the following oil plant buildings sustained major damage, no's 64, , 84 and 96 slight damage to 41, 43, 44, 81, 83 and several workshops stores, unidentified buildings and huts in the labor camp to the south and southwest. No's 8, 25, 47, 48, 51, 71, 105, 108, 112 and 114, photo no. 4022 annotated shows most of the buildings.
Oct. 16th, DB 241 speaks of great deal of repair work observed and new construction in progress. The operational activity seen in the past at the gas plant and elsewhere is not thought to have been associated with the use of part of the Buna plant.

Report G-430, Nov. 29th, 1944 observes the plant as being active; cars are on the sidings and about 100 tank cars are on the rail siding east of the plant area.

Third attack, Dec. 18th, 1944 by 2 B-17's an d47 B-24's Four hundred thirty-six boobs dropped, all RDX filler with 52 regular filler as exception. All bombs 500 lb. size 1/10 nose, 1/40 and 1/10 nose, 1/100 tail, proportion of the two tail delays used unknown. Attack time 11:20 to 12:17; pff system, 22,900 ft. to 24,000 ft. heights. No photographs available yet. Damage throughout the area reported especially on buildings 73, 76, 84, and 104. Extreme active M.T. and pedestrian activity was evident. Repair activity has been intense and some new construction was evident.

Fourth and last attack, Dec. 26th, 1944 by 95 B-24's. Total of 679 500 lb. bombs dropped; RDX filler with 126 with regular filler as exception. Fusing 1/10 nose, 1/40 and 1/100 tail, ration unknown. Time of attack from 12:16 to 12:21 at 22,200 ft. to 24, 700 ft., with pff system. No photographs are available yet. Many hits scored and near misses indicate extensive blast damage. Great operational activity at plant. Following buildings damaged: 9, 65, 73, 76, 77, 84, 89, 99 besides workshops, barracks inside labor camp, welfare building and miscellaneous small sheds.

The last cover was flown 15 Jan. 1945 (no prints available yet). Roof repairs were noted, steam issuing from a number of points. There have been movement and probably turnover of rolling stock.

What Happened to the Perpetrators?

Heinrich Henry Hamann

In 1931 Heinrich Henry Hamann was an independent merchant who joined the Nazi Party. In 1939, he became SS Lieutenant at Nowy-Sacz. And by fall 1943 a short stay in Jasco, the site of the jarmark horse-trading festival near Szebnie.

He was married to a German woman but began a relationship with a Jewish Polish prisoner and was caught by the Gestapo. He was denounced by the SD for racial shame. He then forged her an ethnic German identity and after the war because of her dubious identity, Polish authorities imprisoned her. She was released early due to an amnesty agreement and immigrated to Argentina, where she and Hamann operated a hotel.

In 1966 Hamann was sentenced to Bochum prison for life, for the crime of the murder of hundreds of Jews. He was responsible for liquidation of the Nowy-Sacz ghetto and the vicinity August 1942 where at least 15,000 Jews were deported to the Belzec death camp.15

Josef Grzimek

Born 10/11/1905 In 1943 –1944 December through August he was the Commander of the Ukrainian guard at Szebnie. Here he took part in the mass executions in the forest of Dobrucowa shooting about 1,600 people. Grzimek later directed the action of smoking bodies of victims in wooden grids made of railway track. After the war he was tried for his crimes by a Polish court in Warsaw, January 29th, 1949. He was sentenced to death and he was hung on February 18, 1950.

Amon Leopold Goth

SS Hauptsturmfuhrer Amon Leopold Goth was accused of larceny of Jewish property, which was regarded as property of the German Reich. He was arrested on 13 September 1944 effectively ending his career.

After the war he was extradited to Poland at the request of the Polish authorities and tried before the Polish Supreme Court on charges of committing mass murder during the liquidations of the ghettos at Tarnow,

Krakow, Szebnie and Plaszow. He was sentenced to death in Krakow on 5 September 1946 and was hung on 13 September 1946.17

Bornholt, Johann Claudius - Trial of Bochum, 1966: life sentence + 12 years.18

Hermann Blache

Hermann Blache - Case Nr.571 Oberscharfhrer Hauptsturmfuhrer Blache, Crime Category: Mass Extermination Crimes in Camps, Tarnow. Life sentence + 6 Years.19

Procedure Lfd.Nr.571 act complex: Mass destruction crime in camps accused: Blache, Hermann lifelong + 6 years judicial rulings: LG Bochum 640430 act country: Poland scene: Tarnow, HS ZAL Tarnow act time: 4306-4402 victims: Jew nationality: Polish agency: Detention place personnel ZAL Tarnow procedure article: Single shooting of at least 22 Jewish prisoners of the ZAL Tarnow. Participation in liquidating the Tarnower Ghettos, with which at least 4000 Jewish men, women and children in the KL Auschwitz were removed. Shooting of Jews, who had hidden themselves or their children to escape deportation.

Bloody Mietek

Katarzyński, Mieczysław (1920 – 1948) Kapo Auschwitz-Birkenau -Extradited and executed. Born on 11th November 1920 in Warsaw. Sent as a political prisoner to Auschwitz on 7th, 1941. At first he worked in locksmiths kommando. Then he was appointed as a Blockleiter in quarantine camp in Birkenau, where he was one of the worst sadists. He earned a nickname "Bloody Mietek". On 17th September, 1944, he was transferred do Leitmeritz a sub-camp of KL Flossenbuerg. Here he denunciated other inmates and civilian workers. In February 1945 he escaped from the camp and, after that, he fought along with Czech partisans until May 1945. He was arrested by Polish authorities in September 1945 in Słupca (he used false name Jan Witkowski). During his trial, many former inmates of Birkenau and Leitmeritz testified against him. He was sentenced to death and executed by hanging on 6th July, 1948.

Now It Is Up to You

Some persons are doomed to remember. I am one of them. The fear and anger I felt as a boy living under the Nazi boot has scarred my soul. This book is my final effort to transmute all the horror I have seen and experienced into something good and useful.

Just before I lost my entire family to the gas chamber my father begged me to make sure the world knows what happened to us. Perhaps this is what triggered my obsessive memory of the events of those terrible years and the keeping of those memories for so long. The weight of these memories has been with me my whole life. I found a place deep in my heart and soul to seal each detail so I would not forget.

Memories like this are not easy to express and I have almost waited too long to share them. Now, I am 84 years old with a single purpose – to find a vessel for my memories before it is too late.

During one of the lectures I conduct in schools to foster education about the Holocaust a young girl made a strong impression with her eagerness to learn, her intelligent questions and her sincerity. Carly Shooster was the same age I was when my world was turned upside down. I asked her to represent me in 2045 at the hundredth anniversary Holocaust memorial. She graciously consented. This small event triggered the writing of *The Horse Adjutant.* Carly's father, Stephen Shooster, took on the huge burden and the years-long effort required to tell my story and to see to it that my promise to my father was finally fulfilled. My gratitude knows no bounds.

I am a man who has been visited by both angels and demons. Now at the end of my life the angels have returned.

Leon Schagrin

Three Monuments Honoring the Fallen in Grybow

Israel: Monument on Mount Zion
Honoring mass grave site in Grybow, Poland
fig 146

Three Monuments Honoring the Fallen in Grybow

USA, New Jersey: Monument in Clifton
Honoring mass grave site in Grybow, Poland

For the many saintly martyrs of our hometown grybow Galicia who were brutally slaughtered by the German barbarians three hundred and sixty of these who are resting in one common grave in Grybow we murdered on August 20,1942 This monument was erected by their American land-slept Grybower Ladies and Mens Benevolent Society, Sept. 7, 1947 May their blood be avenged
fig 147

Three Monuments Honoring the Fallen in Grybow

**Poland, Biala Niza: Mass Grave
in Grybow Poland**

Here rest remains of those killed by Hitler thugs
on 20th of August 1942 Jews of Grybow.[23]

fig. 143

The Grybower's Point of View

Kamil Kmak
Student
AGH University of Science and Technology in Krakow
Studying Surveying and Cartography

About four years ago I started writing this book (Stephen Shooster). Because it was about a strange land I went to the internet and reached out for help from a stranger, that is how I met Kamil and because of this my life is richer as well as the story herein.
-Stephen Shooster

Seven decades have passed since that tremendous storm of Nazi totalitarianism brought Poland to ruin. It was the end of a rich and flourishing world of Polish, Jewish, Ruthenian and Ukrainian cultures mingled in the heart of Europe; the Old World. Now who shall bind the shattered glass? Who shall gather the smoke of ashes and bring back the community torn apart? The beautiful land of Poland was forced to be the scene of the most tragic and painful acts of downfall of humanity.

Jews and Poles suffered from Nazi totalitarianism for no reason, just to pay toll to the fantasies of people seduced by evil. Every Polish family lost relatives. They were not exterminated for being Poles, like Jews were just for being Jews, but German Nazism was determined to annihilate Polish intelligentsia: scientists, historians, politicians, officers, teachers, priests and all patriotic movements. Their mission was to destroy the entire Polish culture and make the Poles a nation of slaves. But they did not break the Polish will toward freedom. They were not tough enough, because Poland situated between Germany and Russia, has struggled centuries for freedom. For every help given to the Jews, or hiding

358

the Jews, Polish people and their families were punished with death, like no other nation in German-occupied Europe. And still thousands of brave Polish men and women risked their lives and the lives of their families to help Jews. They are known today as The Righteous Among the Nations. Poles make up more than any other nation when it comes to the total number of the Righteous, and moreover, many Poles did not claim their rights to use this title, because they helped everyone in need, Jew or not, and do not consider themselves heroes just humans of mercy.

The Soviet reign that overshadowed Poland after the fall of Nazi Germany contributed to building a great wall of mistrust between people, including Poles and Jews, and even among Poles themselves. Five decades of Polish subordination to Moscow, from 1945 to 1989, brought about an atmosphere of ongoing suspicion and accusation, leading to expelling Jews who survived the Holocaust from Poland in 1968 by the Soviets. But the Polish struggle for freedom is relentless. Through the efforts of the Solidarity movement and the Polish Pope, John Paul II, Poland once again returned to freedom in 1989 and the Iron Curtain fell. Thanks to those events, Polish-Jewish contacts can now revive, favorably, on the ground of the former common history of Jews in Polish land.

Today many Jewish culture festivals are held, and many books and music are being released. Old Jewish sites like synagogues and cemeteries are being renovated and a new Museum of Polish Jews is being built in Warsaw, documenting almost one thousand years of Jewish presence in Poland. This is expected to be dedicated to not just its terrible end but also the rich culture it created and hopefully a new beginning. The Memory of our Jewish neighbors should be a part of Polish identity we cannot forget.

Kamil Kmak

Kamil Kmak 2010

Why We Tell These Stories

Danny Lieberman
Vice President
Noted Fine and Performing
Arts Educator

I have always struggled to wrap myself around the number 6 million, when it comes to how many Jews were exterminated in Europe during the Nazi regime. Nor can I completely grasp the number 25 million, when it comes to the estimated loss of civilian and combatant lives during World War II. That these figures seem unfathomable doesn't make them untrue. But, because they seem unfathomable, those unfamiliar with the evidence and history are easy prey for the industry of holocaust deniers. We have only to look to Iran. Truth requires an army of ardent defenders with a comprehensive arsenal. Big numbers can make a big impression; but we also need to immerse in the stories and intersect with the biographies of those who lived in that world. Such experiences help to humanize for us an otherwise dehumanized and, therefore, seemingly improbable time.

Stephen Shooster is one of these ardent defenders. He has managed to capture a most powerful story filled with great sadness, perseverance, and triumph. In the first person, he artfully reveals the story of Leon Schagrin, a Holocaust survivor, who navigated treacherous ghetto life as a horse-pulled carriage driver and who then survived three concentration camps. I have read hundreds of books about the Holocaust, and one might think that this would desensitize me emotionally to yet another one. But, I was moved to tears nonetheless, profoundly connecting to Shooster's mission.

As an educator, musician, and past president of the International Make-A-Wish Foundation, I know how essential experiential learning is to the education of young people. Each year my wife Sandy and I lead 82 people on a charity band tour to Europe. Students, ages 11-18, learn that it's "not just about the music."

From all over the United States and Mexico, they arrive in Florida for 4-days of intensive rehearsals, performances, and fun. And then we take the show overseas, performing and touring through the United Kingdom, Holland, Denmark, Germany, Austria, Belgium, and the Czech Republic. The students learn that music is a gift to be shared, a way to open a dialogue, to touch a soul, to bring joy to a sick or impoverished child.

On each trip two experiences always have the most profound impact. The first is when the student performers get to "grant a wish" to a very sick child, on behalf of the Make-A-Wish Foundation of Austria. In that moment, each student witnesses first hand how fragile life can be. The second experience comes when we step foot through the gate of a former Nazi concentration and extermination camp [over the years, the tour has visited Mauthausen, Sachsenhausen, Theresienstadt, Dachau, and Auschwitz-Birkenau].

Perhaps the number 6 million is difficult to comprehend, but when students have a chance to witness in person the acreage of such concentration and extermination camp operations, walk through the barracks into which people were stacked like cords of wood, can see the gas chambers and the cremation ovens used to expedite the "Final Solution," they imagine themselves walking in the footsteps of the millions who lost their lives and the fortunate few, like Leon Shagrin, who lived to share their story.

Leon Shagrin's story, as told by Stephen Shooster, touched me so much, because it helped me recognize anew what has been such a motivational force in my life, whether as a student of the saxophone, piano, and drums, as a leader of Make-A-Wish, or as an Administrator of Fine Arts. In order for the next generation to know how to repair our world – *Tikkun Olam* – we must help them come to terms with our past, and this can only be done well if we are committed to telling the truth, and providing them with the means by which to engage this history first hand. 6,000,000 must stand for something other than a number. It must clearly delineate a period of time, captured so well by Shooster that all people including children must never forget.

Tikkum Olam,

Danny Lieberman

Good Citizen Award

Malcolm Rosenberg

Without Malcolm there would be no book. With little prompting he volunteered to capture the story of Leon Schagrin first hand through personal interviews. Over a period of six months he would visit frequently to find the thread of the story and pull it. I can't tell you how hard this is because our memories order things in an unknown way with snippets of thoughts coming out of order. After his visits he would hand me his notes to stitch the story together. I would put them into order and hand them back to Malcolm to continue the quest.

The process is exhausting both physically and emotionally. Reliving Leon's story is not easy, no one could remain unmoved by realizing what he went through.

When someone asks me what can I do for the survivors I tell them one of the best things to do is just listen.

I raise my cup and toast Malcolm for a job well done!

Stephen Shooster,
co-Author

The Student's View

Moisey Abdurakhmanov
Student

Atlantic Technical Center Magnet High
school, Grade 12

In 1995 Moisey's family immigrated to the United States from Samarkand Uzbekistan by force because they were Jewish. His family was told if they did not leave they would be killed. They left all of their belongings including their home, car and business.

.....

When Leon first came to me, asking me to help him write his biography I was shocked, but also honored. I was shocked that he would choose me, a 17-year-old student, to help write his biography. But, I was also honored that out of everyone he knew, and all the connections he had, he chose me to help.

As Leon told his story of his liberation and his life afterwards, I was shocked at what he experienced compared to his life today. His past contained some of the most hateful things I have ever heard, yet here he is now, willing to tell me his story so that future generations can benefit and not repeat his past.

After everything he had been through, Leon came to America, married, and started up a store. His life picked up, and he moved to South Florida, happy. He joined the South Florida Holocaust Association upon arrival to keep the message alive and tell everyone about the horrors of the Holocaust. After everything that transpired, he still came out with a winning grin on his face. In the years I have known him, known has shown such grace and kindness, I have never seen before. His generosity knows no limits, as he continues to learn and teach everyone he meets. I hope that for the rest of my life, my children's life and my children's lives that no person should die for who they are or for their religious beliefs.

I would like to give thanks for everything that he has done for me, and everything that he has a helped me accomplish. It was because of him that I realized that doing good and making people happy is the best reward there is in life. Leon, thank you for everything you have given to me and the world.

Moisey Abdurakhmanov

Broward County Proclamation - Leon Schagrin Day

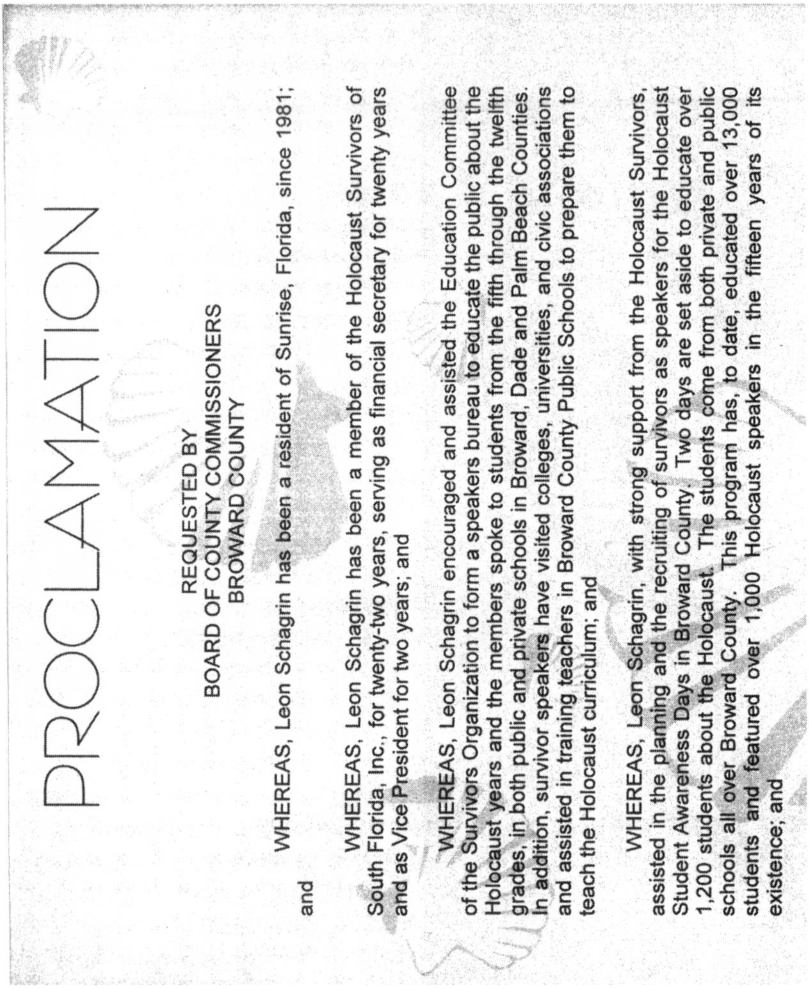

PROCLAMATION

REQUESTED BY
BOARD OF COUNTY COMMISSIONERS
BROWARD COUNTY

and

WHEREAS, Leon Schagrin has been a resident of Sunrise, Florida, since 1981; and

WHEREAS, Leon Schagrin has been a member of the Holocaust Survivors of South Florida, Inc., for twenty-two years, serving as financial secretary for twenty years and as Vice President for two years; and

WHEREAS, Leon Schagrin encouraged and assisted the Education Committee of the Survivors Organization to form a speakers bureau to educate the public about the Holocaust years and the members spoke to students from the fifth through the twelfth grades, in both public and private schools in Broward, Dade and Palm Beach Counties. In addition, survivor speakers have visited colleges, universities, and civic associations and assisted in training teachers in Broward County Public Schools to prepare them to teach the Holocaust curriculum; and

WHEREAS, Leon Schagrin, with strong support from the Holocaust Survivors, assisted in the planning and the recruiting of survivors as speakers for the Holocaust Student Awareness Days in Broward County. Two days are set aside to educate over 1,200 students about the Holocaust. The students come from both private and public schools all over Broward County. This program has, to date, educated over 13,000 students and featured over 1,000 Holocaust speakers in the fifteen years of its existence; and

Broward County Florida, USA
Proclamation - Leon Schagrin Day
fig 123+124

366

Broward County Proclamation - Leon Schagrin Day

WHEREAS, Leon Schagrin, with support from the Holocaust Survivors of South Florida, has made it a priority to provide books and educational materials to Broward County Public Schools in order to facilitate the study of the Holocaust; and

WHEREAS, through strong leadership, well-organized advocacy, and courage, Leon Schagrin convinced the Jewish Claims Conference to pursue a class action suit against the German government for reparations to survivors who never received compensation for their time in the concentration camps. This resulted in the creation of Article II, which has dispersed payment to over 40,000 survivors worldwide and more than 14,000 in the United States alone; and

WHEREAS, Leon Schagrin, with the utmost resolve, took the initiative to lobby the World Jewish Congress, the United States Holocaust Memorial Museum in Washington D.C. and the Polish government regarding a badly neglected burial site in the town of Belzec, Poland. Leon fought to restore this largely unknown gravesite where over 600,000 Jews from eleven different countries lay buried in 20th century Europe. Because of Leon's passion and resolve, The Belzec Memorial has been restored as a proper and dignified memorial and will be dedicated on June 3, 2004; NOW, THEREFORE,

BE IT PROCLAIMED BY THE BOARD OF COUNTY COMMISSIONERS OF BROWARD COUNTY, FLORIDA

That the Board hereby acknowledges Leon Schagrin's many accomplishments and designates Sunday, February 22, 2004, as **"LEON SCHAGRIN APPRECIATION DAY"** in Broward County, Florida.

BROWARD COUNTY FLORIDA

Mayor

Feb 5, 2004
Date

Leon Schagrin Lifetime Timeline

1938	1939-44	1945	1950
Age 10	Occupied Poland Ghetto Concentration Camp Forced Labor	Liberated	Army

Artist's Rendition of Timeline
fig 125+126

Leon Schagrin Lifetime Timeline

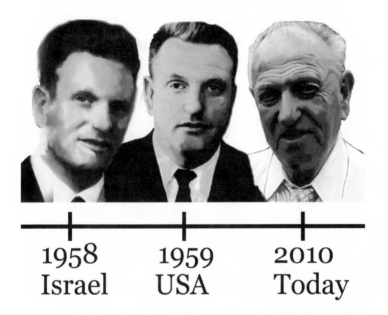

1958
Israel

1959
USA

2010
Today

Thank You

Special Thanks to All of those involved in putting this book together. It is a lifetime achievement making me forever grateful.

To my loving wife Betty Schagrin for her help in overcoming this drama and for her support in writing my biography.

I intend to recommend Righteous Among Nations to the following:

Tadeusz Skrabski & his family - They repeatedly risked their lives to care for my family over an extended period of the worst times imaginable, the Fascist occupation of our community.

Victor Mordarski – Victor, you were a hero.

The Mol family, you are saviors.

My Friends:

Max & Rose Blauner, Max's brothers, Roman and Moshe - Your family is my own. You have helped me in so many ways.

Moses Katz - An *epical* thanks to my closest friend. Our mutual friendship during the worst time of our made it possible to survive.

Joshua Cafri & Pola - My cousins in Israel. You helped me to establish a future.

Thank You

The entire Shooster-Leuchter Family
Herman & Dorothy Shooster
Frank & Agnes Shooster, Jay, Lauren, Adam, Tommy
Michael & Alizabeth Shooster, Forest, Max, Jacob, Logan
Stephen & Diane Shooster, Jason, Jaime, Carly, Cassidy
Max & Wendy Shooster-Leuchter, Joseph, Jessica, Abigail

Malcolm & Sandy Rosenberg

Jim & Deanne Boring

Deborah Raff - JRI-Poland Town Leader - Grybow/Nowy Sacz/Stary
Sacz/Muszyna and JewishGen Shtetlinks Administrator of - Nowy
Sacz/Stary Sacz/Sanok/Bukowsko/Dynow/Brzozow

Sandy & Danny Lieberman
Moisey Abdurakhmanov & Family
Carol & Jim Cederna
Albert & Pearl Nipon and Family
Ethel & Marty Carson
Roman Kent & Ben Meed and the Claims Conference
Dina Axelrod, Board member, Holocaust Survivors of South Florida
The American Jewish Committee for helping to restore Belzec.
Harry & Helen Jonas, my wife Betty's sister, a Survivor of
Schindler's list
Steven Jonas, nephew & Vivian, Shelly, Lola, and Marilyn, nieces.
To all my American relatives and friends, thanks for being with me
during the time of greatest need.
Fran Klauber & her son Adam Klauber.
Rochelle Baltuch and the Staff of the Center for the Advancement of

Thank You

Jewish Education
Broward County Public Schools
Broward County Commissioners
Pepi Dunay, Jewish Federation of Broward County, Yom Hashoah Planning Committee
Steve Feren, Former Mayor of Sunrise
Julius Eisenstein, Honorary President, Holocaust Survivors of South Florida
Miriam Fridman, President of the Holocaust Survivors of South Florida
Esther Haut, Secretary, Holocaust Survivors of South Florida
Rita Hofrichter, Vice President, Holocaust Documentation and Education Center
Holocaust Survivors of South Florida
Rositta E. Kenigsberg, Executive Vice President, Holocaust Documentation and Education Center
Allen Laufer, CPA, Son of Survivors, Board member of the Holocaust Survivors of South Florida
Harry A. Hap Levy, President, Holocaust Documentation and Education Center
Linda Medvin, Multicultural Curriculum Development/Training Special, Broward County Schools
Ken Moskowitz, Director, Jewish Family Services and his staff
Merle R. Saferstein, Director of Educational Outreach, Holocaust Documentation and Education Center - I love you all dearly. May God protect you and may your dreams be nourished by freedom.
Ilene Lieberman and all the commissioners
My associates for Holocaust education programs survivors
Entire board of the South Florida Holocaust Organization
Special thanks to Roman Kent, Sol Kagan, and Greg Schneider and

Thank You

the claims conference in New York for their constant caring and helping of survivors all over the world, including acceptance of our applications and petitions to negotiate for the different compensations available from the German government. With their help the German government accepted many of our petitions. And not just ours; through their negotiations they have helped Holocaust survivors from all over the world, especially in their final years.

My new friends from Poland:
Kamil Kmak and his bride to be Agnieszka Lach
Anna Kurdzielewicz, niece of Wiktor Mordarski and her husband Piotr Kurdzielewicz
Alicja Blicharz, who gave Kamil the photo of Paszek
Dr Jozef Skrabski old photos of Grybow
Jolanta Kruszniewska, photos and advice

Thank You

I owe thanks to many people for helping me keep the promise I made to my father; to tell the story of my life to everyone who would listen. But my dear friend, Fran Klauber, is the one person who stands out among them. I have known Fran for almost 30 years and her list of achievements during that time is impressive by any standard. Fran is the first person I knew who actively promoted the implementation of Holocaust and genocide education and awareness in the public school system. That inspired me to follow her lead and deliver my message to thousands of young people throughout South Florida. Her political involvement brought me resources that would never have been available to me without her assistance. Fran is a former City Commissioner for the City of Sunrise, a ten-year board member of the Holocaust Survivors of South Florida and the first woman inducted into the Sunrise Chamber of Commerce Hall of Fame. Fran is also a second generation survivor.

In 1994, Fran introduced me to her then 23 year old son, Adam Klauber. He was a second year law student and offered to help me draft a petition to The Conference on Jewish Material Claims Against Germany. That Petition, which took many hours to complete, led to reparations being paid to Holocaust Survivors who were previously denied, including me. Adam also spoke to the Holocaust Survivors of South Florida on many occasions always promising that he would do his part to make sure that his generation and the ones that follow will never forget.

Fran, thank you for what you've done for me and for being an inspiration to all who know you.

374

Honoring Leon Schagrin

2-22-2004 Honoring of Leon Schagrin

Fran Klauber - City Commissioner Sunrise
Adam Klauber Att. with his wife and baby
Linda Medvin - Holocaust Education Broward Country
Ilene Lieberman - Mayor Broward Country
Leon and Betty Schagrin
Helen and Henry, Betty's Sister and Brother-in-Law

fig 163

376

NORTH BROWARD
PREPARATORY
SCHOOL
The local school with global vision

7600 Lyons Road
Coconut Creek, Florida 33073
Phone 954.247.0011
Fax 954.247.0042
www.NBPS.org

Thank you leon for sharing your experiences with us. We really appreciated you coming and sharing your story.

Sincerely,

The fifth grade students

[signatures]

Zachary Lopez
Julia Singhal
alex Greenwald
Caroline Skuta
Cassidy Shooter
Zach Plotkin
Giuliano Remigio
Samantha Gould
Iggy Marco
Drew Monaco
Matthew Clark
Matthew P. Uchin
tori Friedman
Aylen Mathew
Heather ager
nathan white
Julia Montalvo
Paris Chisolm
Chris Peter

Memorial Garden

After 20 years of negotiations between the Holocaust Survivors of South Florida Board of Directors, Miriam Fridman President and Star of David a monument was dedicated at the Star of David memorial gardens in Tamarac, Florida, Dec. 14, 2008.

This monument is a memorial to the 6,000,000 Jews killed during the Nazi Holocaust between 1939 and 1945.

fig. 145

378

Never Forget

Jets displaying the blue Star-of-David flew over the Auschwitz-Birkenau concentration camp as slowly as possible following the railroad tracks that led to the camp and crematoriums and then peeled away in a show of Israel's modern might. fig 158

My American Lifeline

Max and Rose Schagrin-Rosen
Rose emigrated in 1921 to the USA. Because of this she was able to send
packages to Poland including clothing, toys and money. In turn they sent
her the only surviving photos of Leon's family. Once Leon emigrated to
the USA she told her family he is to be considered their brother.
fig. 145

My American Lifeline

Rose and Max Blauner
fig. 114

If you lose your
freedom you
are condemned
– Leon Schagrin

The Leon and Betty Schagrin Foundation

The Leon and Betty Schagrin Foundation is a 501c non-profit corporation designed for the purpose of Holocaust Education.

Shooster Publishing 2010

The Leon and Betty Schagrin Foundation
Stephen Shooster, President
954-537-1200
Stephen.Shooster@ShoosterPublishing.com

777 South State Road 7 • Margate, Florida 33068

The Cover

From left to right, top to bottom)

Max Blauner, Survivor
Morris Katz, Survivor

Eli Sommer, Survivor
Kamil Kmak, Polish Liaison

Carly Shooster, Leon's Legacy
Betty Schagrin. Leon's Wife

Rabbi Halberstamm, Tzadick
Frank Shooster, Forward

Danny Lieberman, Afterward
Malcolm Rosenberg, Interviewer

Schagrin Family 1939.

Photo saved by sending it to relatives in America.
Leon Schagrin, age 10, Hersch (dad), Henna in his arms,
Chaja (mom) pregnant with twins, Sister Golda in her arms.[22]
fig 50

Tobi and Josel Schagrin

Leon's Fathers Parents with Uncle Izrael, dressed in his army uniform. He was an Adjutant for a General in the Austrian Cavalry.
Nowy-Sacz, Poland.
fig 51

Tadeusz and Mary Skrabski

fig. 120

Old Grybow Central Square from the Church Tower
fig. 12

Victor Mordarski[24]
fig 121

Leon Schagrin in Polish uniform 1950
fig 122

Leon and Betty Schagrin Wedding Photo[20]
Haifa Israel 1958
fig 112

Leon Schagrin & Roman Blauner
1960 at a Bat Mitzvah for Izak Goldman's daughter
Francis. Izak is a relative that survived from Grybow.
fig. 119

Max Blauner
fig 116

Morris Moshe Katz 2010[27]
Auschwitz tattoo 161274
fig 115

Eli Sommer[26] **2011**
fig 118

Leon Schagrin with Stephen Shooster
fig 110

Leon Schagrin close-up with Panther Tattoo
fig 156

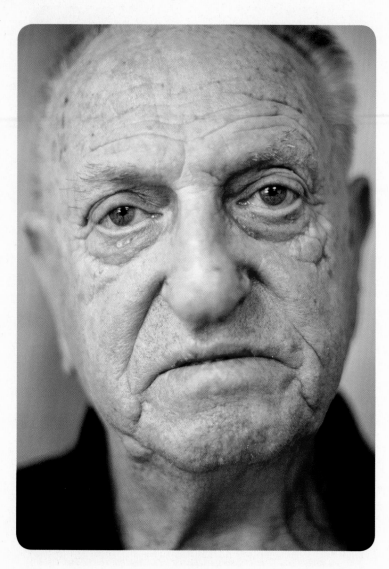

Leon Schagrin Portrait
Age 84
fig 109

**Leon Schagrin with Jim Boring
editing "The Horse Adjutant"**
fig 111

Betty Schagrin lighting one of six candles representing 1,000,000 lost souls per candle
...with Her husband Leon, co-author Stephen Shooster, Linda Medvin, Broward County Public School Holocaust Education and the entire congregation of Temple Sha'aray Tzedek - Sunrise Jewish Center, Day of Remembering the Shoah 2011

fg 159